ADVANCE PRAISE FOR

LOSS OF INDIGENOUS EDEN

"Blair Stonechild offers us, yet again, an interesting and timely read. It is thought-provoking, philosophical, informative, and celebrates the resilience and strength of Indigenous spirituality and our relationships to the sacred. It is grounded in teachings, Indigenous scholarship, and Elders' knowledge. He bravely and critically tackles prevalent ideas, opening up space that can transform discourses related to civilization and ultimately colonization." —DR. KATHY ABSOLON-KING, Associate Professor and Director, Centre of Indigegogy, Wilfred Laurier University

"Provocative and compelling, *Loss of Indigenous Eden and the Fall of Spirituality* offers deep historical insight into the colonialist legacies persisting within contemporary society, illuminating how the enduring values of Indigenous spirituality can provide meaningful paths toward healing and reconciliation. A must-read for all seekers of knowledge." —DR. JESSE ARCHIBALD-BARBER, Associate Professor of Indigenous Literatures, First Nations University of Canada and Past President, Indigenous Literary Studies Association

"When we lose connection to nature is when we become lost, that most times leads to greed, violence and lust for power. Dr. Stonechild has appeared with his writings to consider the spirituality of the Indigenous a key in finding a true path for humanity." —ELDER DAVE COURCHENE, Turtle Lodge International Centre for Indigenous Education and Wellness, and recipient of the INDSPIRE National Aboriginal Achievement Award in Culture, Heritage, and Spirituality

"These chapters completely rewrite the histories of 'civilizations' of religion and the nation states. They do so with great imagination and originality. It is a great scholarly contribution to our Knowledge of the history of Indigenous Spirituality." —DR. DAVID MCNAB, Professor Emeritus, York University and Fellow, Royal Society of Canada, and author of *No Place for Fairness: Indigenous Land Rights and Policy in the Bear Island Case and Beyond*

"*Loss of Indigenous Eden and the Fall of Spirituality* does an excellent job of portraying that Indigenous Spirituality looks after the spirit and interconnection of all life forms and that it is serious this has been lost in Western 'civilization,' which seeks financial profit at the expense of the environment. This tome needs to be read by everyone for the benefit of the Earth." —ANTONIA MILLS, Professor Emerita of First Nations Studies, University of Northern British Columbia and co-editor of *Amerindian Rebirth: Reincarnation Belief Among North American Indians and Inuit*

"Stonechild has written an important book for anyone interested in a comparative understanding of the effects of colonization on Cree spiritual traditions and other Indigenous knowledges throughout the world." —BRIAN RICE, author of *The Rotinonshonni: A Traditional Iroquoian History through the Eyes of Teharonhia:wako and Sawiskera*

LOSS OF INDIGENOUS EDEN

AND THE FALL
OF SPIRITUALITY

BLAIR STONECHILD

 University of Regina Press

COVER AND TEXT DESIGN: Duncan Campbell, University of Regina Press
COPY EDITOR: Rhonda Kronyk
INDEXER: Patricia Furdek
PROOFREADER: Kendra Ward
COVER ART: "Wetigo" by Keith Bird

Lyrics on page 189: "Priests of the Golden Bull" © written by Buffy Saint-Marie, published by Gypsy Boy Music Inc. (SOCAN)

Library and Archives Canada Cataloguing in Publication

Title: Loss of Indigenous Eden and the fall of spirituality / Blair Stonechild.

Names: Stonechild, Blair, author.

Description: Includes bibliographical references and index.

Identifiers: Canadiana (print) 20190218657 | Canadiana (ebook) 20190218746 | ISBN 9780889776999 (softcover) | ISBN 9780889777019 (hardcover) | ISBN 9780889777033 (PDF) | ISBN 9780889777057 (HTML)

Subjects: LCSH: Indigenous peoples—Religion. | LCSH: Spirituality.

Classification: LCC BL380 .S76 2020 | DDC 299—dc23

10   9   8   7   6   5   4   3   2   1

University of Regina Press, University of Regina
Regina, Saskatchewan, Canada, S4S 0A2
TEL: (306) 585-4758 FAX: (306) 585-4699
WEB: www.uofrpress.ca
U OF R PRESS   EMAIL: uofrpress@uregina.ca

We acknowledge the support of the Canada Council for the Arts for our publishing program. We acknowledge the financial support of the Government of Canada. / Nous reconnaissons l'appui financier du gouvernement du Canada. This publication was made possible through Creative Saskatchewan's Book Publisher Production Grant.

*Loss of Indigenous Eden and the Fall of Spirituality is
dedicated to Indigenous Knowledge Keepers and ceremonialists
around the world who struggle to keep their spiritual ways alive.*

CONTENTS

May 2, 23

ACKNOWLEDGEMENTS

— values
— morals
— relationship with
creator

Loss of Indigenous Eden and the Fall of Spirituality is based upon decades of experience working with Elders. In this book I contend that Indigenous spiritual philosophy is a rational and relevant system of beliefs. Speaking about spirituality, I realized the incredible interest and demand for further interpretation of the meaning and implications of Indigenous cosmology. Elders, especially my mentor Danny Musqua, encouraged me to use my academic training to further interpret their teachings within a broader context. One the first Elders I met, Ernest Tootoosis, who talked about living in the Garden of Eden, inspired the title for this book. Our Elders are our philosophers; however, they have not always been able to fully articulate their ideas to members of an audience who can be ignorant, insensitive, or skeptical. I will begin by thanking Manitow for the gifts of Creation and the priceless opportunity to learn. In writing this book I honour our traditional ideals of respect, courage, love, generosity, honesty, humility, and wisdom.

Over more than four decades of working with First Nations Elders, each has assisted me in their own way to overcome the effects of residential school education and to re-see the world from Indigenous eyes. I thank the many Elders I have had the privilege of working with over my years at First Nations University, in particular Danny Musqua, Noel Starblanket, Mike Pinay, William Asikinack, Velma Goodfeather, Walter Linklater, Ernest Tootoosis, and Tyrone Tootoosis. Sadly for humanity, many have passed into the spirit world. Elders prayed for the success of my research, provided me with information, and reacted to my writing. They have provided knowledge and understanding of traditional spiritual culture that has been inexorably fading from public consciousness.

I am grateful to Elder Dave Courchene and Dr. Mark Ruml for reading the draft manuscript and providing me with positive and encouraging feedback, as well as Dr. William Lyon and retired pastor Frank Armistead, who both likewise read and commented on the draft. Jesuit scholar Sami Helewa responded to questions about Islam. I have also had countless opportunities to discuss my ideas with individuals in classrooms, at public presentations, and informally.

I thank my colleagues at First Nations University: Dr. Mark Dockstator, president; Dr. Bob Kayseas, vice-president academic; and Dr. Bettina Schneider, associate vice-president for their unfailing faith in this project; as well as department head, Dr. Jesse Archibald-Barber, and interim head, Dr. Miriam McNab, for their support. The First Nations University of Canada travel funds and Indigenous Studies Research Fund have always been highly supportive of my work.

Thank you to Bruce Walsh, former director of the University of Regina Press, and acquisitions editor, Karen Clark, for recognizing the potential of my book that in many ways treads off the usual academic track and challenges orthodoxies of established thought; Sean Prpick, trade editor; Rhonda Kronyk, copy editor; Kelly Laycock for moving the project along; and Duncan Campbell for his great design work. I am indebted to talented Saulteaux/Cree artist Keith Bird, whose painting inspired by spirituality graces the cover of this book, and to Buffy Sainte-Marie for the use of her lyrics.

Finally, I could not complete this book without the steadfast love and support of my wife, Sylvia, who commented on my writing; my three adult children, Michael, Rachel, and Gabrielle; and my extended family.

May 1, 23

PREFACE

An Ideological Conflict

As a survivor of the Qu'Appelle Indian Residential School, I experienced firsthand the effort to eradicate Indigenous culture and spirituality. The extensive scope of this destructive agenda saw thousands of survivors emerge from residential schools unable to speak their language and detached from their culture and practices of spirituality. As an academic and historian who has worked with Elders for many years, I have had multiple opportunities to reflect on the history of contact with Europeans. What becomes quickly clear is that, over this history, conflicting positions about culture and worldview have long existed. This conflict of ideology—whether it be perception that one belief system is more valuable than another, or whether one culture has the right to declare another inferior and, therefore, justify colonization of its people and their land—stretches back much further in time than contact with Europeans in the late 1400s. I conclude that this problem's roots originate in the very rise of "civilization." Understanding the reasons for this dynamic has become a life-long pursuit.

Indigenous Knowledge: An Ancient System

Indigenous cultures existed in what is now North and South America for millennia prior to European contact. What was the focus of their ideology and way of living? Was it significantly different from that of other parts of the world? Anthropologists have noted the central focus on spirituality and intense preoccupation of Indigenous cultures with spirits and ceremonies. It is evident that nothing else was more important in these early societies than their relationship with the transcendent. It is part of the objective of this book to describe, from the perspective of current Elders, what the traditional spiritual values of these societies were and how those values contributed to viable and successful ways of life.

To that end I wrote *The Knowledge Seeker: Embracing Indigenous Spirituality* in 2016. The purpose of the book was not so much to focus on my story as it was to highlight spiritual teachings shared with me by Indigenous Elders. In particular, I learned much from revered Saulteaux Knowledge Keeper Danny Musqua. The book received positive reception from the Social Science Federation of Canada, which featured my work in its "Big Thinking" lecture series. I was invited by many church congregations to expand on my ideas. But it also received derision from other quarters, one professor labelling *The Knowledge Seeker* as a form of academic dishonesty that amounted to "educational malpractice" that deserved no place in university. It is for those, both supportive and critical, that I felt I had to delve deeper to explain why Indigenous spirituality is important to the world today.

Loss of Indigenous Eden and the Fall of Spirituality posits that the Indigenous world preceded that of modern civilization, that it contained values vital to human survival, and that the significance of ancient beliefs needs to be re-explained for today's world. I discussed many of the ideas contained in this book with my mentor Elder Danny Musqua, and he encouraged me, saying, "You are on the right track." I hope that the concepts put forward in this book will challenge readers and stimulate further discussion.

There are only a few books that seriously examine Indigenous metaphysics. Vine Deloria Jr.'s *The World We Used to Live In* argues that the powers of gifts of Indigenous Medicine Persons need to be taken more seriously. William Lyon's *Spirit Talkers* makes a similar

May 2, 23

case but is based upon forty years of research with Elders and historical documents. Finally, Jack Forbes's *Columbus and the Cannibals* questions modern conceptions of good and evil by contrasting Euro-American and Indigenous spiritual values.

Decolonizing Indigenous Heritage

I have been privileged to know many Elders such as Ernest Benedict, Mike Pinay, Noel Starblanket, and Danny Musqua over the past four decades. I am impressed by how each conversation with them always seems to produce new insights. I owe Elders all credit for what I have been able to rediscover about Indigenous spirituality. Elders encouraged me to use my academic training and knowledge to further articulate their teachings. I have been uniquely blessed and positioned through over four decades of working at First Nations University of Canada to be able to broach a subject as foundational yet challenging as this one.

Over my career I have been fortunate to travel to Indigenous communities across the globe, including to far north Inuit communities, south to Mapuche lands in Chile, east to India to learn about Dalits, and as far west as the Xinjiang Autonomous Region of China where Uighurs are the Indigenous national minority. During these travels, hospitality was always offered—a commonality of Indigenous culture. Listening to Native students from around the globe who come to First Nations University of Canada further confirms that we all share incredibly strong beliefs about the transcendent, and that the fundamentals of spirituality are consistent across the globe. Another shared experience is how this worldview has been suppressed wherever contact has occurred with colonizers. A large part of the reason for penning this book is recognition of the need to decolonize and revitalize Indigenous heritage. It is a vital world legacy that humanity cannot afford to lose.

Truth and Reconciliation

Indigenous spirituality has been historically repressed and ridiculed. Reconciliation is long overdue. *Loss of Indigenous Eden* is a response to the Truth and Reconciliation Commission of Canada, which was established in 2009 to examine the impacts of Indian residential schools on over 150,000 First Nations pupils. The commission heard from over 6,000 individuals in what was one of the most extensive public consultations ever held in the nation. The commission found that the schools' program amounted to "cultural genocide." Outcomes included the devastating breakdown of relationships between student and cultural identity, child and parent, and individuals and their communities. Cultural knowledge, including language and spiritual beliefs, were replaced with alien systems. In Call to Action #48, the commission urgently calls for programs to revitalize Native heritage, including the creation of a new curriculum "for Indigenous peoples' right to self-determination, including the right to practise, develop, and teach their own spiritual and religious traditions, customs, and ceremonies." It is in that spirit that I approach this work. My objective is not to offend or to divide, but to promote greater understanding in a respectful manner.

In order to fully understand the ideological differences that led to residential schools, I found it necessary to examine the widest scope of history possible. What has resulted is an effort to understand how human populations have come to view the world in different ways. The book contends that an ancient knowledge system existed that continues in the form of Indigenous knowledge. Historians tend not to treat the period prior to the "rise of civilization" with much seriousness. In the detailed study of the "trees" of history, an accurate picture of what "happened to the forest" has been lost. The voices of Elders speak to a vision of the world based upon intuition and reflection of their spiritual and cultural knowledge, not the content of books. *Indigenous Eden and the Fall of Spirituality* revisits and reinterprets the history of world civilization. The extent of the subject matter is immense, so I do not claim to be expert in all areas such as religion and philosophy. The book is intended to encourage the reader to reflect and take another look at the nature of the "forest" rather than agonize over the details of each tree.

In a study that covers such a vast range of circumstances and eras, it is impossible to know or cover everything when discussing spirituality and religion. It would take time and resources beyond my means to exhaustively prove every point made. Thus, I beg tolerance for inadequacies that might occur. The main effort has been to assemble sufficient evidence to demonstrate how Indigenous heritage and spirituality have come to be underappreciated. The implications of Indigenous metaphysics continue to remain undervalued in many areas of contemporary Indigenous research. The following is the manner in which I approach the subject matter.

Chapter 1—It is essential to begin with foundational ideas. "Enchanted Creation" explores the philosophy and worldview of Indigenous peoples, mainly among Canada's First Nations, and notes that these apply to cultures in other parts of the world. Fundamental principles include that all created things have spirit, that those essences have to be respected, and that human beings have a responsibility to act as stewards.

Chapter 2—It is necessary to appreciate that a different, and in many ways richer, world once existed. "Indigenous Garden of Eden" describes the type of society that results when harmonious relationships between humans and the rest of Creation are respected—abundance, health, happiness, and a sense of purpose and personal worth.

Chapter 3—The significance of the vast amount of time of human existence prior to the rise of civilization has been dismissed and ignored. "Betraying Indigenous Eden" makes the point that, in comparison to at least 200,000 years of existence of modern man, modern civilization began emerging only about 6,000 years ago—a tiny fraction of the overall time. This was a period of human harmony that reflected living in accordance with Indigenous values. It examines the emergence of ideas of civilization and religion in Middle Eastern and European philosophy. I argue that by defining itself as the central purpose of Creation, human civilization amounted to a rejection of primeval philosophy.

Chapter 4—Something dramatic and traumatic occurred in history that greatly altered human destiny. "Final Conquest of Eden" examines the grand collision between European civilization and the original peoples of the Americas that was the last untouched bastion of Indigenous Eden. I coin the term "ecolization" to describe the Indigenous alternative to civilization.

Chapter 5—Elders maintain that there is a fundamental difference in the way the transcendent was approached compared to today. "Religion Overtakes the World" looks at the differences in characteristics between Indigenous spirituality and modern institutionalized religions, in particular the two largest Abrahamic religions—Christianity and Islam, which have come to dominate the world.

Chapter 6—A fundamental change in attitudes towards relationship with spirit is also reflected in the way thinking about the world has been altered. "Knowledge: Sacred and Profane" examines developments in philosophy, science, and technology that have created modern civilization. It argues that the shift in thinking and living has accelerated the decline of spirituality in general.

Chapter 7—Over recent time, humankind has become frenetic in its obsession over its place and activities in the world. "The Big Rush" examines how modern "civilized" culture is driven by the immediacy of the quests for power and wealth. Greed and exploitation are compared to the concept of the "Wetiko," the force of selfishness that Indigenous societies realized would lead to the destruction of their values and well-being if not combated.

Chapter 8—Human actions are not without consequence. "Harming Our Relatives" looks at the consequences of current policies of resource exploitation and how this has caused damage to our plant and animal relatives in the natural world. It examines how species extinction and climate change could ultimately bring about the undoing of humankind.

Chapter 9—People continue to search for meaning and a better quality of life. "Searching for Healing" asserts that non-Indigenous peoples can be allies in restoring understanding of and respect for the transcendent. It looks at scientific and empirical research that supports Indigenous Peoples' position that there is something vital that extends beyond the physical.

Chapter 10—The historical relationship between Indigenous and non-Indigenous peoples can conceivably be repaired. However, this will require a major refocus and recognition by the dominant culture about Indigenous Peoples, their culture and spirituality. "Need for Global Reconciliation" returns to the Indigenous concept that all events occur in cycles and utilizes the Medicine Circle to make a diagnosis of humanity's sojourn on Earth to this point. It contemplates what the future might hold and concludes that a global reconciliation with Indigenous Peoples and their spirituality is critical for the survival of humanity.

CHAPTER 1
ENCHANTED WORLD

When one hears the term "enchanted world," one is drawn to ideas of fairies, elves, and talking animals. In the enchanted world, now consigned to realm of imagination, spirits lurk in every corner—in trees, in animals, and even in rocks. In fables, one can magically communicate with such spirits. Some are mischievous, others malicious, but most of them are benign. We think such a world only belongs to un-reality and that no sane person can take it seriously. Yet, this is precisely the type of world that Indigenous Peoples perceived and learned to live in. They successfully navigated such a world for hundreds of thousands of years prior to the rise of today's concept of civilization.

Noted Lakota Medicine Man, Fools Crow, describes communicating with a rock: "I talk to it like a person, and I let the rock talk back to me. It tells me where it comes from, what it has seen, what it has heard, and what it feels. When we are finished, I have a whole new picture of that rock. Doing this expands the way I behave towards rocks and towards other things, and my mind grows."[1]

Today, the dialogue about Original Peoples is based upon science and rationalism. Archaeologists are preoccupied by how they evolved from simians. This approach stands in contrast to Indigenous stories of how our peoples were placed on this land by the

Creator. But the scientists will remonstrate, we have the proof—just look at the bones and fossils and geological strata. However, perhaps it is the scientists who are missing the point. Traditional Indigenous thinkers are not particularly interested in quibbling about the details of whether people arrived by foot or boat or otherwise. Indigenous philosophers are concerned about what they perceive to be a higher reality: that spiritual forces are and have always been afoot in the human story. The ancient accounts, derived from intense contemplation and prayer, tell us that people are late arrivals to the created world. The oldest human stories of arrival on Earth are not about God creating the world in seven days but, rather, speak about coming from the stars. Moreover, we are here for a reason—to engage in a learning experience. There is something sacred about origins that archaeologists, let alone modern intellectuals, do not take seriously.

Whatever the account, people have been on Earth for at least 200,000 years and perhaps for as long as 500,000 years according to geneticists. They may have been in the Americas for as long as 100,000 years. This period of existence before written history is generally referred to as "primitive," "prehistoric," and "uncivilized." However, these prehistoric inhabitants should be more appropriately recognized as Indigenous. I bristle when I hear cultures such as those of the Sumerians, Egyptians, Greeks, and Romans being referred to as ancient. Having arisen a mere 6,000 years ago places their history in about the last 3 percent of human existence. At best, they should be referred to as cultures of the recent past. "Ancient" should refer only to that vast swath of experience that preceded the rise of so-called civilization.

Can we accept that "primitive peoples" were thinking beings? If so, what would their view of the world have been? I realize that the ideology and spiritual values of "prehistoric" folks is similar to the philosophy and practices of Indigenous Peoples across the world.

First Peoples across the globe value their connections to the land and see this as a sacred obligation. Rituals of welcoming and for creating strong relationships and ceremonies that recognize the power of the transcendent and promote forgiveness and healing were Indigenous tools for creating social cohesion. Protocols for entering the territory of others effectively governed relationships between groups. These were the ancient equivalents of borders and passports. The Indigenous ideology of harmony with all created things meant that the environment was respected. Despite all of this, things were not perfect and people made mistakes. However, with their spirituality, they could eventually find their way back to the "Good Path."

We Came from the Stars

My mentor, distinguished Saulteaux Elder Danny Musqua, who was employed at First Nations University of Canada for over twenty-five years, shared his deep understandings of spirituality. Musqua is of a unique breed of individuals who have received the ancient teachings of the Saulteaux people directly from their Elders; teachings that have been transmitted through generations over millennia. According to Mosôm Danny, our people are beings who came to Earth "from the Stars to be men."[2] Mosôm elaborated on the motives for and process of human arrival on Earth.

> The old people say that a question was asked by the spirits after they were created: "I wonder what it would be like to be physical?" And thus Kise-Manitow, the Creator, responded: "You have asked that question, therefore you shall experience that. If that is what you want to know, then those of you that want that conscious knowledge of the physical universe must go down there, must go down into the essence of my being." The Creator then dreamed the universe into existence to answer the spirits' question.
>
> The Creator, which is the woman within God, came out and became the physical essence. By giving life to the four corners of the universe of time, the heavens, the stars, and everything else were born. The Creator brought order to the universe, and we have to learn to live within that order. The spirits were created within the mind of God and everything in the universe that God created has spirit essence. After the physical world was created, time began. The universe continues to give birth: rebirth to the stars and to the star systems

within our world and our universe. And it continues for all of the spirits who participated in that question.

The Creator is both spiritual and physical, the physical being a manifestation of its creativity. It is male and female, father and mother. It was with the female mother aspect of his being that he created the physical world. She gave birth to the world and everything in the universe and will continue to give birth until those spirits who have come into the physical world have obtained all the knowledge that they originally sought.[3]

According to Native American scientist, Gregory Cajete: "After myths about animals, the second largest group of Native myths are those about the stars. In all of these stories, there is the deeply felt sense that humans do have a direct and ancient relationship with the heavens. Humans are also seen to benefit in terms of moral under-standing and ethical behaviors through their interaction with the heavens."[4]

Tribal peoples all over the globe have stories of coming from the stars. Lakota writer Dr. A.C. Ross provides some examples.

The Dakota people also have an origin story connected with the stars. The story is that we came from seven stars and that we were put in the Black Hills. Research identified the stars as the Pleiades. . . . The Osage have an origin story telling that, at one time, they lived in the stars. 'We were pure and noble people. Then we came onto the earth and became flesh and blood.' In a similar way, an Iroquois origin story relates that they lived in the heavens. Then they, too, came to earth and became flesh and blood. A Navajo origin story tells that at the beginning of this age when they emerged, they discovered a god already here. They called him Dark God. They asked him where he came from and he said, 'I came from Delyehe, the Seven Stars.' . . . The Aztecs also believe they came from the Pleiades.[5]

Cree science educator William Buck echoes Mosôm Danny's words: "We originate from the stars, we are star people. The genesis mythologies say this is where we come from. We come from those stars, we are related to those stars. Once we finish doing what we come here to do, we get back up to those stars. The Pleiades are a constellation known in Anishinaabe as 'Hole in the Sky,' the place of opening between the star world and Earth."[6]

Star origin stories, among the oldest accounts of human emergence, all agree on one basic theme: that people need to be grateful for and respect the gifts of the Creator.

> The Pueblo creation story is essentially that: Humans came into this world, their place, after having evolved through three other worlds of being. Before they could come in, they sent messengers to ask the powers of this world if they could live here. As the people received the message that they were indeed invited to come into this earth, they were very happy. Their messenger, a sparrow, explained the rules they must follow, and those rules dealt with proper relationships.[7]

The biblical story, which portrays humans as having been originally created as part of Earth, is at odds with Indigenous stories that do not say that people were created here but as having arrived "from the stars." Why should this account of origins not be accorded the same respect as the biblical story of God creating the world in seven days or as scientific theories that life has evolved from biological soup and that humans are nothing more than intelligent apes?[8]

Covenant with the Animals

According to our Cree and Saulteaux stories, animals already existed on Earth at the time of our arrival. They had their own families with quasi-human qualities. Wolves and beavers, for example, display wonderful characteristics of being able to raise and take care of their offspring and extended community.

Wîsahkecâhk, our Elder Brother, was a semi-divine being who assisted humans in coming to Earth. He was the Cree God of knowledge, a trickster known for humorous feats of transformation, and provided instructions to people on how to behave. He was the one, it is said, who created Turtle Island after the time of a big flood. According to legends he enlisted the help of animals. The beaver dove into the floodwaters and then the muskrat followed. The muskrat drowned but had a lump of mud on his paw. The Trickster blew on the mud and created the land.[9]

The Wîsahkecâhk stories describe how, when people arrived, a sacred covenant was entered into with the animals. Animals willingly made themselves available as food. In times of crisis, they could make their location known in a dream—in early times, humans and animals could communicate telepathically. In return, inhabitants showed their appreciation for the animal's sacrifice, often through prayers or by leaving tobacco. For their part, animals could benefit from benevolent contact with humans. However, because of abuses and a lack of respect by humans, the relationship is severely damaged. Animals now distance themselves and are harder to hunt.[10]

Elder Gordon Oakes describes one Creation story and hints at the role played by Wîsahkecâhk.

My grandmother spoke of a previous civilization before this one. The people of that ancient civilization were given far greater power by the Creator than this current civilization. For example, people could fly. Those ancient people led themselves into a life of disrespect and they began to abuse their way of life.

At the time of Creation, there existed four good Grandfather Spirits who were responsible for that civilization. As that ancient civilization became more chaotic, our Creator decided to discontinue them by causing a great flood. After the flood, Grandfather Spirit took some mud, and from it he molded some men. Then our Creator reminded Wîsahkecâhk that he had provided him with a sacred life-giving whistle, the women were created by our Creator and were spiritually placed on Earth to join the men.[11]

The succeeding new civilization relied on our loving Grandfather Spirits to help them as they were bestowed with less power than the previous civilization. Those four Grandfather Spirits came from the four directions to love this new civilization and answered their prayers to teach them how to survive. The people could then still fly, and they tried to fly upwards in hopes of meeting the Creator directly for more direction. The Creator instead took away their ability to fly and gave them many languages and moved to settle throughout the Peoples' Island according to their linguistic groups. Through the power of the Creator, the four Grandfather Spirits bestowed these people with many sacred ceremonies and prayer lodges through which they could pray to the Creator and through which they could preserve their oral history and teachings.[12]

Such myths and legends are sacred and are taken very seriously, having been received through supernal revelation. They are not to be understood literally, but in symbolic and archetypal terms.

Inquisitive Spirits

The fundamental precept to understand and appreciate, Elder Musqua reiterated often, is that we actually are spirit beings who are on a physical journey as humans. Mosôm went on to explain why human consciousness came to inhabit the Earth.[13]

Spirits are originally occupants of the spirit world and have always existed in the spirit world. These spirits are all creations of the ultimate being, the Creator. After these spirits express the desire to increase their knowledge by experiencing the physical world, the Creator and Grandfather Spirits, who themselves do not live in the physical world, work together to create it. The Creator made the physical world in such a way that the spirit beings going there will have to conform to the laws and limitations such as time and space.

There is spiritual meaning to all of the things that the Creator brings into existence. This knowledge is what those spirits come to Earth to seek. That knowledge is part of the Creator and is one with the Creator. Humans seek that knowledge, and once they achieve their purpose, they need to eventually find their way back to the Creator and the spirit world, their real home. Their time in the physical world is limited and temporary, a mere travelling through the physical world as part of an infinitely long journey of spiritual development. But that they ultimately return to the spirit world is unquestionable.[14]

According to this teaching, humans were originally spirit beings. But they wished to experience physical life, as the physical is also an aspect of the Creator. This account of Creation is brilliant in its simplicity since all have a moment of birth and live through a constantly changing physical world until ultimately arriving at the moment of death. Postulation of an etheric realm implies something significant about what happens before birth and after death. Danny Musqua's version stood in stark contrast to what I had learned in school and heard in church. It is refreshing, resonating with a sense of intrinsic truth. It addresses Creation and the purpose of life in a fulfilling, loving, and meaningful manner.

Mosôm became more specific, going to great lengths to describe the process involved.

The old people say that Ahcahk[15] (the human soul) comes and puts shrouds on the fetus for the first seven weeks. The shroud acts like a blanket over the fetus. When the body is fully formed the spirit then enters through the top of the head into a "well of thoughts." Once Ahcahk decides to take this fetus as its earthly vehicle, the spirit imprints its journey deep within one's memory system. Then the physical journey that it wants to take on begins. Ahcahk goes to the centre, to the heart, to become the living force of that body.

The soul that is going to take this body has to make the decision to enter that body. Most of the time when it is preparing, for seven weeks, Ahcahk does not make the decision to enter that body. The first thing that it does is go into the "well of thoughts." It goes deep into one's mental capacity and imprints its journey and the purpose it must fulfill. When it has finished imprinting its journey, it enters the heart, which is the centre of the body. But, before Ahcahk enters there, the

Grandfather Spirit shuts down all remembrance of the spirit from whence it came. Ahcahk is forced to start its journey. It has to teach and discipline this body about the spiritual will of the Creator.

Prior to birth the spirit knew everything about the spiritual universe from where it came. When that spiritual doorway is shut Ahcahk has to go into the same state as the body that it has adopted. Its human vehicle is childlike and the spirit also becomes childlike. The spirit can fulfill its purpose and mission in this earthly life only through this physical body. Ahcahk has to struggle with, and win, the body over to its purpose. The body does not have any inkling about spirituality. However, the body comes to realize that the spirit motivates it, and it begins to understand its purpose in relationship to the spirit that occupies it. So gradually the body responds to its purposes in life.[16]

Mission in Life

The notion that spirit exists is key to understanding Indigenous spirituality. The purpose for experiencing physical life, Mosôm Danny explained to me, is to learn from it, and such learning occurs over a series of reincarnated lives. All things, plant and animal and inanimate, have spirit essence and all interact in a web of interrelationships. It is through the interaction of energy that beings learn. However, deep inside, we yearn to ultimately reconnect with our etheric origins.

Earthly existence comes at a cost. That price is the loss of memory and knowledge of Ahcahk's incorporeal nature. This process occurs in order that the soul will become totally focused on its mission in the physical world.[17] The Grandfather Spirit "shuts the doorway" to the numinous universe, casting a veil over that memory. Ahcahk enters the physical world, a helpless infant who must struggle to learn every lesson and law of physical life, from eating and sleeping to walking and talking. The soul, locked into the physical body, is challenged to rediscover its origins through looking inward. Danny Musqua says:

The teacher is Manitow itself. Spiritual changes occur when one begins to act on one's spirituality. One has to go back into the recesses of one's mind through the silence of prayer. Meditation is called 'sitting in a dream state in a conscious way.' You shut out the world. You use moments of peace to delve into the well of thoughts and think and reflect. That is where you discover what your journey is. One acquires that through the visions, dream states, the insights that come from the spirit.

Manitow says, 'You go down into the physical, and then you come back to me. You will go through a quagmire of knowledge systems that are down there. However, I will give you tools to find your way back to me. These include Seven Disciplines, Seven Virtues, Seven Great Laws, Four Forces of Creation, and Four Great Spiritual Laws.'

The purpose of spirituality is to discover the relationship that the Creator has with the universe. Spirituality enables human beings to get an understanding of their journey on this path and purpose. Once you find out what that journey is within yourself, your understanding becomes clearer. Ever so gradually you research your memory system. The experience becomes intense and your enthusiasm builds. The spirit that wants to complete its journey urges you on.

The prophecy of knowledge given to the Old Ones was earned through long practice and arduous individual effort. The greatest pain you have to accept is the fact that you are limited. You cannot find your way back until you sacrifice that time to understand. You find that only with self-analysis, self-research, examining your good and bad experiences.

You learn how to pray through the directions of the old people, and especially through the ceremonies. Ceremonies will lead you through the challenges of the disciplines. The answers are locked within those ceremonies.[18]

Mosôm Danny confirmed that physical life is intended to be a challenge.

Now the spirit finds itself faced with a unique challenge. It has entered into a physical body and has to live within a physical world. It finds that one has to struggle to learn things and to achieve goals that it has set before itself. But how does it do that? The answer is that the spirit must learn to work with the body, to understand its limitations and to understand how the body must be trained and prepared to meet the spirit's challenges.[19]

One has to conquer this body, to make it understand its real purpose, which is to be the servant of the Creator. The physical body is merely a tool, like a suit of clothing, that each of us as spirit beings has had given to us exclusively for use during our journey on Earth. The body is not who we are, it is not our identity, though we identify so closely with it. But as we learn to fit into this body, we need to discover its abilities and limitations as we strive to grow and develop.

Entering the physical world presents a troubling phenomenon: separation into individual bodies, each with its own artificial sense of self. One's ego then needs to discover through interaction what appropriate interactions and relationships are, in other words, lessons to be learned. While on Earth, Ahcahk explores all types of knowledge systems as it determines the appropriate behaviours needing to be followed.

Spiritual Tools

Mosôm Danny carefully covered the important lessons called the Seven Disciplines. These disciplines are key to achieving control of one's vehicle, the body. The answer to one's purpose is right there in front of you, but it is your responsibility to find it, he informed me.

The Seven Disciplines that are necessary to complete one's spiritual journey are fasting, sharing, parenting, learning, teaching, praying, and meditating. They each constitute entire teachings and have a specific set of practices. Mosôm suggested that one learn these disciplines over the course of seven incarnations.[20]

Fasting is a form of sacrifice that disciplines the body and helps it to focus on one's quest. Physical deprivation enables one to place more focus on one's spiritual side. Without some sort of sacrifice, advancement is not possible. Sharing is a fundamental aspect of positive relationships that includes generosity and service. Sharing strengthens the bonds of affection and respect between individuals and within the community. Through parenting, one learns responsibility by caring for the weak, sharing one's resources, and imparting one's wisdom. Learning in innumerable areas is the fundamental reason for pursuing the experience of physical life. In teaching, one guides those who are less experienced or need advice and help. One can teach simply through example. Mentoring is one of the roles of the Elder. Praying is entering into a sacred space where one can focus on communication with the spirit realm. Prayer and participation in ceremonies reminds one of the requisite to achieve healthier relationships and plays a central role in healing. Prayer is an especially effective tool calling for spiritual assistance in genuine humility and acknowledging the pitiful nature of human beings. Meditation is an advanced tool that involves serious reflection in a sacred or ceremonial setting in order to understand one's path. Time needs to be taken to create a relationship with the supernal world. Meditation helps one to understand dreams and visions. Mosôm explains that

> Your spiritual questions are answered through prayer and meditation, especially meditation. Meditate and then you will be able to get your answer. Your dreams become reality through your meditation. You will get answers and sometimes you may not be aware of them. Or perhaps you are afraid to talk about them. You should find an Elder who can interpret them for you. But sometimes you just have to take the answer and interpret it yourself because there is nobody else. Sometimes you have to take the answer and go off with it. They say you should go off with it and pray. Go to Sweat Lodge Ceremonies a couple of times. And the answer will become evident. You will get your answer and sometimes it comes suddenly.[21]

During the practice of meditation, a person retains consciousness while transitioning into dreaming, a process similar to lucid dreaming. Mosôm acknowledged that many dreams simply reflect preoccupations with waking life and do not have any special significance. The old people say that if a dream comes three or four times, then it is meaningful.

Standards of Behaviours

Behaviour involves feelings about, and dispositions towards, others. It is central to how we interact with family and community. When one seeks to be guided as to what is appropriate or inappropriate, one turns to the Seven Virtues: humility, respect, courage, love, generosity, honesty, and wisdom. In traditional society, each of the virtues is tantamount to a law in itself. Living up to them sets a high standard, which, when attained, leads to personal and spiritual contentment. The Seven Virtues are an intertwining and mutually enforcing set of guidelines that, if followed, create a positive social and psychological environment. Failure to adhere to these virtues creates a loop of negative consequences. The guidelines are flexible and emphasize the positive as opposed to strictures such as "Thou shalt not kill, thou shalt not steal," etc.

Humility is humbling oneself and recognizing that no matter how much one thinks one can do, it is little compared with the universe of possibilities. Humility is one of the most basic and foundational of virtues. With humility, humans acknowledge that they are the recipients of the gifts of Creation for which they need to be grateful. Despite our unique abilities, humans are no greater in the eyes of the Creator than a blade of grass or an insect and are the most helpless creation in terms of dependency on plants and animals for sustenance. Therefore, our non-human relatives need to be treated with respect. Nor should people think they are capable of creating a better world than the Creator has provided. Only kind and thoughtful stewardship of the Creator's gifts can lead to improved relationships with the natural world. Pride, which is a lack of humility, causes us to persist on going down an unhealthy road despite innumerable warning signs. With humility, one finds the ability to admit mistakes and embark on healing.

Respect flows naturally from humility. Respect creates trust with others and self-esteem in oneself and promotes honesty. Respect includes empathy towards others, creates positive role models, and encourages others to behave in their best manner. Showing respect for the beliefs and rights of others is a form of encouragement in which positive relationships will grow. If one does not show respect, one may not receive respect in return. Respect also includes recognizing the validity and legitimacy of other plant and animal life-forms. Respect is an essential pillar upon which good relationships with all of Creation are built.

Courage does not involve only physical bravery but also includes relationships. Having courage involves doing the appropriate thing, even if it hurts oneself. Courage recognizes one's deepest convictions, allowing one to rise above one's egotistical and selfish tendencies. The individual overcomes fear in order to do what is difficult or necessary to repair relationships. Failure to act out of fear and cowardice weakens one's resolve and convictions. With courage one becomes increasingly stronger and able to help others through example. It takes courage to walk the Good Path.

Love is to be unconditional and given freely even when others may not seem to deserve it. Love is the general attitude that recognizes that all are intrinsically connected. Physical existence and separation are illusory. One puts the interests of others above one's own, such as in ceremonial prayer that serves the purpose of appealing for help for others rather than oneself. Love encompasses and reinforces respect, generosity, humility, and courage. It is the general ingredient that ties beings together in a life-enhancing cycle of positive coexistence. Love results in peace.

Generosity involves sharing, especially with the needy such as the elderly and infirm. Generosity has the benefit of strengthening relationships because it fine-tunes one's sense of empathy and helps to create love and trust with others. Generosity is another form of courage. One gains wisdom through realizing that there is more benefit through generosity than from apathy or selfishness. Those who are generous have increased emotional strength and become role models. Generosity is essential to a life-enhancing philosophy and culture.

Honesty includes being true to oneself by recognizing who and what we are as spiritual beings. Honesty and truth require courage and reveal true knowledge. When honesty prevails, people are able to function optimally in a trusting and supportive environment. One becomes a role model for others and strengthens community trust and cohesiveness. Honesty keeps the individual from stumbling off the Good Path while dishonesty weakens one's personal integrity and trust. Deception and mistrust can become contagious. Finally, the truth cannot be hidden from the spirit realm, as Manitow hears all thoughts.

Wisdom is knowledge of the difference between what is proper and improper and appreciating the consequences of our actions. Wisdom is the cultivation of cumulative practical knowledge that not only enables one to remain on the Good Path but also serves as a beacon for others. With wisdom, the individual fosters foundational values such as humility and generosity and cherishes the value of knowledge. One instills peace, confidence, and joy in others. With wisdom one recognizes the critical importance of acknowledging and respecting the guidance of the transcendent. That person is looked to for help and advice in staying on the Good Path.

The Seven Virtues are mutually reinforcing codes of conduct. They were so important in traditional society that they attained the level of laws. If virtues are undermined, relationship ties, the invisible bonds that hold a community together, are weakened. As ties unravel, the community becomes susceptible to unhealthy and destructive actions. Theft, insult, or murder may lead to others' resorting to similar counteractions. These energy exchanges feed upon one another indefinitely, resulting in dysfunctional communities. Individuals become more concerned about their wants than with the welfare of the community. When values were transgressed, sanctions were imposed, the most severe being exile or even death.

Heart versus Head Thinking

The distinction between thinking with the head and thinking with the heart is that when one thinks with heart, the sanctity and importance of positive relationships are always paramount.[22] Thinking with the head emphasizes differences, sorting into categories of better or worse, often for the purpose of gaining individual advantage.

Such an approach might be called objective or impartial, but the unity of relationship takes second place to the particular interests of the individual or the group. In this sense, head thinking lacks sensitivity and holism. Appeals arising from the heart are more powerful than those arising from the head, especially in the context of relationships. Indigenous people often revert to heart mode when making important decisions.

Sacred Learning

In traditional times, transmission of supernal knowledge was carefully supervised under prescribed circumstances. An individual had to demonstrate genuine interest through use of appropriate Protocol and engagement in ceremony. Addressing the most sacred questions was a mature undertaking and not to be embarked upon lightly. According to Elders, the central challenge of life is the task of learning appropriate relationships—not only between people but also with all other created things that we regard as relatives.[23] The laws governing human behaviours manifest in the Great Law of Peace and Harmony, and standards of behaviours such as the Seven Virtues revolve around the quest to learn respectful relationships.[24] Teachings of Elders are a practical ethic that can be applied in daily life.

The first responsibility of spirits who came to occupy humanoid bodies was to learn to control them. Even after 200,000 years, people still have trouble gaining control over the body's appetites and desires. The next major responsibility was to develop positive relationships with the existing denizens of Earth, the plants and animals. This is why ceremonies to communicate with animal and plant spirit guardians are important. These beings were gifts of the Creator who could be allies to humans in the quest to learn about physical life.

Mosôm Danny emphasized that the struggle to learn can be a painful process.

What we learn about on this Earth is knowledge. The Creator put order in the universe of time. We must learn how to live in that order. Therefore, knowledge and the Creator are one. Ahcahk was in the presence of Manitow before it arrived here. Manitow's abode is right there inside of you. The spirit inside of us has become caught in the darkness of time. The only tools it has to find its way back are intelligence and brain-power. To know Manitow, you will have to reach back into your mind. Lost in darkness, Ahcahk will cry a lot of times. It feels like it is stuck in the bowels of hell. It wishes that it had never asked the question about the physical world. Until it finds the answer and completes that journey that is imprinted in its mind, it will have to continue to search. Your tears will fill an ocean for the amount of pain and suffering that the spirit will experience because it is lost. Along its pathway there are a thousand distractions. The body has a thousand wills. Yet, the spirit in you has only one will—to go back to where it came from and reunite with the Creator.[25]

The world provides the stage upon which to learn basic lessons, among them the fallaciousness of individuality and the pitfalls of selfishness. Lessons are learned through mastering various avocations, including that of parent, learner, and teacher. Traditional knowledge is based upon years of rigorous and disciplined training of the mind and body. Developing spiritual gifts or abilities is analogous to developing physical or intellectual abilities. Professional athletes spend hours and days over years, repeating a skill until it is honed to perfection. Intellectuals such as professors spend long years in educational institutions, reading, researching, discussing, and writing about a particular topic of interest.

Spiritual training is comparable to any professional area, be it law or medicine, that requires years of rigorous study, discipline, and proper training. In a similar vein, Indigenous holy persons who seek to develop that relationship with the transcendent spend much time fasting, praying, engaging in ceremonies, and meditating. These practices do lead to tangible results. Today, few seek high achievement in sacred pursuits because they see others pursuing materialism, doubt that concrete results are possible, and want to achieve immediate rewards. When the sacred is ignored, it withers, much as unused physical and intellectual abilities.

Spiritual Unity

The principle of wâhkôhtowin is that all created things are related. It stems from the concept that all originate as spirit beings but manifest as physical entities. Everything is to mutually support everyone else's life mission. All aspects of life have a numinous dimension. Plants, animals, and even stones have such essence. Everything lives in an interrelated web of life, and whenever beings interact, there is an exchange of energy. These energy exchanges can be positive or negative.

To Indigenous people, the belief in the transcendent is not something separate from everyday life. All aspects of life are viewed as having a spiritual dimension and plants and animals possess their own form of consciousness. Even rocks are not regarded as insensitive, but as beings in the same manner that humankind are people.[26] The stone is considered special because of its longevity and as an entity that does not depend on other life forms to exist. It is witness to the events of long spans of time. Powerful knowledge can be accessed through the spirit of the stone, such as knowledge of events at a distance or that have occurred in the past. Medicine people sought stones that have special qualities of shape and size and sometimes appeared to an individual in a dream.[27]

Just as ants and animals are connected by a unified consciousness at a superior level, so are humans. While we all appear to be individual egos, we are all unmistakably human in our consciousness. We all have languages, feelings, families, and so many other characteristics that mark us all as human. We are like leaves on a tree—all seemingly separated but in reality all joined to the same trunk. It is only our ego that gives us the sense of separateness.

Kinship among animals, reptiles, birds, and people, in the Indigenous way, was a conception shared by virtually all tribes. Ironically, of all the creatures, we are among the most vulnerable, being entirely dependent on plants, insects, and animals for survival.

Principle of Stewardship

As spirit beings coming to occupy human bodies, people possess a form of free will and intelligence that is superior to that of plants and animals. In return for the gift of experiencing physical life, all that the Creator requires is that humans act as stewards. Our superior intelligence can be used positively to create mutually beneficial relationships, and to influence plants and animals who can benefit from our greater awareness and ability to manipulate the environment.

Wanting to understand the mysteries of the world, Medicine Persons, the ancient explorers of the incorporeal, underwent rigorous preparations through ceremony—cleansing, fasting, and praying. They supplicated the Grandfather and Grandmother overlords of Creation to grant them answers. The responses came in powerful dreams and visions in which spirit spoke to them directly. Medicine Persons understood that the gift of ceremony includes the transmission of laws and instructions to humans. They discerned that the Creator's perfect love gives birth to perpetual life-giving and life-sustaining forces found in all aspects of Creation.[28]

> The earth may die a hundred times but the universe will not stop until all the beings who wish to experience physical life have done so. The end of time depends not on this earth but upon the heavenly realm. It will not end until all those who wanted to experience the physical essence have all come and occupied a specific body, then found their way back to spirit. The Creator gave humans perfect knowledge systems to discover and use and intelligence—brainpower greater than that of all the animal species. As an individual, one is greater than all the animals put together—that's how important we are.[29]

In the pre-contact Americas, this attitude led to an environment in which resources were abundant even without modern resource conservation and distribution practices. If there were shortages, it was not perceived as being due to overhunting or overuse but as a repercussion for abusing relationships. Imbalances were attributed to some sort of ethereal punishment and would quickly lead to a change of behaviours by the community.

Spiritual Awakening

Mosôm teaches that people must come to terms with the existence of limitations of physical life. We must learn to overcome various challenges the human body is presented with, whether physical, emotional, or mental. The mental world provides conceptualization of what we perceive to be reality; however, it has its limitations because it is founded upon assumptions based on observation of the physical world only. The mind sees exterior appearances and manifestations and entertains our physical needs and desires. It does not readily connect with insight gleaned from our inner consciousness.

After one's birth, Ahcahk goes into a type of dormancy and needs to be reawakened in order to reconnect with the incorporeal. The more spirit is ignored or mistreated, the more it forms a shell, making it more difficult to reach. One becomes more materialistic, arrogant, and unfeeling as one's reverence for life withers. This disassociation can lead to selfishness, greed, and treating other beings as mere objects.

In traditional life, children were made aware that they were spiritual beings from the time they could begin to walk and understand speech. As one approaches adulthood, the desire to know more about the divine might motivate that individual to embark on the seeker's path. One explores the celestial realm through dreams and visions and works to cultivate strong relationships with the Grandfather and Grandmother âtayôhkanak. As they become more invested, they use proper Protocol such as offering tobacco to seek guidance from Elders who are further along the sacred path. The Wise Ones advise that if one prays with a good heart and is truly humble and in need, âtayôhkanak will take pity and intervene to help.

Spiritual Senses

Scholar John Mohawk points outs that two "systems of knowing" can coexist. "On the one hand there are dreams and visions and on the other hand there's a responsibility to maintain a clear vision of reality. Those two streams of thoughts and reactions have to live cooperatively together. The idea that the spiritual and secular can live side by side is extremely important at this time."[30]

Ancient sages realized that physical senses were not the only ones that exist. By looking inward, individuals can use their inner senses. These are experienced during vision quests, dreams, meditation, and in ceremonies. They bring abilities to communicate with plant and animal spirits, and Ancestors. Such skills allowed communication with others located at a great distance, and the ability to locate medicines and game. Using those gifts helped people to continue to understand the Creator's purpose and to trust in the benevolence of Creation. Developing inner senses was considered a part of normal human development.

Mosôm Danny and other sages explain that spiritual insight arrives as revelation obtained after difficult struggle to consult the supernal world. It requires belief, sacrifice, discipline, and participation in ceremonies. Sacred knowledge always originates with personal consultation with the transcendent. Responses to questions can be startlingly and inexplicably accurate.

Revered Lakota Medicine Man, the late Fools Crow, described his technique of communicating with the ethereal.

To reach full communication with Wakan-Tanka and the Helpers, I must isolate myself from all distractions, including intruding thoughts, and create a quiet place where I am fully open to Them and focused on the matter on hand. The black cloth enables me to do this in a very effective way. Darkness allows my mind to take over, because it can see far beyond what my physical eyes can see. Have you noticed that images stand out very well against a dark background? When the wrapping is on me, my senses are keener and come alive. Darkness helps what I feel and sharpens my hearing for spiritual sounds. Even whispers become like shouts. And if a patient is with me under the same blanket, we are floating around in a mood that makes us think of spiritual things and the Higher Powers. Then we are more open to Them. These are some of the reasons why I and some of the other medicine people sometimes cure or heal at night, and why the vision quester's greatest visions usually come to them at night. Sun is good, light is good. But during the daytime we see with our physical eyes and it is harder to concentrate on spiritual matters.[31]

Visions and supernal revelations are how Indigenous ceremonialists investigate the deeper meaning of life. It is their form of scientific exploration, although it has a different methodology. Replicating experience is possible, although the experience is highly individual. Mosôm indicates that we are able to understand the divine messages and metaphors according to our state of personal evolution. Advanced Elders have the power of inner sight, which means they have mastered the ability to communicate with the spiritual realm through visions and dreams.

Non-Interference

The Creator gives each individual a unique mission in life. Such missions are a spiritual journey that only the individual truly knows. Interference with another's sacred journey interferes with their learning and puts one in a position of becoming responsible for negative consequences. It is incumbent on humans to respect Manitow's will and follow this higher authority. If one transgresses divine law, it is that individual's responsibility to provide restitution and seek healing. With this approach, it is possible to preserve a community's unity and integrity. This approach is radically different from the practices of the contemporary justice system and its impersonal laws that generally do not result in healing. Instead of punishment, Indigenous communities simply pitied the transgressor, as loss of personal relationships was just as effective as corporal punishment. Worse, the offender could be exiled—cutting off the relationships that are vital to an individual's survival.

Mosôm elaborates: "There's no greater truth for each of us than what each of us knows from our own experience. We must respect that in each other and not criticize what another experiences. We listen and we learn. And we don't just blindly follow what an elder says but first make sure that what he says is something that has made sense for you."[32] Tony Sand, another Elder at the First Nations University, reaffirms Musqua's words. "What happens in the lodge is your own business and only you know why you are here and that is between you and the Creator. Your experience in this lodge is yours. . . . The story of what happens here is your story. . . yours to tell if and when you wish."[33]

Continuous Healing

Medicine gifts are considered special and great care is taken to ensure that these abilities are only used for the good of the community and not for selfish purposes. Healing practitioners are able to obtain visions and dreams connecting them to spirit powers that may deign to assist in healing, hunting, or other challenges. The consistent exercise of these gifts guaranteed the persistence of a healthy society.

Failure to continuously heal results in the insidious breakdown of the invisible bonds that keep communities healthy and can lead to a relentless downward spiral. Indigenous communities worked constantly and diligently to prevent evil from taking root. Wetiko, the closest Cree concept to the devil, was a force that always lurked in the background but could be defeated with appropriate ceremony. The Cree did not spend a lot of time focusing on notions of evil, because that only gave it more power and legitimacy. Sometimes it took generations to heal rifts between communities or nations but maintaining focus with persistent spiritual effort eventually brought about reconciliation and peace.

Spiritual Evolution

The Creator desires that people learn by experiencing this world. The message Mosôm gave that meant more than anything else was that, in reality, we are spirit beings: There is more to life than what we see and the life we experience in our physical bodies is temporary. We assume these physical frames during our earthly journey, upon which we have embarked more than once. One really comes from spirit and returns to the same source after a sojourn on Earth.

At the end of life, those who have lived their life according to proper relationships look forward to joining their Ancestors in the afterlife.[34] Preparation for death includes fasting, meditation, and ceremony for the purpose of facilitating the journey of the soul to the spirit world. The soul is present during the wake for the dead, so stories, humour, and prayers for restitution or blessing are uttered. Too much grieving is discouraged, as it can impede Ahcahk from embarking on its journey.[35] Mosôm said that death is a very good teacher that brings about deep reflection.

After passing, Ancestors greet one, then there is a review and reflection on one's life. Our soul records every detail of thinking, including everything good and bad. Because the Ancestors' consciousness continues in the spirit world, a great deal of effort is invested in maintaining contact with those who have passed into the incorporeal realm. Feasts and ceremonies are held annually to honour the deceased "on the other side." Individuals who did not lead a good life go to a spirit place where there is confusion and difficulty. Others who lost their way but tried to live properly will be in a dream-like void. These souls do not remain in these states forever, and prayers and ceremony can assist them.

Another meaningful message is that death is a natural end of one cycle that opens the door to another. The incorporeal does not have the strictures of time and space found in the physical world, hence, existence is far easier and more pleasant. It is while on Earth in human form that we face our most difficult challenges. Once these life relationship lessons are learned—the original life lessons humans came to exist for—we as spirit beings move on to other evolutionary challenges, Mosôm concluded.

Universal Indigenous Ideology

Although there are many names for the Creator and variations in ceremonies across the Indigenous world, the underlying nature and principles of spirituality are the same. Protocols of welcoming such as the Sacred Pipe Ceremony commonly used across Turtle Island welcomed visitors into one's community in a sacred way. No significant private or public event could be properly initiated without the employment of the pipe and prayer. It is used to solemnly seal political, social, or economic agreements such as treaties by inviting Manitow to witness the transaction.

Sacred stories of the intervention of the supernal in Creation are found in all Indigenous traditions. The story of the origin of the Haudenosaunee (Iroquois) False Face healing society is an example. It is said that while Shonkwaia'tison (Creator) was preparing to populate Earth with humans, another entity called Ethisoda was wandering about claiming that the world was its creation. To correct the matter, the Creator challenged Ethisoda to a contest. Whichever could move a mountain the furthest would have its claim confirmed. They agreed that the backs of the claimants were to be turned away from the mountain. The pretender went first, and, to the Shonkwaia'tison's surprise, Ethisoda managed to move the mountain a bit. The Creator needed to do something spectacular and so moved the entire mountain very close to the pretender's back. The startled imposter turned to look, causing his face to strike the rock and become deformed. Shonkwaia'tison was concerned about leaving this charlatan among the humans so decided to remove it from the Earth. But the spirit pleaded to remain and in return promised that it would use its healing powers to help people whenever they were in need. When Shamans needed help, they only had to create a mask in Ethisoda's likeness and pray. The Creator agreed and ever since then the Haudenosaunee have used the False Face Ceremony to repel illness and evil.[36]

The Cherokee understood the universe to be overseen by transcendent forces. Visions, dreams, and healing were gifts of Yowa, the Creator. The Cherokee venerate only one Creator while recognizing that many spirit beings such as those of the wind, of the corn, and of the deer assist Yowa. In Cherokee tradition, the plants saw the illness and suffering in humanity and so created medicines that could treat every ailment, allowing harmony to be restored in the world. In contrast, the evil Winago, equivalent of the Cree Wetiko and Anishinaabe Windigo, threatens to prey on people and consume their souls.[37]

The name Hopi means "People who live in the Correct Way."[38] One is to live in accordance to the guidance of the Creator, Tawa, who deemed that humans are to respect all created entities and live in peace with them. Tawa, the sun deity, created the world out of empty space. Beings called Kachinas aid the Hopi to ensure they are living in the correct way. Through ceremonies, the Hopi gain power to help keep the world in balance. Spider Woman serves as an intermediary between the supernal and ordinary world much as Wîsahkecâhk did for the Cree. The Hopi have great reverence for the feminine and the deities of earth and plants are represented by nurturing female spirits. The males have their own ceremonial roles that interface with the Kachina spirits. A world of chaos develops if humans ignore Tawa's directives. Those who live according to the Creator's design move on to an even more promising existence.[39]

Mistakes could be made in Indigenous Eden. In an environment where volcanoes, earthquakes, and drought-induced famine are regular occurrences, the Aztec became apprehensive about their surroundings. Human sacrifice increased when political rivals exiled Quetzalcoatl, the Aztec deity of knowledge, and this led the Aztec to stray off the Creator's intended path. Obtaining captives who became the main source of sacrificial victims was one of the principal motives for conflicts in the Aztec world. Subjects of sacrifice were treated reverentially and willingly and bravely faced their fate. This was seen as a show of respect for the gods that would earn them a lofty place in the afterlife. Sacrificial subjects freed by the Spanish objected that they would rather have been sacrificed than be enslaved.

When one hears of the Aztecs, one cannot ignore the prevalence of sacrifice. Thousands could be sacrificed each year and as well there were animal offerings. Few outsiders understand the importance of sacrifice as an element in the Indigenous spiritual quest. In Plains cultures, this took on the form of flesh offerings such as during Sun Dances. Offering an aspect of one's body was considered to be the highest and most powerful form of offering. The Aztec believed that such extreme gestures were necessary to propitiate the deities, whose acquiescence enabled the Sun to continue to rise every day. As the end of the fifty-two-year cycle of being approached, the need for sacrifices increased to ensure the world would continue into the next cycle.[40]

Such actions were ultimately due to fear and ignorance of the inner workings of nature. However, such activity, no matter how misguided, demonstrates the how seriously Aztec culture treated the necessity to meet what they perceived to be celestial imperatives.

Yet, Aztec knowledge seekers would eventually have discovered the physical reasons for volcanic eruptions, earthquakes, and movements of the planet. One contemporary Elder indicated that Aztec leaders had been warned by their soothsayers that the practice of human sacrifice was wrong and that it would lead to their ultimate demise. The prediction came true when the Spanish, who perceived human sacrifice as the work of the devil, arrived and used the sacrifices as a pretext for destroying Aztec society.[41]

In South America, Inca philosophy revolved around the sacred. The Inca went to great lengths to thank the spirits of the plants during ceremonies. Prayers and ceremonies beseeching the spirits for a successful harvest lasted for days. Developing this hallowed relationship with plants enabled them to become among the most prolific producers of vegetables in the world. Incan philosophy did not promote ruthless exploitation of plants as commodities for commercial purposes. They stored and traded their produce and engaged in barter rather than monetary transactions. Their primary objective was to produce sustainable food for the population while maintaining balance with the environment.

At the southernmost point of the Americas, among the Mapuche, the creative force Ngenechen manifested a world in which ancestral spirits coexist with human, animal, and other essences of nature. People are to live in stewardship over the land. Machi medicine practitioners were fluent in herbal remedies as well as ceremonies to "ward off evil" and initiate healing.[42]

My experiences meeting Indigenous Peoples from all parts of the globe, including Canada, Africa, India, China, and Australasia, suggests that their belief systems and practices are fundamentally similar. Living with a certain set of values led to the creation of environments that engendered social harmony and fostered non-interventionist relationships with the natural world.

CHAPTER 2
INDIGENOUS GARDEN OF EDEN

The biblical Garden of Eden is conceived of as a place of pristine beauty and harmony.[1] In this place of plenty, humans were perfectly content, charged only with safeguarding the Tree of Life. When I began teaching at the First Nations University of Canada over forty years ago, one of the first Elders I encountered was Ernest Tootoosis. Ernest would often say, "We used to live in the Garden of Eden. And we never abused the gifts of the Creator."[2] I admit that I did not fully appreciate the meaning of this statement back then. With hindsight, I understand that Tootoosis was referring to the era of Indigenous hegemony, when the belief in the supernal was strong, respect for the validity of existence of animals and plants was embraced, and health and well-being flourished. All things were in balance and harmony because people did not place themselves and their interests above that of the rest of Creation.

The word *Indigenous* derives from a Latin word suggesting having birth roots in a geographical area. The United Nations defines Indigenous Peoples as communities, peoples, and nations having a historical continuity with pre-invasion and pre-colonial societies that developed on their territories and who consider themselves distinct from other sectors of the societies now prevailing in those territories. Indigenous Peoples are determined to preserve, develop, and transmit to future generations their ancestral territories and their ethnic identities as a basis of their continued existence in accordance with their own cultural patterns, social institutions, and legal systems.[3]

It is estimated that Indigenous Peoples constitute as many as 370 million, or 4 percent, of the world's population.[4] The definition of continuous occupation of their lands could also apply to others, such as the majority Han Chinese; however, the Han are not included in the definition of Indigenous because they are not considered to be marginalized or oppressed. In Europe, some groups can also trace long ancestral lineage to land; however, they do not practise traditional ceremonial connections to it. In locales such as Indonesia, which groups should be considered native to the land is contested because several migrations have occurred over recent centuries. Finally, Indigenous hegemony becomes weakened through intermingling with new arrivals.

For the purposes of this book, the term Indigenous is applied to those peoples who have maintained the fundamentals of their culture and beliefs. This includes connection with the spiritual essences of these places, be they plants, animals, or sacred sites such as mountains. This is not to suggest that Native people could not become geographically mobile. For example, the Iroquois migrated from the southeastern seaboard of North America to the Great Lakes region, as did the Dene from what is now northern Canada to the American southwest, where they became the Navajo. In such cases, however, those tribes were careful to cultivate sacred relationships with their adopted environment, often with the assistance of neighbouring inhabitants.

Indigenous Peoples did not pursue the conquest of others' territories exclusively for commercial or military gain. The notion that lands could be dispossessed and sold without regard to sacred obligation was inconceivable. It is a gross misconception cultivated by outsiders that Indigenous Peoples were warlike by nature or had little ethical concern for the rights of others and, therefore, happily engaged in indiscriminate bloodshed and looting. Outside observers interpreted events through their own cultural biases and were only too willing to find ways to portray tribal societies as inferior. The historical record shows that, upon initial contact, Aboriginal Peoples were hospitable to newcomers, at times saving their lives.

Indigenous life was based upon spiritual convictions that recognized that the human sojourn on Earth presented them with opportunities to learn and benefit from the gifts of the Creator. Maintaining proper relationships with other created beings was paramount. These worldviews produced healthy societies capable of long-term sustainability and uplifting cultures that promoted life. This does not mean that everything in Indigenous Eden was perfect. People made mistakes. However, through adhering to their sacred beliefs, Indigenous people could ultimately heal and overcome their differences.

A detailed study examining every Indigenous practice around the globe as it has existed over the centuries is well beyond the scope of this book. I draw upon Aboriginal cultures of North America with which I am most familiar to illustrate the general nature of Indigenous spiritual ways. Contact with Native scholars and students from across the globe has reinforced my argument that a common ideology underlies our societies. Following these practices has produced societal achievements based not only on human achievement, but also on respect for and living in harmony with all of Creation. Likewise, the portrayal of Indigenous Eden is not any more idealistic than the representation of current civilization.

The Great Law

The Great Law of Relationships, also known as the Great Law of Peace[5] or Law of Harmony, has its roots in the Great Principle that humans are spirit beings on a physical journey. Spirit, having assumed physical form and function in the separateness of space and time, faces the imperative to preserve unity among all created things. In Cree, the doctrine miyo-wichetowin calls for laws of relationships that create accord among all created beings.[6] This philosophical concept explains why it is important to create positive familial and community relationships as well as connections with the natural and spiritual realms. The original laws guiding what humans are to strive for are grounded in a profound understanding of the Great Mystery gleaned from visions, dreams, and reflection.[7]

Saulteaux Elder Campbell Papequash succinctly sums up how this principle works. "There is a natural law. It is the law that everyone is ruled by, including all things in the creation. It is an absolute law. It is a law that has no mercy. It is a law that will always prevail. The basis of this great law is peace. And peace is a dynamic force. Peace takes a lot of effort. It is harder to keep the peace than to have war. For the wellbeing of all, there must be harmony in the world to be obtained by the observance of these laws."[8]

Mosôm Danny went to great lengths to explain that when we enter the world dominated by time and space, we must abide by limitations imposed by earthly existence. Taking on physical consciousness means that we become psychically disconnected, thinking of ourselves as individuals. All created beings interact with one another, and the challenge of learning through life experience is to discover the appropriate and positive relationships necessary to restore spiritual harmony. Relationships exist in four realms: with the Creator and the spiritual; with the natural environment, including land and animals; within the human world, including values necessary for successful marriage and community relationships; and, finally, within ourselves as individuals.[9]

Seeking Harmony

Of the four elements of being—physical, emotional, intellectual, and spiritual—the last is the most important as it is the milieu from which humans originate. It is also the most illusive when it comes to realizing meaning in physical life. Indigenous Peoples have always sought guidance and incorporated spirituality into everyday life through rituals such as the cleansing Sweat Lodge and using the Sacred Pipe for communication with the divine. Ceremonies such as the Vision Quest and Thirst Dance provide even more direct connection. Some wonder about the frequency and lengthiness of rituals, thinking they are not an efficient use of time. But one of the most important functions of ceremony is to constantly remind people about their true nature as spiritual beings and to reinforce our

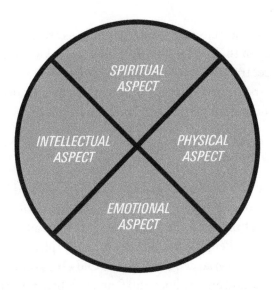

Figure 1: Medicine Circle—Four Quadrants of Being

understanding of our role in Creation. Using ceremonies and Protocols to enable the individual to attain self-control and ultimately learn to live in balance cannot be rushed—it takes time. There are complex Protocols for communicating with the Grandfather Spirits and for receiving sacred knowledge. Ideas of the transcendent were introduced and taught to the very young as soon as they were capable of listening.

The ethereal world precedes the physical and influences all other aspects of existence. The Creator is above all and beyond our ability to fully comprehend, but is addressed in Cree with the endearing term Kitche Manitow (Benevolent Father) characteristic of a familial connection. Earth is nikâwînân askiy (our mother). Such relationships imply reciprocal responsibilities.[10] In their prayers, First Nations Peoples acknowledge "all our relations," reflecting ties not only among humans but also to the natural and supernal realms.

Listening to Elders, I came to realize how highly focused traditional cultures are on the sacred. One only needs realize the extent to which ceremonies are practised daily, seasonally, and at important stages of life. There is a daily prayer when the sun rises in gratitude for a new day. There is a ceremony at the time a baby is born and when a child takes its first steps and so on. Ceremonies are deemed essential to keeping open the connection with the ethereal world. These practices are so central that ritual is conducted whenever any major development occurs in individual or collective life, be it health-related or political, in order that matters will unfold in a "good way."

Harmony with the Land

Pimâcihowin[11] is the concept of connection to land and its ability to provide livelihood. It is part of the reciprocal responsibilities to honour and respect ties with the natural world. Such attitudes explain why Indigenous Peoples did not historically place emphasis on ownership and material acquisition. The Old Ones say that spiritual respect for the land and its flora and fauna will bring prosperity.

Sacred legends speak of a time on Earth before humans arrived when animals were rulers of the Earth. Animals were beings that possessed their own particular characteristics. Some were powerful; others were fast or brave or clever. These beings communicated with one another in nearly human-like languages. They led quasi-human lives with families and home activities. In early times, people could communicate with animals, but this did not endure as relationships with humans evolved.[12]

In Cree sacred mythology, humans were late arrivals to Earth and changes occurred when they arrived. The semi-human deity called Wîsahkecâhk aided this transition to a world that would include humans. This trickster was partial to people, favouring them in their interactions. It enjoyed deceiving animals and even held them somewhat in contempt. Wîsahkecâhk's fundamental role was to help usher in humans' tenure on the planet.

As part of a grand arrangement, the animals agreed with Wîsahkecâhk that they would place themselves in a serving role to humans, offering up their bodies as food. In appreciation, whenever an animal is taken in hunt or by trapping, a small offering such as tobacco is left as a token of thanks to the animal's Grandfather Spirit. Hunters made this gesture to ensure continued good will with animals and to guarantee the animal's availability as food when needed. If First Nations hunters encountered difficulty finding game, they would enter into ceremony and petition âtayôhkanak to reveal an animal's whereabouts. This method is considered reliable as long as respectful relations between animal Grandfathers and humans are maintained. In return, the animals also learn from their interactions with humans.

Elder Ernie Benedict elaborates on this relationship.

> In the English language animals are not given a gender, unless they are a pet or something, it is always it. In Indian you are always referring to something as people, the way you would refer to a person, he or she. Animals are people to the language, that makes a difference to the way you actually treat them too, which means also, when a hunter perhaps prays before a hunt he will ask that the certain animal will be kind to him, allow himself to be killed because he needs that, as the books say. That is the way of all life, he will give his life for another. That is very often mentioned in the old prayers and the old-time hunters.[13]

The product of respectful relationships with the land and its flora and fauna was abundance. Plants, including medicinal herbs, flourished. Animals such as bison, deer, passenger pigeons, and other game were plentiful. They were abundant because there was respect between the human population and the resources they relied on. Rarely would resources be over-utilized, as hunting was not driven by exploitation and human over-population. The economic ethos of Indigenous societies was based upon respect for the existence of other life forms and the belief that such creations did not exist simply for human exploitation and profit. Once notions of domestication, trade, and profit became predominant, the door to unfettered exploitation and dwindling resources was opened. This is not to say that famine or over-exploitation never occurred in Indigenous societies. However, when it did, the Law of Relationships would lead them to question whether their actions were the problem and adjust their ways accordingly.

Ceremonies for Healing and Harmony

Ceremonies can be held to mark the passage from one phase of life to the next or for healing. But one of the most important reasons for rituals is to constantly remind people about our true identity, place in Creation, and responsibilities. Ceremonies also constantly refresh connections to the transcendent. A common requirement for observance is to have clear intent and to adhere to proper preparation and Protocol, including prayer and sacrifice. Spiritual development is the result of preparation, hard work, struggle, and a sincere search for meaning.

Upon birth there is a Greeting of the Newborn Ceremony. Later, there is a naming ritual during which an Elder asks the spirit world to identify an etheric protector for the child. At puberty, a Vision Quest Ceremony marks a young person's embarking on the sacred path to establish a relationship with the supernal and to obtain revelations about their mission in life. One obtains insights in a vision or dream that provides personal direction. The vision quest requires fasting, isolation, prayer, and concentration. Similarly, those who wish to find herbal remedies could have plants pointed out to them in a dream. Some medicine people suggest that those who have never experienced a vision are somehow lacking.

A Pipe Ceremony is held whenever visitors are welcomed, important decisions are to be made, and ventures are to be embarked upon. Campbell Papequash elaborates:

In the early days of the Aboriginal people, no altar was ever complete without the sacred pipe. It was used at every function, at all spiritual gatherings and ceremonies. In the pipe ceremony, the four orders of life and beings are represented: earth, plant, animal and man. Earth, whose elemental substance is rock, made up the pipe. Tobacco, a plant, was the sacrificial victim. Animal was symbolized by the feathers or fur which was appended to the pipe. Man was the celebrant.[14]

Lodges are sacred gatherings for ceremonial activities such as praying, singing, learning, or healing. The physical structures are not permanent but are erected in special locations. One engages in a ritual of purification before embarking on a sacred endeavour such as the Vision Quest or before leaving on a long journey. The Sweat Lodge symbolizes the womb of Mother Earth and is for cleansing through symbolic rebirth. There is singing and praying while water is poured over glowing hot rocks, producing steam.[15]

Learning lodges are convened so Elders can discuss issues among themselves or assist in educating young people about the transcendent. The lodge involves fasting for up to four days during which participants pray and meditate. They reflect on, and gain insight into, their gifts and challenges in life. The lodge plays an important role in arriving at consensus about metaphysical revelations. The Wise Ones would meet, pray, and discuss the meaning of supernal messages until consensus was reached. Learning about the transcendent is better described as a process than a religious practice.

An important way to begin connecting with the inner realm is through seeking a vision. Many do not know what a vision is, never having experienced one. A vision occurs when one experiences a powerful non-physical experience as if it is real while being fully conscious of the experience. One can recognize this experience because of its vividness and lasting impact on memory. Such sight can provide answers about "real" or earthly matters that cannot otherwise be rationally obtained. For example, the vision may reveal an event that will happen in the future, or it may provide meaningful information about something that has happened at a distance.[16]

A ritual was held upon a boy's achieving manhood by a display of bravery such as horse capturing or counting coup. Developing the virtue of bravery is a spiritual task that is not embarked on or continued with in the absence of prayer and ceremony.[17]

The kosâpahcikan (Spirit Lodge), commonly known as the Shaking Tent Ceremony, is convened primarily when an individual requests assistance to find a missing person or objects or to obtain information on health concerns. This lodge provides the opportunity to consult âtayôhkanak (spirit helpers). The convener, a Medicine Person, is concealed from the audience. The Medicine Person is bound in a gesture of submission to the supernal, and the lodge is put into darkness. After prayers and songs invite in disincarnate entities, their presence can be felt. The shaking of the tent signals the entry of the âtayôhkanak. They may move around and talk with those in the lodge, sometimes speaking in different tongues while answering questions.

The Thirst Dance Ceremony, also termed the Sun Dance, is a central ritual held at the summer solstice in June, when the sun is at its strongest. Settlers referred to the rite as a "rain dance" because of their interest in conjuring for rain. Thirsting refers to the sacrifice of abstaining from food and fluids. The ritual's overall purpose is to pray for renewal of life and nature's bounty. Plains tribes took advantage of the occasion to gather together to discuss political issues and hold communal activities, including arranging marriages.

The Anishinaabe (Ojibway) Mitewiwin is a highly respected medicine society where seekers progress to higher levels of attainment as they master esoteric teachings and ceremonies. Mitewiwin provides a moral code as well as spiritual accountability mechanisms. Accomplished members are able to prophesize and heal. Advanced levels of Mitewiwin that deal with healing involve complex Protocols to deal with serious illness.[18]

Foundation of Family

Family is the strong foundation of human relationships. The first phase of human development actually occurs before birth when Ahcahk chooses its parents. Children were considered to be special gifts from the Creator to be cherished, and they have great sensitivity to spirit. The newborn straddles both the ethereal and physical realms. Upon birth, memory of the disincarnate becomes dormant so that recollections do not interfere with focused physical learning.[19] When a child is born, an Elder prays over him or her in ceremony. An appeal is made to the âtayôhkanak for protection for the child. The child is given a sacred name, and Elders speak about challenges in life.[20]

As soon as a child can walk, he or she is told that everything has spirit and that interconnections with all beings must be respected.[21] Teaching about the sacred begins in earnest at seven or eight years of age. The child is made aware that one must listen to and obey parents and grandparents in order to learn principles of behaviour. Children also learn through observation, honing their senses to become more aware of their environment. Parents or grandparents ask children to describe what they saw over the day. It is important for parents to provide good examples and to be kind and truthful to maintain trust. Stories stimulate a child's imagination and make one aware of interactions. By age seven, children begin to learn practical skills.

In adolescence, boys and girls begin to prepare for adulthood. After puberty, they are urged to leave immature childhood behaviours behind. One is taught to honour plants and herbs that can be used for healing. Hunting and obtaining food are tied to thankfulness to the spirits of the animals. When a boy kills his first game, there is a community celebration and the meat is shared. A boy's first feat of bravery is an important sign of maturity and earns him respect with older braves. The Vision Quest is a significant act that symbolizes the creation of ties with the transcendent. Around age twelve, a boy retreats to a sheltered lodge away from the camp. Over four days, the seeker fasts and prays in anticipation of a special message from âtayôhkanak. Girls are required to fast only, as it is understood that they already have a direct connection to the Creator through their ability to engender life.

In young adulthood, one becomes increasingly independent. Preparation for marriage includes learning skills required for parenthood. Elders speak about controlling one's feelings and about responsible relationships. In adulthood, the focus is on marriage, parenting, and providing for family. It is important that a couple live in harmony. One's spouse is considered a "companion on the path of life." Marriages are often pre-arranged, but it is also possible to find a partner through love. Both families support the union, with the male's parents constructing the lodging and the woman's providing the furnishings. Trust must exist between the partners or possessiveness will ensue. Other couples can offer advice to help mediate conflicts. Eventually there has to be give and take between marriage partners. Compromise requires understanding, maturity, and self-sacrifice. If all attempts to resolve differences fail and the pair has to separate, the man's possessions are put outside the door.

Females are particularly vital to maintaining stability in the family. Their hearts have to be strong because they inherit important responsibilities of caring for the sick and elderly. Women have their own rituals such as Moon Time and Name-Giving Ceremonies, and they play important roles as mediators. A mature couple has confidence in their ability to guide children and grandchildren. They enjoy the fruits of child rearing and harmony.[22] Elderhood is rewarding as one imparts wisdom and can conduct ceremonies. Wisdom is acquired as people demonstrate that they have successfully navigated life. Older community members can advise others on what succeeded or failed for them. They can speak authoritatively about the history of the community and issues that arose.

Gender Balance

Mosôm Danny described Creation as beginning with the female essence. Similarly, he maintains that human life began with woman who became lonely, so the Creator made man to provide her with companionship. This stands in contrast to the biblical account of woman being created from Adam's rib. In Mosôm's teachings, an ideal relationship is one in which the complementary roles of each gender are respected. The sexes are different but equal in value. Elders compare the relationship to that of the wings of a bird—each must play its role in order for flight to occur. Male Elders speak highly of the female role, acknowledging the vital responsibilities of women in raising and nurturing children, maintaining the family, and caring for the aged.

Katsi Cook notes the importance of the female spirit in traditional Indigenous worldviews: "Of the sacred things that there are said to be about this [Creation], woman is the first environment; she is an original instruction. In pregnancy, our bodies sustain life. Our unborn see through our eyes, the baby feels, too. At the breast of women, the generations are nourished. From the bodies of women flow the relationships of those generations, both to society and to the natural world. In this way, our Ancestors said, the earth is our mother. In this way, we as women are the earth."[23]

Over his life experience, Noel Starblanket has come to appreciate that women are not weak, but are strong, valuable, and important.

A female spirit is very, very powerful. The true spiritual old men will ask very humbly to be like a woman, who is life, the only life-giver after the Creator. To be able to be like them—to be humble, to be kind, to be grateful, to be forgiving, to be tolerant . . . all those good things that women have. True spiritual old men will pray like that, I've heard them. . . . A lot of people in ceremony will say it's up to the women to carry us men, it's up to the women to heal our spirits, our wounded spirits of our communities. . . . It's up to us men to help those women, to put them back up on the pedestal, because they are greater than we are. We in our spirit world don't believe in equality. We believe the women are greater than us. . . . The women are the lodge keepers, they are the fire keepers. We always say our home fires, or our lodges—the women are in charge of that. The women are in charge of our communities. They are in charge of our children, the grandchildren. They are in charge of the Old Ones and they are in charge of the warriors. To the men, they are in charge of the leaders. They will help these men—the men are simply the spokesmen, as they were in the signing of the treaties.

I always use this dichotomy: The women are life-givers, they are healers in charge of the well-being of the community. So their job is to nurture life and bring life and to take care of it. The men on the other hand are life-takers. They go to war—they take other human beings' lives. They kill animals for food—they take animals' lives. They take trees and water. They take those lives so that these things can give life to human beings. That's the difference between men and women. That's why those teachings of those Elders are true and that the women are indeed greater than men. The sooner men realize that, the sooner communities will heal.[24]

Dakota Elder Eva McKay echoes Noel's words:

A woman has a very important role in the family. That was to be the mother and grandmother, because women were stronger than men, they took on very difficult roles which the man could not. The man was just the provider; the woman kept the fire going, women bore babies, raised babies, and were the teachers. They played a very important role in the family. Women took part in decision-making traditionally, they were accepted. Today you hardly see any females in these First Nations organizations. Women always seem to be in the background.[25]

Outsiders often wonder why the genders have different ceremonial roles. Protocol involves distinctive arrangements that acknowledge male and female differences. The intent is not to discriminate but to balance male and female abilities so they do not conflict. For example, the Pipe Ceremony is tied to male spirituality; therefore, females sit around the perimeter. On the other hand, females hold ceremonies in which males play peripheral roles.

In Cree society, women are the law keepers, which should not be a surprise given the high regard accorded to them. Someone breaking the law would be brought before the female Elders' council to answer for the transgression. Women owned the teepee, which gave them considerable power over the household.[26]

Individuals of one gender do exhibit qualities of the other. Such individuals can be valued because of unique abilities they have, something understood to be a gift. Elders also acknowledge that individuals are reborn in different lives as male and female. It is interesting that psychologists today recognize what Indigenous Peoples have always known: Each person inherently possesses both male and female attributes.[27]

Respectful Politics

Holy people say the Manitow created Turtle Island (North America) as a place where a life of peace and harmony could be built upon traditions and teachings.[28] The Creator's laws are natural laws. Community relations, including those with outside groups, are to be based on the laws of relationship. An example of their application was seen in First Nations' approach to treaty negotiations. The old people predicted that it was the will of the Creator that foreigners would come and that we were all to live together. They believed that the newcomers would understand our ways.[29] Elder Peter Waskahat states: "Elders from different tribes say they knew about the coming of the Whiteman long before he arrived. They say the Elders and the holy men among them prophesied that men would come with different ways and that these men would want to live among them. Long before the arrival of the Whiteman, the First Nations discussed how they would live with them."[30]

The Cree call the overriding doctrine governing all relations wâhkôhtowin. It affirms that everything is a unity under the Creator, a state symbolized by the circle of life. Miyo-wîcehtowin is the principle of "having good relations" among humans who are to conduct themselves in such a way as to achieve harmonious life.[31] As a ritual of adoption, the Pipe Ceremony was used during treaty negotiations. First Nations pledged to create a kinship relation with outsiders; their promise was witnessed by Manitow. White people are referred to as kiciwâminawak (our cousins). A term used by Cree Elders to describe treaty is iteyimikowisiyecikewina, or "arrangements inspired by our Father Creator."[32] Creation of familial relationships is reflected in First Nations' terminology, such as the term Great Mother for Queen Victoria. A family relationship created the expectation of reciprocal behaviours and responsibilities.

The Haudenosaunee (Iroquois) Confederacy is an example of the brilliance of Indigenous politics and how spirituality enables political healing. The concept of the Great Law of Peace was carried to the Iroquois nations by Huron visionary Deganawida and his spokesperson, Hiawatha. The Iroquois were embroiled in damaging internecine warfare. Deganawida received a vision that the Iroquois should "throw in their weapons to bury any greed, hatred and jealousy."[33] The brutal practices of warfare would be replaced by peaceful dialogue. This message was a recovery of their spiritual principles and practices, which they had forgotten. The five warring groups, Mohawk, Oneida, Onondaga, Cayuga, and Seneca established a confederacy under which each was assigned a certain number of representatives. The confederacy influenced creators of the United States constitution, including Benjamin Franklin, Thomas Jefferson, and James Madison. They included the phrase "We the people, form a union, to establish peace, equity and order" in the preamble to the United States constitution. The Indigenous symbol of bound arrows as a sign of strength and concepts of representative government and individual freedom are also features.[34]

Controlled Conflict

A common path for development of courage among males was the path of a warrior, or, more accurately, brave. The role of the brave was primarily defense of the community rather than aggression towards outsiders. The path emphasized ethical training more than learning how to use weapons. During a Vision Quest, a period of deprivation and prayer, powerful âtayôhkanak could appear in dreams or visions. They imparted songs, rituals, and amulets that the individual could turn to for strength and protection. For example, Cree leader Big Bear, although not physically large, carried a bear paw and claws in his medicine bundle that accorded him "bear power."[35]

Thomas Mails, a Christian minister who became interested in the ornate regalia of warriors, realized how unique the First Nations' concepts of war and soldiers were. The object of war, Mails discovered, was not to kill or conquer territory. Young men could raid other nations to take horses or perform brave deeds, proving their courage and claiming their right to the status of manhood. The path of becoming a warrior or a brave involved a long process of developing proper relationships, beginning with the sacred. Young men engaged in controlled conflicts in order to develop personal qualities of bravery. To prepare, one went into ceremony for purification to petition the incorporeal for protection and to learn Protocols of warfare. When a man encountered a brave from another tribe, they followed a procedure for combat. It was more honourable, once one had the upper hand, to "count coup" than take an opponent's life.[36] Cree writer Harold Johnson notes: "If we had anything like war between us, it was about killing the differences between us more than it was about killing each other. It was more important to show bravery than it was to kill."[37] Unfortunately, the advent of the gun made warfare much deadlier and unforgiving as many died in protecting territories and trading interests.[38]

Powerful Ceremonies

One of the most dramatic ceremonies is the Spirit Lodge, more commonly known as Shaking Tent. It is so named because the lodge shudders as âtayôhkanak arrives in response to a Medicine Person's plea. In the age without telephones, computers, or other devices, this ritual was an effective communication tool. The individual conducting the Spirit Lodge Ceremony is tied securely with ropes and wrapped in a hide. Sounds such as the flapping of birds' wings, small lights, and shaking of the lodge, which is firmly secured to the ground, signal the arrival of âtayôhkanak. At the end of the ritual, the ceremonialist is released from his bindings, the knots still intact. Sir Cecil Denny, an officer of the Canadian North-West Mounted Police, reported this experience among the Blackfoot in 1879.

The medicine man was seated wrapped in his buffalo robe at the side of the teepee smoking one of their long medicine pipes. He paid no attention to us. Everything was still, while outside from the main camp sounded beating drums where dances were being held. We sat this way for quite a time when I was startled by the ringing of a bell above the top of the lodge. I could see nothing, and the medicine man made no move. Presently the teepee began to rock, even lifting off the ground about a foot. When it is remembered that such a tent as this consists of a dozen long poles crossed at the top, wide apart at the bottom and covered with heavy buffalo robes making it impossible to lift one side, as I now witnessed, for these teepees are built so that no ordinary wind could blow them over. And remember the Indian did not touch the tent. After some time the rocking motion ceased. I hurried outside to see if anyone had been playing tricks. No human being was in sight near us; the moon was clear and you could see a long distance. I returned and resumed my seat. The tent began to rock again, this time so violently that it sometimes lifted several feet on one side so that both I and the interpreter could plainly see outside. My interpreter was thoroughly frightened, and I was not much better.[39]

Renowned artist Paul Kane, who travelled through western North America in the 1850s, related this account:

> The medicine man, one of whom is generally found in every brigade, gets inside and commences shaking the poles violently, rattling his medicinal rattle, and singing hoarse incantations to the Great Spirit for a fair wind. Being unable to sleep on account of the discordant noises, I wrapped a blanket around me and went out to the woods, where they were holding their midnight orgies and lay down amongst those on the outside of the medicine lodge to witness the proceedings. I had no sooner done so than the incantation at once ceased, and the performer exclaimed that a white man was present. How he ascertained this fact I am at a loss to surmise, as it was pitch dark at the time, and he was enclosed in a narrow tent, without any apparent opening through which he could espy me, even had it been light enough to distinguish one person from another.[40]

George Nelson was in charge of the Hudson's Bay Company post at Lac la Ronge in 1823 when he wrote a memoir of his experiences and describes his first encounter with Indigenous "conjuring."

> I don't know whether I should relate a circumstance that I had done by an old Indian at his house. I had sent two men to our house for rum. They had been gone 7 days beyond the time they thought they would be, and 3 days beyond what I expected. I therefore employed this old man, who, report said, never failed speaking truth. His way was after everybody had retired to rest—he would have no spectators. How he done I know not, probably it was an inspiration, or vision in his dreams; but the Indians said his familiars [spirit helpers] appeared to him, or told him, what he wanted to know. The next morning he told the people: 'They will be here by noon— they slept last night at such a place. They have had a great deal of trouble—they were near drowning, and are very hungry. But they are well, and bring the rum!' All he said turned out

to be so correct that those who had been up thought he had followed them.[41]

Nelson went on to hire "conjurers" over the years in similar circumstances. He concluded:

There are many in the civilized or Christian world who absolutely and positively deny this power of theirs as being absolutely impossible and at best but absurd and idle stories. Many of these things related to these Conjurings I acknowledge to be so; but at the same time I am positive and as firmly persuaded of the truth of the assertion 'that they have dealings with some supernatural spirit,' as I am convinced that I live and breathe in air; unless, indeed, we chuse [sic] to acknowledge and believe a certain sect of philosophers (of the last century I believe) who wish to tell us that we only imagine ourselves alive. And I am by no means inclined to acknowledge myself as superstitious; I am convinced of this from reason, argument, comparison; in short from analysis.[42]

Another individual, J.G. Kohl, witnessed a Shaking Tent Ceremony hosted by a Medicine Man who later converted to Christianity. Thirty years after the ritual, as the former ceremonialist lay dying, Kohl asked him as a Christian to say truthfully whether trickery had been used. The former ceremonialist replied:

I have become a Christian, I am old, I am sick, I cannot live much longer, and I can do no other than to speak the truth. Believe me I did not deceive you at the time. I did not move the lodge. It was shaken by the power of the spirits. I only repeated to you what the spirits said to me. I heard their voices. The top of the lodge was full of them, and before me the sky and wide lands lay expanded. I could see a great distance about me, and believed I could recognize the most distant objects.[43]

Skeptics strongly attack any notion of spirit as lacking in reality. Not knowing precisely how the transcendent operates, they are afraid and wary of what they cannot comprehend. Some fear that the unseen might be used for evil. Others resent the intangible because they feel humanity is condemned to a meaningless existence. This should not deter asking the question whether miraculous healing was possible when those in Indigenous Eden were in harmonious relations with all existing things. Events claimed to be miraculous are controversial due to the difficulty of studying them objectively. However, they are essentially the inverse of unexplainable catastrophes that occur in our contemporary materialist environment. The "curses of civilization" is one way to describe the opposite of the miracles of Indigenous Eden.

Miraculous Healing

Most non-Indigenous people are incredulous at the mere mention of miracles. However, several accounts from the past by reputable witnesses make a compelling case that powerful healing gifts did indeed exist. Historical examples included above were compiled by eminent Indigenous scholar Vine Deloria Jr. in his final book, *The World We Used to Live In: Remembering the Powers of the Medicine Man,* and by anthropologist William Lyon, who toiled for over four decades to compile his impressive tome *Spirit Talkers: North American Indian Medicine Powers.*[44] Deloria was convinced that the power and legitimacy of American Indian heritage lay in its spirituality, yet he was mindful of the need for objective proof. He collected the witness accounts because he was aware of the biases of priests who treated amazing feats of medicine people as works of the devil or of scientists who considered miracles fraud.

The Knowledge Seeker: Embracing Indigenous Spirituality recounted observations again, not just because they are first-hand accounts by individuals of integrity, but because they raise the question of how such phenomena might occur. Good and evil are uniquely human creations. Is there potential for dramatic healing in an environment such as Indigenous Eden, where everything is harmonious and peoples' mental and psychic health is optimal? Would the dynamics of energy and healing be different than in a world where humans declare themselves to be dominant and are not in harmony with the natural or supernatural?

Spirituality in Indigenous cultures is ultimately about connecting with the transcendent. Personal attainment is highly valued. "If an Indian has no Manitow [spirit] to be his friend he considers himself forsaken, and has nothing upon which he may lean, he has no hope of any assistance and is small in his own eyes. Those who have been thus favored possess a high and proud spirit."[45] The Sauk "believed that no one could succeed in any undertaking without divine or supernatural help of some kind."[46]

The mysterious and miraculous is not something that was restricted from ordinary life.

> Some of their stories convey a world filled with strange and mysterious experiences—happenings that cannot be satisfactory [sic] explained to our rational minds. These unexplainable events may tempt us to beg for understandings that reveal an access to a supernatural power and magical tricks. Yet [healers] Otavia's and Joao's non-ordinary lives have nothing to do with supernatural mastery or elitism. Their glimpses of a world with expanded horizons are common for people whose hearts are open to a huge love, a love that breaks through all boundaries of reason and rationality. Yes I am saying that when a person is in the purest love zone, extraordinary experiences take place naturally. It is a consequence of being open to spirit in a pure, heartful way.[47]

Demonstrating Healing Gifts

There are historical examples of displays of miraculous healing whose purpose was to demonstrate the presence of supernal authority. One method was to create injuries such as the immersing of arms into boiling water or creating self-inflicted wounds that would then be restored to a healthy, normal state. Other medicine practitioners transformed themselves into the shape of animals. Medicine Persons gave demonstrations, not to flaunt their abilities or gain personal adulation, but to reassure their community that the connection to the transcendent was real and strong. One such demonstration was the ability to make plants grow miraculously, as reported in *The New York Times* in 1922.

> He [Zuni Medicine Man] takes a grain of corn from the medicine bag at his waist, thrusts the sacred arrow into the center of the sand square, withdraws it, drops the grain into the opening, and carefully smoothes down the sand. Resuming his seat, all the assembled chiefs light their pipes and smoke in silence. If the Great Spirit condescends to answer the prayer of the medicine man, as generally happens, the grain of corn will sprout and send forth a shoot. After an interval of fifteen or twenty minutes the sand seems undisturbed. Soon slender light green shoots of sprouting corn appear above the surface. The plant rises naturally and rapidly during the day. By the next sunrise the silk and tassel appear. By noon the ear and stalk have reached full maturity.[48]

Dr. William Brigham, who became the director of ethnology at Bishop Museum in Honolulu in 1888, was among the first to officially suggest that medicine powers are genuine. After observing the ability of Hawaiian kahunas to walk over molten lava, he concluded:

> There is no mistake. The kahunas use magic in their fire walking as well as in many other things.... It took me years to come to that understanding [of the reality of medicine powers] but it is my final decision after long study and observation.... It has been no easy task for me to come to believe magic possible. And even after I was dead sure it was magic I still had a deep-seated doubt concerning my own conclusions. You may say for me that I gave my word as a student and a gentleman that I would, and had, told the exact truth about what I saw and did.... There must be some sort of force used in exerting this control, if we can recognize it.[49]

Healing is not always dramatic and may need to take place over a period of extended and consistent effort. All people have the inner potential to heal and be healed but must pray and have faith that is strong through prayer, meditation, and dreams. When treating an individual, healers embark on a process of diagnosis in which they ask âtayôhkanak to grant them insight into the nature and root of the illness. Then they determine which Medicine Person holds the appropriate treatment or healing ritual.[50] The healer is merely a conduit for Manitow and the etheric world, so subjects must also be clear of mind and firm in their conviction in order to be restored.

Spiritual Illness

The Old Ones acknowledge the damage that negative relationships can wreak. Illness can be dysfunction brought about through broken relationships that result in evil. However, Elders state that Satan does not exist; evil exists only as long as humans fail to recognize their spiritual responsibilities and fail to overcome shortcomings.[51] They realize that mainstream society, which is in the depths of materialism and secularism, fails to adequately value our interconnectedness to others and everything around us. Soul sickness can manifest itself in forms such as substance abuse, abusive relationships, family dysfunction, anti-social behaviours, mental illness, and suicide.

Healing is restoration of harmony. Accord can be achieved only through acknowledging and respecting the supernal. Mosôm maintains that our relationship with the supernal world is just as important, if not more, than the relationship with the physical world. Those who have lost connection with the transcendent have become unbalanced and susceptible to various harms and dangers. We can witness many of these consequences in greed, callousness, criminality, and self-destructiveness. Humans need to regain balance in order to achieve self-healing.

All relationships include a feedback system, and all actions bring consequences. Elder Jimmy Myo states:

> We have laws as Indian people and those laws are not man made, they were given to us by God. . . . But in my law if you do such a thing [breach a sacred undertaking], even if no other human being is aware of it, you will always carry that for the

rest of your life. Some part of it here on earth, you will pay for it, something might happen, you might lose something more important than what you stole ... our law says that the amount we do not pay here on earth, when we die we will pay for it.[52]

Some might think that tribal life filled with ceremonies was boring and not very enjoyable compared to contemporary lifestyle. Yet, there was a much greater sense of individual purpose in Indigenous life. There was less stress since matters of importance would be dealt with when, and only when, the time was right. Most energy was spent in maintaining personal and social relationships through cultural activities such as singing, storytelling, and dancing. Europeans perceived this approach as laziness. However, in Indigenous thinking, preserving sacredness and social unity was the foremost priority. Cultural activities were a tremendous source of entertainment and mirth. Personal and financial gain were not priorities: there was no sense that one had to "keep up with the Joneses." There was little physical or mental illness due to poor lifestyle or lack of social support because culture, ceremony, and relationships helped people maintain a healthy balance in their lives.

Accomplishments of Indigenous Eden

The fruits of harmony and cyclical increases of abundance for future generations led to some of the healthiest and most harmonious societies on the planet for millennia. Over time, Indigenous Peoples would have been perfectly capable of making the scientific and technical developments that are taken for granted today, except that they would have been achieved within a context of spiritual wisdom rather than personal gain. However, their development would have been achieved only after considerable reflection and deliberation, and not driven by wealth, power, or prestige.

In 1492, the Americas had some of the most sophisticated civilizations on Earth in terms of resource husbandry. The population of the two continents is estimated to have been as high as 112,000,000,[53] constituting about 20 percent of the world's population. This compared to a European populace of 60 million, which was wracked with wars, plagues, and social unrest. The world's most massive pyramid loomed at Cholula, Mexico. The Aztecs had institutions of higher education called calmecac that taught spiritual knowledge, systems of astronomy, mathematics, architecture, religion, and healing. The sophisticated Aztec calendar included twenty-two cycles of fifty-two years each, which, when completed, constituted a cosmic cycle of creation and destruction.[54]

Monuments to the Heavens

Teotihuacan, a pre-contact city of 125,000, was one of the largest urban habitations in the world at the turn of the millennium. It was a peaceful centre of multiculturalism and a testament to the efficacy of Indigenous relationship building, both at the public and personal levels. Ironically, little is known about the original occupants of the pyramid complex or even if Teotihuacan was its original name. Destruction of Indigenous records by Spanish authorities did not help.[55]

Today the awe-inspiring pyramids of Teotihuacan loom over the arid plains forty kilometres northeast of Mexico City.[56] Called the City of the Gods, Teotihuacan, like other ancient pyramids and monuments, honours the heavens. Upon arriving at the site, one makes one's way past ubiquitous vendors selling obsidian carvings of the gods of the Pyramid of the Sun and Pyramid of the Moon. Ornate blankets and paintings depict the feathery serpent Quetzalcoatl, intermediary between the heavens and earth and god of knowledge. Climbing the steep 250 steps to the top of the Pyramid of the Sun gives one a sense of the once great splendor of this civilization. One can only marvel at the social organization and technical skills required to create the vast array of pyramids that stretch four kilometres along the Avenue of the Dead (more appropriately, Avenue of the Spirits). At the north end of the avenue lies the smaller Pyramid of the Moon. To the south, in the area once frequented by artisans who produced masks, figurines, and ornaments of jade, quartz, or obsidian, stands the Pyramid of Quetzalcoatl.

Along with being home to some of the largest pyramids in the world, Indigenous lands in what we now call southern North America were dotted with sacred sites that paid homage to the empyrean. It is believed that the three main pyramids at Teotihuacan are aligned to accord with the three central stars of Orion in a manner similar to the pyramids at Giza.[57] Solar projection of the Sun Dagger in Chaco Canyon, New Mexico, reveals the summer solstice, spring and fall equinoxes, and the cycles of the moon.[58]

The Mexica, a marginal tribe, arrived at Lake Texcoco around 1250 CE, having chosen the site through a sacred vision where an eagle perched on a cactus while devouring a snake. There they founded Tenochtitlan, site of modern-day Mexico City. The Spaniards marvelled at its wide clean streets with ornate buildings and botanical gardens that stood in contrast to some unsanitary disease-ridden centres of Europe. With an estimated 200,000 inhabitants, Tenochtitlan was bigger than Paris, the largest city in Europe, which had a population of 185,000 at the time.[59]

The Aztec lived in a region where cataclysmic volcanic eruptions and devastating earthquakes occurred. They understood that they had previously undergone four apocalypses and were living in time of the Fifth Sun. Their Supreme Being, Ometeotl, had four sons, including the warlike Huitzilopochtli, the reigning deity of Tenochtitlan. According to their beliefs, the brothers fought at night, and only if things were in balance would the sun rise again. It was a dark age in which their deity of knowledge, Quetzalcoatl, was in exile. In the battle of light against darkness, if the sun failed to rise from the depths of the darkness, famine and death would come. In order to fortify themselves for the battle against the dark, the "gods" required steady offerings of life-energy. This became the justification for human sacrifice. The people were seized with fear in a world that seemed intent on destroying them at the slightest whim. The Aztecs pursued the Wars of the Flowers with neighbouring city-states for the primary purpose of obtaining captives who were used as sacrificial victims.

Unfortunately, the Aztecs and their place in history are most often associated with gruesome accounts of human sacrifice. However, the spiritual meaning and role of this ritual needs to be understood. The Aztec ritual was an extreme extension of flesh offerings that were a widespread practice in the Indigenous Americas. Taking a small cutting of the flesh as part of a ceremonial offering was regarded as one of the most personal and powerful sacrifices that could be made to secure supernatural favour. The more powerful the nation, the greater its responsibility for maintaining reciprocity with the otherworldly. That sacrifice, however, was carried to an unhealthy extreme in Meso-America.

Spaniard conquistadors immediately associated human sacrifices with torture and wickedness, though similar barbarity occurred in Spain during the Inquisitions. The Catholic Church found human sacrifice abhorrent and ascribed it to Satan—justification to annihilate Aztec civilization.

Tenuous Cities

Tikal on what is called the Mayan Riviera is one of the better-known ancient religious centres found throughout Mexico. The magnificent centres had impressive pyramid temples including astral observatories, as the Maya were avid observers of the sky. The El Caracol observatory at Chichen Itza was used to monitor the movements of Venus, understood to be the embodiment of Quetzacoatl.[60] Mayans also claim achievements in mathematics, such as the concept of zero.

Around 900 CE, Mayan cities collapsed and became so overgrown with vegetation that some are only now being uncovered. It is a spectacular example of the disintegration of a major civilization with little apparent cause. Archaeologists theorize that their demise had to do with the area's climate and fragile water resources. Over-population began to overwhelm the Mayan's relationship with the natural habitat. This brought about increased risk that humans would damage their surroundings and over-exploit nature. Such actions carried consequences such as, entire Mayan communities vanishing. Because they had a good understanding of what was going on, the Maya accepted nature's agenda rather than fighting against it.

Cahokia, near modern day St. Louis, had a population of about 20,000 at the time of contact in the 1600s. It was the largest pre-contact habitation north of Mexico and was about the same size as London in 1100 CE. A large ceremonial mound reminiscent of Meso-American pyramids dominated the settlement, following a 4,000-year tradition of mound building. The structure was the equivalent of a ten-storey building and its base was as wide as that of the Great Pyramid of Giza. Cahokia was a hub of continental trading networks. Mounds of the Adena culture, found throughout the Ohio Valley region, were places of interment. Objects including pipes, pottery, and bracelets, were included with the burials. The existence of such sites over much of eastern North America is proof of widespread cultural interplay.

Inca civilization reached a remarkable level of achievement. Tawantnsuyu, the Inca domain, spanned almost the entire west coast of South America. A transportation system that included roads and bridges extended nearly 4,000 kilometres and tied the region together. Messengers delivered goods and conveyed diploma-cy.[61] Perhaps the greatest Inca achievement was the proliferation of agricultural and medicinal plants that they cultivated or harvested. These included potato, tomato, maize, quinoa, peanuts, peppers, and coca leaves. The Inca developed terraces with aqueducts, creating an agricultural revolution that produced an astonishing variety of foodstuffs and medicines. Agriculture was carefully blended with the natural environment. Extracts such as quinine, impressive walls constructed with massive tight-fitting rocks that withstood earthquakes, and a highly organized system of record keeping were among other accomplishments. Their economy flourished on barter alone and did not employ a formal currency.

The Gate of the Sun, part of an extensive sacred site at Tiwan-aco in Bolivia, predated the Inca. At 13,000 feet elevation, it was the highest city of the ancient world. Tiwanaco was a powerful cer-emonial centre that commanded reverence and attracted peaceful pilgrimage from the large surrounding area. The site showcased the arrival of the sun as it shone through the Gate of the Sun during the winter solstice.

Fruits of Stewardship

Amerindians made achievements in science and technology compa-rable to that of other parts of the world. Advances in architecture and astronomy reflected sacred inquiry about humanity's place in the universe. Meso-Americans developed three calendars, including a 365-day calendar, a 260-day calendar based upon the orbit of Venus, and a Long Count calendar marking progression through a fifty-two-year cycle after which the renewal of creation occurred.[62] The difference in the approach of Amerindians and colonizers, however, is that Indigenous advances were not driven primarily by human ambition or profit; they were accomplished within a context of sanctity where humans behaved as stewards of nature. Compared to contemporary society that measures success in terms of exploitation of nature for economic growth, Indigenous societies gauged their progress in terms of health and harmony.[63]

Indigenous Peoples of the Americas were the world's most successful cultivators, for example nurturing 3,000 varieties of potato.[64] They developed three-fifths of crops now cultivated worldwide. Julio Valladolid Rivera, a Peruvian expert on "ritual agriculture" emphasizes their traditional technique of collaborating with nature.

> In the Andean concept of life, everything is alive—the hills, the stars, the rivers. Everything is alive. And everything is our family. Even the dead are alive.... The whole family including the hills, the rivers, and the dead, with affection and respect raise their plants, their animals, and their countryside. Everything is raised. But not only do people raise the plants with affection and respect, but also the plants raise them. This wisdom is the valuable thing they have, taken into consideration with Western thought, taking into account the survival of life on earth.... The agriculture of the future will resemble more the agriculture of the first peoples than the commercial agriculture of today. The conception of life must be reinvigorated because it is the guarantee of maintaining life on the planet.[65]

Gregory Cajete elaborates on the involvement of the supernal: "Native farmers 'negotiated' with their gardens and with the spirits of nature on their garden's behalf. They negotiated with the sun and rain for just the right amount of warmth and moisture to ensure their harvest. They negotiated with insects, birds and other animals on behalf of their gardens. Prayer and ritual were applied to request the goodwill of various other living energies that comprised the greater community in which the gardens were placed."[66]

A multitude of healing aids and cures that revolutionized the modern practice of medicine were developed while its Old-World equivalent amounted to little more than alchemy. Andeans discovered that quinine derived from bark relieved the symptoms of malaria. Aspirin, a derivative of the willow tree, alleviated headaches and other discomforts. In the Andes, the Quechua make widespread use of the coca leaf as a therapeutic plant. Derivatives of cocaine, including Novocain, have become staples as anesthetics for surgery. Indigenous Medicine Persons also employed treatments that included tourniquets and trepanning of the skull.[67]

Upholding values of respect for all and maintaining the Protocols for healing kept the Indigenous world in relative harmony for millennia. Such a strategy was intended to provide advantageous conditions for countless future generations. With their reputation as healers, it was a cruel irony that Old-World diseases would strike the greatest blow to Indigenous societies: Tens of millions perished from alien diseases within a few years of contact.[68]

Another unrecognized area of Indigenous contribution is in politics and administration. Indigenous societies found ways to balance personal liberty and collective responsibility. European systems, in comparison, were marked by a rigid structure based upon power and wealth. Benjamin Franklin recognized the wisdom of Haudenosaunee governance and advised the founders of the United States to adopt their model of the Great Law of Peace. Thomas Jefferson was also strongly supportive of the Indigenous model for creating a federal system in which each state had an equal voice.[69]

Economies of Abundance

Traditional economies were fundamentally different from their European counterparts because of the principles of sharing prosperity and distributing wealth versus accumulation and greed. In the words of Cree Elder James Carpenter:

I have never heard Native people say that they own the land. The land is for us to use and to live, this is where the food is, fish, rabbits, otter or any other animals for food. We know when freeze-up will happen. The Native person will know what he will need in order to hunt and fish. Whenever he meets another Native person on the land and if he has an abundance of fish, he will invite the person to fish there with him or he will tell another person you can trap with me where there are weasel, muskrat, and otter. That's what the Native person says to his fellow Natives. The Native person treats the other with love. The Native person will not say to another person 'Don't trap there.' He will never say to another person 'That is my land.'[70]

The Potlatch, a mechanism of social organization found among northwest coast cultures, was based on the principle of giving away wealth. This ceremony could be held at significant junctures in the life of a community, including births, weddings, political agreements, or deaths. It also functioned as a means of rectifying wrongdoings and bringing about collective healing. Goods distributed could include food, blankets, household items, canoes, and even more valuable items depending on the purpose of the potlatch. The more generous gained status and created ties of gratitude. Missionaries and government officials sought to have the Potlatch banned as a useless and wasteful activity that inhibited civilization. This resulted in the passing of an amendment to the 1884 *Indian Act* that included imprisonment for up to six months for participation in a Potlatch.[71] Other groups, including the Cree, held give-away events but they were less overt and extensive.

A Culture of Life

One could describe the totality of experience in Indigenous Eden as a "culture of life"—one that promotes meaningfulness, well-being, and respect for all life. Some might think that traditional life must have been tedious. There were no televisions, computers, fast cars, or money to spend! Yet observers, such as explorers who had early contact, reported very happy and contented populations. The reasons for the contentment were appropriate, respectful, and positive relationships, not only among individuals and groups, but also with the natural and supernatural environments.

Early colonists and missionaries criticized their charges as being lazy. They accused them of spending too much time in allegedly useless ceremonies and in dances and singing described as debauchery. But these outside observers missed the point. The amount of time spent in such activities was important for constantly refreshing Indigenous Peoples' connection to the numinous and to remind them of their place in Creation. As well, ceremonies played a key role in healing individuals and groups. The emphasis on social activities such as sharing, dancing, or storytelling contributed towards social cohesion and harmony. What is not entertaining or fulfilling about positive social environments or vibrant activities like singing or dancing? Indigenous Peoples had little to worry about when they were in harmony with their cosmos.

Vulnerability of Indigenous Eden

Aboriginal societies were not perfect utopias. While Indigenous Eden enjoyed a high level of harmony, it had its imperfections and vulnerabilities. The Cree and Anishinaabe had no concept of the devil and hell; however, it was possible to go off the Good Path and commit serious errors. Cree and Anishinaabe societies grappled with the most dangerous force that threatened their world and all of its hard-won accomplishments. This threat was Wetiko (Windigo in Anishinaabemowin), a fearsome monster who was said to freeze human hearts, transforming them into ravenous, greedy cannibals.[72] Essentially, the force of greed represents the lower self, that which becomes preoccupied with individual over collective good. It values the benefits of the material world over those of spirituality. So dangerous was Wetiko that, if unaddressed, the person who had succumbed to it was banished or even killed. Its destructive influence could not be allowed to spread. This spirit of greed was the closest Cree and Anishinaabe people had to a devil. But given the right treatment, Wetiko could always be kept at bay and eventually vanquished.[73]

What has been termed "Wetiko psychosis" was not a mental illness as portrayed by psychologists but, rather, was the personification of selfishness that destroyed family and community bonds.[74] Wetiko was associated with the activity of European traders: "You [trader] will introduce the Windigo who will cross the Atlantic and consume human flesh."[75] In an incident on Hudson's Bay, the killing of European traders was reported. Those traders had hidden a cache of food from their starving Indian companions. While observers might see this as an act of brutality, from the Indigenous point of view a severe violation of the Law of Relationships had been committed.[76] An individual who put his own welfare before that of the collective was deemed possessed by the fearsome Wetiko. That person suddenly became voraciously greedy and dangerously cannibalistic. The traders' murders were not something personal. They were the result of the spectre of selfishness and greed that had to be eliminated lest it infect and inhabit others. In Indigenous thinking, succumbing to this evil would be catastrophic to social harmony.[77]

One could describe today's devil as Wetiko who can no longer be vanquished and has, therefore, become an ever-present and inescapable fixture of today's moral landscape. What purveyors of history are loathe to admit is that if the original cultures of the Americas had been allowed to continue unmolested or if the newcomers had been more respectful, a far healthier and more stable civilization would have emerged.

Spanish conquistador Hernán Cortés marvelled at the grandeur, cleanliness, and social order of the Aztec capital Tenochtitlan, which stood in stark contrast to some European cities of the time. People were well nourished with the many varieties of foodstuffs, such as potatoes, which would eventually become staples around the world, as well as tomatoes, chili peppers, and quinoa. Spanish conquistadors came across Inca rooms waist-high in gold. However, the magnificent accomplishments of the Indigenous Peoples of the Americas was not respected and little of their legacy is acknowledged today; it has been relegated to the dustbin of history.

Following European contact and the devastation of virgin soil, epidemics eradicated 95 percent of community populations at one fell swoop. The loss of agriculture, combined with violence from conquest, caused the Indigenous population to fall to a shadow of its former size. Today, only six million of Mexico's nearly 100 million people self-identify as Indigenous. A similar situation prevails in Brazil where only 900,000 of the country's 200 million people are counted as Indigenous. The strength of Indigenous Peoples of the Americas lay in their relationship with their land, something that would guarantee longevity and prosperity for millennia. However, that birthright was stolen by outsiders who usurped the land's resources for their own selfish goals of power and wealth. Can the calamities that brought about the end of ancient ideologies and cultural ways be traced to the emergence in the Old World and the phenomenon of "civilization"?

CHAPTER 3
BETRAYING INDIGENOUS EDEN

Having examined the characteristics of Indigenous Eden, it is instructive to contrast that with how development in more human-focused civilization unfolded. According to archaeologists, modern humans, *Homo sapiens*,[1] appeared as far back as 200,000 BCE. Others contend that DNA analysis indicates that these origins could go back even further. They theorize that the human population was initially miniscule and tenuous at about 15,000 individuals due to adverse climatic conditions such as drought. It was only around 70,000 years ago that people began to thrive and their numbers expanded. These ancient folks were little different in appearance from people today and would not stand out in a modern crowd. Common sense tells us that "primitive" persons must have been able to make effective decisions that enabled them to survive for millennia and, therefore, would not have been the empty-headed subjects that imperialists made them out to be. They must have had an ideology that effectively framed their interaction with the world for the at least 190,000 years that preceded "civilization."

Prehistoric or Indigenous?

What do we know about the thinking of "primitive people"? Most of us have seen stereotypical representations of prehistoric cavemen walking around making grunting sounds, carrying clubs, and occasionally whacking others over the head. But, in fairness, these early humans deserve more credit than that. Phenomena such as mortuary rites and cave paintings that clearly set people apart from animals began to emerge at least 35,000 years ago. What makes sense from the Indigenous point of view is that these early folks were spiritually aware, revelled in the gifts of the Creator, and were abundantly respectful and thankful for their existence.

The term prehistoric is also incorrect because it implies no history when, in reality, early humans simply did not record history according to modern standards. Indigenous Peoples had oral methods of keeping track of events and had prodigious memories for such details. It is likely that in the earliest years of human existence our Ancestors felt so beholden to the physical world around them that they barely thought of altering or dominating it. Thus, for their first 165,000 years on Earth, humans attempted to harmoniously fit in with Creation so there was nary a trace left of their activities. There was no domestication of plants or pets—everything was to be respected exactly as the Creator intended. Then we, as distant observers, begin to see the stirrings of self-consciousness. Ancient people began leaving handprints on cave walls and making rudimentary images of animals. But why did they do this?

From a traditional perspective, which is essentially a spirit-centred consciousness, there must have been some justification for creating such images. Perhaps the Ancients had simply dreamed that they could and should do these things. In Indigenous tradition, all inspiration emanates from the spirit. Perhaps the birth of humanity can be likened to the birth of an individual. An infant's initial experience and awareness of life is one of being overwhelmed. Gradually one becomes more aware of one's surroundings and becomes more capable of navigating those surroundings. How one decides to behave in a new environment depends increasingly on that individual's maturity.

Anthropologist Claude Lévi-Strauss speculated about the "primitive intellect":

I see no reason why mankind should have waited until recent times to produce minds of the caliber of a Plato or an Einstein. Already two or three hundred thousand years ago, there were probably men of similar capacity. . . . Certainly the properties to which the savage mind has access are not the same as those which have commanded the attention of scientists. The physical world is approached from opposite ends in the two cases: one is supremely concrete the other supremely abstract; one proceeds from the angle of sensible qualities, and the other from that of formal qualities.[2]

Lévi-Strauss was giving a more balanced portrayal of the primitive mind than others have. The Ancients could be practical when needed. He pointed out that while early people would have a similar potential to humans today, their ideology and motivations would have been entirely different. Indigenous people would agree with anthropologist Ashley Montagu, who astutely observed that "prehistoric man was on the whole, a more peaceful, cooperative, unwarlike, unaggressive creature than we are, and we of the civilized world have gradually become more and more dysfunctional, more aggressive and hostile, and less and less cooperative where it matters most, that is, in human relations. The meaning we have put to the term 'savage' is more correctly applied to ourselves."[3]

Denigrating Prehistoric Peoples

We have all seen the cartoons about prehistoric peoples. In a Carpe Diem cartoon (Figure 2) that appeared recently in my local newspaper,[4] the leader of the pack gives his followers disastrous instructions to pursue the berries over the cliff because he failed to distinguish between hunting and gathering. Really? These jokes, while intended to evince a chuckle, are also offensive in that they play an insidious role—to discount, minimize, and obliterate the notion that ancient "pre-civilized" peoples had any credible thought or philosophy. Not only are prehistoric people seen as stupid, it is also suggested that they displayed the worst of human traits, such as brutishness, as in cartoons of the caveman knocking his female partner over the head. One begins

FIRST DAY AS LEADER OF THE PACK AND A NERVOUS GROGHULT MAKES THE CLASSIC MISTAKE OF CONFUSING HUNTING WITH GATHERING.

Figure 2: Cartoon ridiculing primitive humans. SOURCE: © 2017 Niklas Eriksson/Bulls, Dist. by King Features Syndicate, Inc.

to suspect that this crude portrayal of prehistoric humans served not only to set them apart but also to wrongly paint them as intellectually and morally inferior to today's civilized person. Prehistoric peoples are no better understood by the civilized world than Indigenous Peoples are comprehended today.

Common sense dictates that these early folks were conscious and made deliberate and intelligent responses to their environment. One should prefer descriptions by experts who state that prehistoric people looked so much like us that one could not pick them out of a crowd today. Discounting their intelligence and integrity is not only a slight against Indigenous culture, it is also a disparagement of our Ancestors, including those of us who are "civilized."

Prehistoric life would not have been a utopia, and archaeologists are quick to point out examples of discovery of an ancient human apparently killed with a weapon. Some people see this as proof that the Ancients were all just like us today. If humans today can be brutal, it must have started with our Ancestors. However, in the Cree/Saulteaux tradition, individuals whose behaviours had become destructive were understood to be possessed by the evil spirit personified by Wetiko and were dealt with quickly, sometimes killed. This not only protected the physical, but also the spiritual welfare of the collective. There is no reason to believe that prehistoric peoples did not have a highly developed moral sense.

Another example is often cited to suggest that ancient peoples lacked respect for the environment. About 11,000 years ago, around the time of the Clovis hunter culture, many of the large mammals of North America died off.[5] The extinctions happened very suddenly, leading some scientists to conclude humans must have decimated them. These disappearances included mammoths, horses, camels, and armadillos. Archaeologists arguing against this notion observe that for prehistoric people to have killed them would have required a monumental and sustained slaughter. Other species of small mammals and mollusks not hunted by man also went extinct in the same era. Close examination reveals that many of the large animal extinctions occurred prior to the arrival of the Clovis hunters. The fossil record does not, in fact, support the hypothesis of large-scale hunting. Many paleontologists believe that climate change following the last ice age is the more likely culprit.

But the portrayal of ancient humans as indiscriminate hunters fits in nicely with those who want to reinforce the stereotype of prehistoric hunters as wanton and cold-blooded killers, just as many of today's sportsmen are. It is a tradition of demonizing ancient cultures to imply they could not have had a moral sense or respect for their fellow creatures. "The overkill hypothesis lives on not because of archaeologists and paleontologists who are expert in the area, but because it keeps getting repeated by those who are not," claims archaeologist Donald Grayson.[6]

From an Indigenous perspective, localized overhunting may have occasionally occurred. But this does not place the situation in the same category as unfettered exploitation of animals for sport or profit. Indigenous Peoples always regarded animals as our spiritual kin and did not desire that they be harmed. It would certainly appear to be contrary to prehistoric hunters' ideology to overkill. If anything, they would have understood the importance of creating harmonious relationships and constantly refreshing those relationships through ceremony to ensure that their animal relatives thrived.

A television documentary called *Origins: The Journey of Mankind: Spark of Civilization* begins by showing a group of prehistoric people fleeing in terror from a pack of wolves.[7] This scenario is revealing for a couple of reasons. In the Cree tradition, we regard the gifts of the Creator as acts of benevolence. It was the beneficence of the Creator that sustained us. Our value system was one of respect, bravery, and love. We would not have seen wolves and nature as threatening. In fact, wolves are honoured in many cultures for their characteristics of caring for their offspring and family structure. This does not mean that animals cannot be dangerous; they were to be treated with respect. When animals were hunted, their spirits were thanked through prayer. In this manner, humans managed to maintain good relationships. And animals, being conscious in their own right, would not perceive humans in a negative light.

The humans in the documentary had succumbed to fear because they did not have a positive relationship with nature. The absence of bravery grew out of a lack of trust in the Creator's benevolence. The group looked unkempt, as if they never cared for themselves. Rather than reflecting Indigenous views of nature, the fearful actions portrayed in the show seem to exhibit more the type of reactions that a Hollywood scriptwriter who has never spent a night alone in the woods would have. It is a ridiculous portrayal of prehistoric peoples and is, frankly, very insulting.

The documentary promotes the idea that some of the Ancients did become fearful of nature; therefore, it became an enemy to be subdued. In order to accomplish this, it was necessary to create civilization. One needed to not only protect people from nature, but also to ensure that nature never became a problem again. This attitude gradually led to disengagement and contempt for nature. As that conquest of nature progressed, people began to increasingly believe that they had the God-given right to "fill the earth and subdue it."[8] Whatever happened, it was not in accordance with Indigenous spiritual values.

Early World Population

Archaeologists believe that civilization blossomed around the urban centre, Ur, in Sumeria, around 4500 BCE. Ur is considered the earliest example of urbanization with a population of around 80,000, including slaves. It was a premier centre for trade in its heyday and was surrounded by eight-metre-high earthen ramparts. Some scholars believe Ur was the birthplace of the patriarch Abraham of the Old Testament. Laws of Ur were similar to, but preceded, Babylon's Code of Hammurabi, which advocated an "eye for an eye and a tooth for a tooth." From a tiny number, those considered to be part of civilization and no longer Indigenous grew until they became the majority of world population around 1820 as indicated in Figure 3.

200,000	BCE	0 of 15,000	0% non-Indigenous
6,000	BCE	80,000 of 12 million	1% non-Indigenous
1492	CE	60 million of 550 million	11% non-Indigenous
1820	CE	800 million of 1.6 billion	50% non- Indigenous
2018	CE	7.3 billion of 7.7 billion	95% non-Indigenous

Figure 3: Growth of Non-Indigenous World Population[9]

The Idea of Civilization

A major study sanctioned in 1963 by the United Nations affiliated International Commission for a History of the Scientific and Cultural Development of Mankind investigated the origins of human civilization. The study involved a multitude of scholars, including: "art critics and artists will be needed as well as of art historians; of anthropologists and students of comparative religion as well as of divines and theologians; of archaeologists as well as classical scholars; of poets and relative men of letters as well as of professors of literature; as well as the whole-hearted support of the historians."[10] Significantly, the study reveals the authors' perception of how human civilization arose.

> The opening of any full history of man must be its Book of Genesis, the story of man's creation. . . . The creature who has now changed the whole face of habitable earth will be seen coming out of Africa only a little better equipped than the apes that were his poor cousins. . . . For the very many thousands of years before man was fully man in his physical and mental capacities, his way of life, his culture, remained that of the natural world. This part of the History will therefore carry man on to the time less than 10,000 years ago when he began to establish himself as a farmer on certain favored regions of the Old World. Here is the proper point at which to hand on the story to those who can tell how once man had achieved

the agricultural way of life which is still the basis of our existence, his mental powers could flourish and put out rich and various fruits of human civilization. . . . At the beginning of it all, position is rather different, for in looking back we do not see a stretch of human history leading up to our point of continuation, but instead an immense vista of natural history. A tremendous perspective of landscape and living forms, but not a glimmer of science or culture.[11]

The study favours the theory of evolution that maintains that humans evolved from animals. "What will prove most important to remember is that our species did not only inherit from its past its bodily equipment, dominated by its subtly elaborated brain, but also highly charged emotional centres and all of the strange ancient furniture of the unconscious mind. Man emerged bringing with him hate, fear and anger."[12]

Civilization, as conceived by the study, is clearly predicated upon a rebellion against nature, specifically a rejection of and separation from the natural world. "While in many parts of the world, Europe among them, the hunters merely played the passive role of adjusting their habits to forest conditions, in some regions of south-west Asia men *were inspired to counter-attack against nature* [emphasis added] and make the momentous revolution in human history that accompanied the domestication of cattle, pigs, sheep and goats and the cultivation of wheat and barley."[13]

Subsequent scholars who write about the history of the world and the rise of civilization continue to use this interpretation.[14] They write about how humans gathered near rivers, began to domesticate animals, and aggressively cultivated the land about 6,000 years ago. The philosophy behind Indigenous approaches of respecting the validity of plants and animals in their own right is swapped for human control and economic advantage. Developing agriculture over long periods of time, humans began to claim parcels of land as their own and to acquire property, which implies some form of recognized ownership. A new type of human-centred web of life emerged. Vanished is the idea that humans are the most dependent of creatures, needing to be respectful and non-interfering with the Creator's gifts.

The word *civilization* itself centres on the root *civil*, which implies a behavioural compact between humans only. This makes sense as civilizations developed in conjunction with urbanization, a divorce from nature where groups of individuals assert their power not only over nature but also against individuals or groups viewed as competitors for limited resources. This mindset of dominating nature and exploiting resources and needing to maintain order among the civilized becomes the defining characteristic of civilization.

Ancient cultures prior to 6000 BCE are excluded from the definition of civilizations. This suggests the need for a word to distinguish those groups that refused to follow the so-called civilized path. I propose the word *ecolizations,* which reflects the idea that a compact of society should be holistic, including the interests of all created plant, animal, and spirit relatives. Among Indigenous Peoples, final authority always rested with acquiescence towards the spiritual worth of Creation, interrelatedness of life, and ongoing consultation with the supernal. "Uncivilized" is a compliment, as it indicates those who did not betray Creation by placing themselves above it as exploiters.

What Is Ancient?

One constantly hears the terms "ancient Egypt," "ancient Greece" or "ancient Rome." In context of overall human existence, societies like the Sumerians and Egyptians that are touted as the first civilizations are not really ancient but are only recent. The Sumerian civilization is the earliest documented, going back 6,000 years. Given a human presence of 200,000 years, that civilization emerged in the last 3 percent of the human epoch. This places them in the recent past. Only peoples who lived during the previous 97 percent of time should properly be labelled ancient. Granted, Sumerians did invent the useful tool of writing in about 3000 BCE. Their initial beliefs included deities associated with the sun, earth, water, wind, and agriculture and their priests mediated between terrestrial and cosmic forces. However, their deities became increasingly concerned with the impact that humans were having on life. Interestingly, the first recorded wars occurred in Sumeria; it should not be a surprise that the Sumerians also had a god of war.

The original Persian belief system, Zoroastrianism, flourished about 4,000 years ago. In it one can see the foundations of Abrahamic religions. In the Persian worldview, there was only one Supreme Being, but it was acknowledged that humans had been granted free will. Along with the privilege of free will came responsibility for one's actions. That included caring for and protecting the natural world. There was only one true path that could be followed, and it required good thoughts and actions. Conforming to the true path ensured happiness, and disobedience allowed evil to enter society and cause chaos. Living a life of evil resulted in consignment to a hell-like place of darkness and discomfort in the afterlife.[15]

Along with increasing onus on human responsibility for their actions comes peoples' need to police their own behaviours. The Code of Hammurabi, said to be the template for the modern legal system, originated in Babylonia around 1750 BCE. It included nearly three hundred laws that are best described as an eye for an eye and tooth for a tooth approach. For example, law 196 reads: "If a man destroy the eye of another man, they shall destroy his eye. If one man break a man's bone, they shall break his bone. If one destroy the eye of a freeman or break the bone of a freeman he shall pay one gold mina. If one destroy the eye of a man's slave or break the bone of a man's slave he shall pay one half his price."[16] Punishments varied according to one's gender and status, such as a free man or a slave. Such systems took positive relationships and accountability based on interaction with spirituality and increasingly placed them in the hands of elites to adjudicate.

Philosophy of War

Primitive war is described as involving raids and massacres. It is thought these raids were not well organized but were impulsive and included participants who were untrained. Again, this analysis shows profound ignorance of Indigenous practices. On the Plains, raids were a cultural institution intended to allow young men, and occasionally women, to hone and develop the virtue of bravery. The object was not to kill but to demonstrate bravery and skill. Counting coup was a gesture that showed that a brave literally held another person's life in his hands.[17] But it was accepted practice and more honourable to spare that life. Moreover, since developing bravery was a spiritual exercise, participants prepared themselves by undergoing cleansing ceremonies and rituals that could invoke the assistance of protector spirits.[18] History records that as European traders introduced guns and trade goods such as alcohol, violence spiralled out of control as Indigenous Peoples became dependent on the goods.[19] When epidemics struck, inflicting far more casualties than warfare, Indigenous philosophers believed that the Creator was punishing people for transgressions against their original laws.

When Indigenous Peoples fought conflicts, it was largely to prevent others from violating ancient values or to attempt to correct aggression and other negative behaviours. These were also exercises to demonstrate personal bravery as already indicated. Such occurrences were interpreted by civilized colonizers as being wars of conquest or to dispossess others of their resources. Researcher Joshua Mark theorizes that war mentality should be blamed entirely on the perceived unpredictability of tribalism.

> War grows naturally out of the tribal mentality . . . they usually view outsiders as dangerous and conflict against them as normal. . . . The coming of civilization therefore brought the need for organized bodies of shock troops. The tribe mentality always results in a dichotomy of an 'us' versus 'them' and engenders a latent fear of the 'other' whose culture is at odds with, or at least different from one's own. This fear, coupled with a desire to expand, or protect, necessary resources, often results in war.[20]

In a similar vein, another writer declared: "Pre-literate societies, even those organized in a relatively advanced way, were renowned for their studied cruelty."[21]

Civilization and Superiority

The rise of civilization has been accompanied by new ideologies that extol virtues of human strength, beauty, and superiority. Prime examples are the Greek theory of natural slavery that justified domination of the "uncivilized," and the actions of the Roman Empire in subjugating and supplanting Indigenous cultures throughout centuries of conquest.[22] Discourse justifying such actions pervades European philosophy and religion. It's most recent manifestation, the Enlightenment or Age of Reason, glorified human intellectual ability to the point it has become the ultimate solution and the substitute for spirituality.

The collapse of Indigenous ecolizations is consistently portrayed as having occurred because their systems were inferior. These societies were, in fact, wiser in the sense of spirituality and respect for human and natural relationships. Their strengths lay more in peace making than in devising methods to undermine and overthrow weaker peoples. Ecolizations collapsed not because they were inferior, but because of relentless persecution and dispossession by those addicted to aggression, greed, and lust for power. Original peoples could not stoop to the level and tactics of the oppressors lest they become just like them. All they could do was try to heal themselves.

The lack of comprehension of how ecolizations work together to promote balanced living through harmony and healing that is based upon spiritual traditions is appalling. Indigenous Peoples employed extensive mechanisms to ensure peaceful relationships between tribes, including intermarriage, engaging in welcoming and generosity, and sharing spiritual knowledge. The accusation that tribal peoples, who were acting to protect their legitimate interests, were barbarous is an example of the projection of behaviours of purportedly civilized peoples onto others.

Violence was not inherent to Indigenous cultures and is still resisted in modern civilization. Studies have found that during the American Civil War 90 percent of muskets found on the battlefield had not been fired, though the reasons for this may be complex. In World War II, only 20 percent of American servicemen actually fired at the enemy.[23] Most combatants are not in combat out of desire to kill but out of duty or having been coerced. Training for combat often involves the dehumanization of the other; some service members are able to destroy without remorse, but many others develop traumatic stress and other psychological illnesses.

Their inability or lack of desire to kill discounts the theory of violent human nature.

Ashley Montagu was one of the few theorists to buck the trend of positing inherent violence. He argued that childhood and socialization are primary factors in determining the propensity for societal conflict. Warfare is a product of human culture and history. He notes that societies that do not promote aggression are more peaceful than those that encourage it.[24] Indigenous philosophers would agree with that point of view.

Civilization and Oppression

Greek culture and philosophy glorified humankind's thought and fine art. However, while they are touted as the creators of democracy, such achievements only benefitted Greek citizens, who perceived that their civilization was superior. In reality, it was the slaves whose resources and labour made Greek prosperity possible. In fact, Indigenous cultures demonstrated more democratic and egalitarian characteristics.

Greek philosophers redefined the world in terms of order versus chaos, the latter being what they viewed as nature not under control. The idea that people are not born equal is endemic to Greek and Roman thinking. These societies were the first to embark on significant campaigns to subdue so-called uncivilized peoples, eventually controlling over half of the then known world. Using the philosophical theory of natural slavery, tribal peoples were subjugated in the belief that it was the proper place for the non-civilized. In other words, the seeds planted by the civilizing endeavour brought some cultures to perceive themselves as inherently superior to Indigenous populations.

The Greek Sophist thinking was the first to squarely focus on the human condition and meaning. Protagoras summed it up in his saying: "Man is the measure of all things." He believed that humanity must perfect itself, a narcissistic approach that demonstrated little humility.[25] Socrates was skeptical of the Sophist approach, asking pointed questions such as "What is true knowledge?" Socrates became a thorn in the side of Greek society for questioning the new morals, was charged with undermining civility, and sentenced to death.[26]

Aristotle is credited with creating the science of logic. He taught that one who practises such logic needs nothing more than one's mind, which makes that individual not only self-sufficient but also superior.[27] Aristotle espoused the proposition called the Theory of Natural Slavery. In his treatise *Politics*, he explains that a slave, common in Greek society, is "anyone who, while being human, is by nature not his own but of someone else...he is a piece of property."[28] Aristotle continues: "They are in this state if their work is the use of the body, and if this is the best that can come from them—they are slaves by nature. For them it is better to be ruled in accordance with this sort of rule." This justified the dominance of some humans, in this case civilized Greeks, over others. While Socrates was hesitant, Aristotle heartily indulged in "eating of the fruit of the Tree of Knowledge of Good and Evil." The Spanish and other colonists later used this logic to justify enslaving Indigenous Peoples around the world.

In 343 BCE, Aristotle became the teacher of Alexander of Macedonia, later known as Alexander the Great (356 to 323 BCE). Among other things, Aristotle impressed upon his student that the Greeks were superior to all other people. Alexander was an attentive student. By age eighteen, he was commanding troops and quelling rebellious city-states. By age twenty, he had become head of the Greek army. Seeking to conquer, plunder, and enslave Persians, Alexander attacked Persian King Darius, killing tens of thousands and selling survivors into slavery. He repeated this pattern time and again in the eastern Mediterranean, Egypt, Babylon, and India.[29] Alexander's depredations were unrivalled up to his time. From Aristotle's point of view, his student was a glowing success.

However, from the perspective of the Indigenous Seven Virtues (fasting, sharing, parenting, learning, teaching, praying, and meditating), Alexander violated virtually every value. The ancient Greeks had lost humility, believing that their limited knowledge and reasoning somehow gave them special privilege. They had lost respect for others. Love was not for others, but for the power and wealth of their own. They were generous only to themselves, distributing goods stolen from those who had been conquered. They were not honest in the vein of the Socratic tradition. Observers marvelled at their aggressiveness, believing it to be connected to courage. However, the courage of the Seven Virtues is doing the right thing, even when it is to one's disadvantage. Finally, the Greeks had lost wisdom. In their philosophical musings, they began focusing more on the material than on the spiritual and lost their appreciation for the fundamental importance of positive relationships. Like other civilizations of this nature, they "lived by the sword and died by the sword." Greek and Roman practices, inevitably forced upon conquered Indigenous populations to pacify them, set the template for later civilization.

Roman Subjugation

Rome grew into an urban centre of around 80,000 before, like Ur, they sparked aggressive behaviours towards neighboring cities. The mythological founders of Rome, Romulus and Remus, violently fought over power, setting the tone for Roman behaviours. Mars was widely worshipped as a god of war. Nobility and stature were obtained through the cult of manhood and the ruthless exercise of power. Romans began to intimidate smaller centres, forcing them to join their endeavour or be destroyed. After defeating their main competitor, the Carthaginians, the Romans believed they could control the entire world. Subjugating weaker groups and forcing them to become allies was their primary empire-building strategy.

The Romans were following in the footsteps of Alexander the Great. While they could not boast the philosophy and refinement of the Greeks, they took great pride in their virulence and lust for power. Historian J.P. Balsdon notes: "The Romans were God's own people in fact. Spaniards had the advantage over them in point of numbers, Gauls had physical strength, Carthaginians in sharpness, Greeks in culture, native Latins and Italians in common sense; yet Rome had conquered them all and acquired her vast empire because in piety and appreciation of the omnipotence of the gods . . . Romans were a master-race."[30] Romans were infatuated with the art of warfare and honed their military skills to the point where it was guaranteed that "barbarians" could not withstand their calculated military tactics.[31] So certain were their emperors of their place in the universe that they declared themselves to be gods.

Rome was fully committed to the guiles of materialism—fine food, clothes, public baths, and entertainments of chariot races and gladiator fighting. As with the Greeks, taking slaves was justified and widespread. A common benefit of conquest, slaves were engaged as household servants, labourers, business employees, prostitutes, or gladiators. The Coliseum epitomized the cruelty of Rome's rule. It served to demonstrate how Romans held the power of life and death not only over human vassals, but over wildlife itself. Drunk with power and wealth, morals degenerated to the point where intrigue, betrayal, fratricide, and matricide were standard behaviours at the highest levels of society.[32]

Tribal peoples were seen as inferior. The Gauls were "not clever ... highly incredulous and they were braggarts ... they were impetuous and improvident" but "collapsed quickly if faced by resolute opposition. . . . The British were hardly civilized and were inhospitable, only better than the Irish who were without any redeeming virtues."[33] The Romans believed that all their wars were just and that they were doing conquered peoples a favour by bringing civilization to them. "When Rome conquered a foreign people, it did it for that people's own good."[34]

The Romans found the perfect combination of aggressiveness and military efficiency and tactics to inflict maximum damage on opponents. This unleashed a potent force that conquered the then known world. In their way were Indigenous ecolizations that only wanted to exist harmoniously on their own territory. Their cultures were not a threat to Rome; however, they stood in the way of Rome being able to exploit their resources. Beginning with Julius Caesar (100 BCE to 44 BCE) and extending to the Holy Roman Empire's Charlemagne (742 to 814 CE), Rome embarked on fierce campaigns to subjugate all people within their reach.[35]

The Romans exploited Indigenous proclivity to create peaceful relationships. But after building relationships and taking control of a region, they divested the local population of its wealth and resources. Julius Caesar, conqueror of the Gauls, began his conquest by attempting to buy allegiances. When leaders refused, he agreed to meet them on the pretext of making peace and then ambushed and mercilessly slaughtered them.[36] In one notable campaign, Caesar embarked on a genocidal massacre of Germanic tribes near the Meuse River. The tribes had petitioned for a truce, but Caesar gave the order to slaughter all—as many as 200,000 men, women, and children.[37] Caesar is reputed to have killed a million people and enslaved another million during his campaign.

In Britain, Celtic tribes agreed to become allies with the Romans in return for protection, but would find themselves exploited and ruthlessly put down if they rebelled. Indigenous Peoples could not fathom the deceit and brutality that "civilized peoples" were willing to employ in order to establish dominance. Back in Rome, far-flung Indigenous tribes were described as backward and ignorant, and deserving of subjugation.[38] Over the centuries, Rome conquered North Africa and Spain, and later Greece and the Balkans, Egypt, and Mesopotamia. The Romans created sophisticated administrative mechanisms to monitor and control the population and resources of the vanquished. Matters remained peaceful as long as subjugated peoples appreciated the benefits of the empire, whether that be prosperity or the distractions of entertainment for the citizenry. Any threat to the established power structure was dealt with quickly and forcibly. Conquered peoples were subjected to Roman ways and were required to pay tribute and supplement the ranks of the military.[39] The "protection" rendered to vassals resulted in Rome's version of peace under the sword: Pax Romana. The promise of calm and prosperity would continue so long as the population remained docile.

Template of the Pax Romana

Conquest by Rome and its successor, the Holy Roman Empire, ushered in an entirely different set of values from those of Indigenous Peoples. This would also be true of the other Abrahamic religion, Islam. The two traditions later became major competitors in global expansion and the subjugation of the original populations.

Caesar's successor, Augustus, perfected the skills of deceit and treachery. Others, like Caligula and Nero, demonstrated the depths of greed and cruelty they could sink to, such as committing matricide. Killing members of one's family was not an obstacle to ambition. Intrigue followed upon intrigue as aspiring emperors fought for control. Such acts were inconceivable in Indigenous societies.

Jewish beliefs as reflected in the Tanak, which forms the basis of the Old Testament, reveal the strong emphasis on lineages of chosen people with whom God had entered into a special covenant. While the image of humanity was increasingly included in the portrayal of deities, Judaism created a new religious vision with man appearing in the form of God. As prophecy would have it, the Jewish people were much persecuted by Babylonians, Romans, and others and suffered historical diaspora. Inspiration to write the Old Testament began while in captivity in Babylon. Much of its purpose was to preserve Jewish identity and create hope for future redemption. It was not intended that Jewish beliefs be spread to others. The Old Testament reflects the struggles that Abraham and his descendants faced in terms of living up to the terms of their agreement with God, particularly as expressed in the Ten Commandments.

In contrast, Christianity, following a more open interpretation of Abrahamic belief, placed more emphasis on healing approaches of love, forgiveness, and relationship building. In this sense, the teachings of Christ, although essentially monotheistic, were an effort to reconnect and rekindle the spirituality and ethics of Indigenous Eden. However, the drama of Christ unfolded under the gaze of one of the most rapacious cultures to evolve up to this point of history—the Roman Empire. This would dramatically affect Christianity, propelling it into a global religion. A century after Christ's death, Christians were one of the most persecuted groups in Rome. Christ's teachings were the antithesis of Roman values. The Sermon on the Mount reveals the core of Christ's moral and ethical teachings.

Blessed are the poor in spirit,
for theirs is the kingdom of heaven.
Blessed are those who mourn,
for they will be comforted.
Blessed are the meek,
for they will inherit the earth.

Blessed are those who hunger and thirst for righteousness,
for they will be filled.
Blessed are the merciful,
for they will be shown mercy.
Blessed are the pure in heart,
for they will see God.
Blessed are the peacemakers,
for they will be called children of God.
Blessed are those who are persecuted because of righteousness,
for theirs is the kingdom of heaven.[40]

The Sermon on the Mount hearkened back to Indigenous values of love, humility, respect, generosity, courage, honesty, and wisdom. These were an ideological threat to Rome, which was why adherents of Christ's teachings were regularly tortured to death.

Emperor Constantine, who assumed power at a time of crisis in 306 CE, attributed his key victory at Milvian Bridge to a vision from Christ. He interpreted it as the signal that he would prevail. He forbade the persecution of Christians and paved the way for the creation of the Roman Catholic Church. He engaged in the redemptive ritual of baptism as he lay dying. Constantine's personal motivation involved revulsion at his barbarity, having killed his own wife and son. He desired to be redeemed of these sins even though such behaviour was endemic in Roman society, a symptom of its moral rot.[41] Constantine's adoption of Christianity eventually led to the acceptance of Christianity as the empire's official religion. However, the faith took on the trappings of a Roman institution, with all its pomp and hierarchy. Once embraced by Rome, Christianity gave the empire new vitality. It standardized the beliefs of the far-flung empire, something that was seen to foster greater stability.[42] The Council of Nicaea, called by Constantine in 325 CE to define Catholic doctrine, reflected Rome's preoccupation with control. Roman Catholicism would become a new avenue for the persecution of Indigenous Peoples of the Americas and other places. It ushered in a regime of power, wealth, and control that paid handsome dividends for its beneficiaries but bore little resemblance to the original teachings of Christ.

Emergence of Islam

Pre-Islamic Arab tribes held Indigenous beliefs including in an array of spirits connected with natural objects of stones, plants, and animals. They had a reputation as fierce defenders of their land. The Kaaba, a cube-shaped shrine in Mecca, was the focus of worship for these tribes prior to its transformation into a major Islamic pilgrimage centre. Islamic scholars refer to the pre-Islamic period as a time of ignorance on the premise that people practised polytheism rather than monotheism.[43]

Over the centuries, Arab tribes witnessed the aggressive and domineering machinations of the Roman and Persian Empires. They had access to knowledge of the Tanak with its teachings about Adam, Abraham, and the other prophets, and they were aware of Greek and Egyptian influence. Muhammad's message of Islam responded to the need to create a unifying vision for his people. He laid claim to the entire Abrahamic tradition, maintaining that Adam, Abraham, Jesus, and other biblical prophets were precursors of Islam. Arab scholars also embraced Greek ideas, including condoning slavery.

The pre-Islamic population of tribal peoples, Jews, and Christians initially resisted Muhammad's religious movement. However, through a series of battles and occasional setbacks, the prophet managed to secure alliances and gain a foothold. The early spread of Islam was often at the point of a sword, but also through intermarriage and the granting of economic and legal privileges. Within a century of Muhammad's rise, Islam's dominance spread across northern Africa and into southern Spain.

Like the Roman Empire, Islam spread through conquest and extracted taxes and tributes from its subjects. Laws towards Jews and Christians who were "Peoples of the Book" were more lenient than those towards polytheists who did not recognize Allah. Islam became another Roman Empire of sorts, subjugating the vanquished, converting them to Islam, and exploiting their territories and resources. This demonstrated the characteristics of a Wetiko civilization—human-centredness, use of violence, exploitation of resources, restriction of freedom of spiritual quest, and creation of society based upon wealth and power.

By the end of the first millennium, Islamic hegemony had spread rapidly across North Africa. Egypt was 99 percent Christian when invaded by Islamic armies in 639 CE. Egyptians were given three choices: to convert to Islam, to pay jizya (tax levied on non-Muslims), or to fight and be killed. Eventually Egypt became 90 percent Muslim. Economic and military power grew as Islam spread through Christian Syria and Persia, displacing original religions such as Zoroastrianism. In some regions, as occurred with Christianity, conversion to Islam included synchronistic beliefs that combined elements of Muslim and Indigenous practices.

Islam became a faith that competed with Roman Catholicism. Like Rome, its early expansion revolved around the dynamics of power and wealth, with Islamic rulers expanding their territory through military conquest. Further to the east, Islam made inroads through trade and conquest as far as India, Malaysia, and Indonesia. Today, Christianity and Islam, the two major Abrahamic religions, dominate global religions. Their ascendancy has come largely at the expense of displacement of Indigenous Peoples.

Clashing Faiths

By 716 CE, Islamic conquest reached across North Africa from the Byzantines to as far south as Spain, where Islamic influence would remain for the next eight centuries. This was the beginning of rivalry between Christianity and Islam, both of which stemmed from Abrahamic roots. Christian fervour had heightened around 1000 CE in anticipation of the millennial return of Christ. However, in 1009, Muslim Caliph Al-Hakim demolished the Church of the Holy Sepulchre in Jerusalem, a major pilgrimage site that marked the site of Christ's crucifixion, burial, and resurrection. In Europe, stories circulated about depredations against Christians in the Holy Land. By 1095, the Holy Roman Empire had organized a campaign in response.[44]

While there was indignation at what was happening in Jerusalem, Europeans were largely ignorant about the societies of the Middle East.[45] In an attempt to mend relations, Pope Gregory VII promoted the notion of a just war to restore Byzantine authority. He appealed to the vanity of the nobility who, in turn, recruited fighting men, often peasants who were forced into service. Nobility who zealously fought for Jerusalem were promised that all of their sins would be forgiven. As many as 60,000 crusaders embarked in 1095, travelling 2,700 miles by land. They came from across the Holy Roman Empire, primarily France.[46]

Crusading forces, although often poorly organized, managed to capture bastions such as Antioch on the way to Jerusalem. However, it wasn't until 1099 that they succeeded in capturing Jerusalem after 450 years of Muslim control. By then, they were a much-reduced force of about 25,000 due to dissention and defections. Soldiers experienced gruesome sieges involving catapults, breaching walls with ladders, massacres, torture, burning, and beheadings that led to high mortality.[47]

In the face of Christian success, it took nearly a hundred years for Muslim opposition to coalesce around Salah ad-Din Yusuf ibn Ayyub (Saladin), a Muslim sultan. He retook Jerusalem in 1187, which reignited crusading fervour under Richard the Lionhearted. In 1189 Richard assembled 219 ships with 7,000 men. After a series of inconclusive battles and dwindling resources, he withdrew but struck a treaty that allowed Christian pilgrims to visit the holy land peacefully.

Subduing Indigenous Europeans

The Celts are ancient Indigenous people who once occupied much of Europe from the British Isles, east to Turkey, and south to Italy and Spain. Like Aboriginal Peoples across the world, their medicine practitioners, the Druids, used ceremonies to mediate between the temporal and spiritual worlds. They perceived that spirit existed in all things and that humans experienced cycles of incarnation. The divine was manifested in nature, and people were an integral part of nature, so the natural world was not to be conquered but, rather, to be lived with harmoniously. Humanity was one functional part of nature, and all parts had to work cooperatively together. Druids had the responsibility of conveying the wisdom of their Ancestors and keeping spiritual practices alive. Healers called Wicce became the basis of the idea of the evil witch. Stonehenge, a Neolithic creation that predated the

Druids is indicative of an even more ancient worldview that took into careful account the movements of the sun and stars. [48]

The word *pagan,* meaning peasant or country-dweller in Latin, was a derogatory term used by the Romans to describe those who were uncivilized and inferior. Paganism was pantheistic, recognizing various spirits associated with nature rather than a religion that arose through the revelation of a prophet.[49] Druids played important roles as guardians of knowledge and adjudicators of disputes. Today the pagans call their religion the Ancient Way.[50] As is standard in imperial efforts, Roman officials went to great lengths to portray the Celts as barbarians in order to justify their subjugation. The Roman Empire pushed the Celts out of their territories and decimated them in a series of crusades. Today, remnants of Celtic culture are located in Ireland, northwest France, and outlying areas in Europe.

German and French former vassals of Rome eventually overcame their overlords. However, they did not abandon the religious and state apparatus of Pax Romana and became the new oppressors of Indigenous Peoples. Holy Roman Emperor Charlemagne (742 to 814 CE) used brutal tactics against the Germanic pagans to consolidate Christianity's hold on north-central Europe. He waged a thirty-year campaign against the Indigenous Saxons "marked by pillaging, broken truces, hostage taking, mass killings, deportation of rebellious Saxons, and draconian measures to compel acceptance of Christianity."[51] Charlemagne introduced civilized education in the form of arts and literacy and laid the foundation for Christian Europe. He launched a series of six Northern Crusades against the remaining pagans of Europe, directed mainly at the Finns of Scandinavian descent and the Baltic states of Latvia and Lithuania.[52]

In 1147 Pope Eugenius III declared that crusades against the pagans, primarily in the Baltic states, was justifiable. "We utterly forbid that for any reason whatsoever a truce should be made with these tribes, either for the sake of money, or for the sake of tribute, until such time as, by God's help, they shall be either converted or wiped out."[53] These crusades employed Germans who had returned from the loss of Jerusalem to Salah ad-Din's forces in 1187. The Indigenous pagans were no match against the assault and pillaging tactics learned during Middle East clashes. Incentives offered to crusaders were the usual promises of spiritual salvation and possession of conquered lands and booty. Tribes who agreed to convert were offered protection. Those who refused were exiled or destroyed. The crusades met stiff resistance, including the Lithuanians' defeat of the Teutonic Order crusaders, which resulted in the end of the Northern Crusades in 1410.[54] Pagans retreated to remote areas where they could practise their spirituality in obscurity and peace. While history records these details, what many Christians rarely admit is the influence of pagan beliefs on Christian rituals, including Christmas and Easter.

Europe in 1491

A Great Famine occurred in the early 1300s due to colder than normal climate conditions. Church leaders blamed bad weather that caused crop failures on the behaviour of wicked people. Witches were often the targets of blame as it was thought they could manipulate the weather. Throughout the medieval period, childbirth was difficult and perilous, and mothers sometimes died of exhaustion. Infant mortality was almost one third in children under seven. Among the perils people faced were malnutrition, smallpox, measles, whooping cough, tuberculosis, and influenza. Much of this was caused by unsanitary conditions in urban centres that had long become divorced from their natural surroundings.[55]

Agricultural pastoralists dominated the economy of the Old World in the 1400s. In medieval Europe, 80 percent of the workforce was engaged in subsistence agriculture.[56] Environmental conditions were challenging, and people struggled to survive on marginal crops of wheat and other cereal grains from which they made the gruel famously disparaged in literature from Shakespeare to Dickens. While resources such as gold, silver, and slaves were incentives for imperial endeavours, the introduction of New World foods—the potato, tomato, beans, corn, and chocolate among others—revolutionized the Old-World diet. Such vegetable crops were less labour intensive and produced more consistent crops. Improved nutrition ushered in an explosion of the European population: from 100 million in 1650 to almost 600 million in 1950.[57]

The Black Death plague of the fourteenth and fifteenth centuries is estimated to have killed up to one half of Europe's population. Bacterium carried by fleas and rats caused oozing swellings all over one's body and was easily spread through sneezing or spitting. Death came within a few days. Once again, it was believed that the ravage was due to God's anger over sin, for which Jews were most often singled out.

There were few places of public lodging, and travellers faced the risk of being robbed or killed. Violence was endemic and took many forms, including street brawls, feuds, assault, rape, and murder, sometimes over the most trivial of things. People could easily be caught up in social and political intrigues and criticizing political and religious authorities for the conditions could result in imprisonment, torture, or death. Wars, both smaller, local feuds and large campaigns, affected many people. For example, the Wars of the Roses in 1461 claimed nearly 30,000 lives.[58] One was fortunate to avoid environmental and social hazards and survive to the age of forty.

Europe in the Middle Ages had been influenced by the expansion of the Roman Catholic Church for centuries. The Church was fervently fighting crusades against Muslims in the east and pagans in the north. Its enthusiasm for vanquishing heathens later carried over into its contact with the Original Peoples of the Americas. Population estimates for the world in 1492 reveal that approximately 60 million lived in Europe and the Middle East. Yet, for all of their civilized impacts, those who persecuted Indigenous Peoples accounted for little more than ten percent of the world's population.[59]

Survival of the Sami

The Sami of Scandinavia (along with the Basques of northern Spain) are one of the few surviving Indigenous Peoples of Europe today, numbering approximately 50,000. Somehow, despite the pressures of encroaching civilization, they manage to retain many elements of traditional culture and remain semi-nomadic reindeer herders. In Samiland, one is impressed by the lavvo, a tent that resembles a teepee with a structure built upon poles with floors covered by birch twigs and reindeer fur. A fire in the middle provides heat like the teepees on the Canadian Plains. As evidence of their close ties to the land, the Sami employ numerous words to describe various types of snow, such as powdery, recent, encrusted, etc. The Sami understand that spirits are associated with everything, including animals and plants, places, and Ancestors. Their medicine practitioners use a drum to enter a trance and become intermediaries between the physical and transcendent worlds.

The Sami have been dominated by different nation states over their history. Children were placed in Norwegian residential schools designed to acculturate them to the dominant society. As a result, they speak the national languages of Norwegian, Swedish, Finnish, or Russian. The Sami have also adopted Christian celebrations, including Christmas and Easter. Yet, they cling tenaciously to their own culture and spirituality, dressing in their colourful traditional outfits with ribbons of red and yellow woven into a dark blue background. The increased acceptance of Sami culture by Norway is evident in the opening of the Sami University in Kautokeino.[60] That the Sami can continue practising their way of life while coexisting with modern society is a promising sign.

Ecolizations Elsewhere

Major human cultures, particularly in Asia, developed sophisticated social and economic systems, but did not subscribe to the same human-centred ideology as in the European tradition. China and India, although featuring so-called civilized attributes, including agriculture and advanced technologies, did not follow Abrahamic monotheism. They were advanced societies that still acknowledged the presence of spirits of nature and Ancestors. Such cultures were content to remain within their own spheres and were not committed to world domination.[61]

Indigenous populations in Asia, such as Indonesia, can be difficult to identify because of the complexities of centuries of migration. Ultimately, the definition of Indigenous can be distilled down to a set of values. Most early immigrants brought their Aboriginal ethics with them. On the other hand, populations of the Middle East and Europe, while Indigenous in terms of historical linkage to their original lands, had lost connection to their original spirituality.

The majority of the world population was Indigenous until the 1820s when they began to be outnumbered by industrialized peoples. The 1820s are also remarkable for a couple of other reasons—the embrace of rationalism and the rise of industrialism. In a mere two hundred years since Wetiko civilizations became predominant, world environment and stability has been dramatically impacted by these ideologies. Modern civilization is really just a blink of the eye in terms of humanity's time on Earth.

Destroying Indigeneity

Disdain for prehistoric peoples is part of a long ideological war by civilized peoples to distance themselves from ancient Indigenous ideologies. While the world's scholars are transfixed by developments in Mesopotamia and Egypt, where the attack on nature began, little interest is given to the millions of ancient peoples who lived in brilliant harmony with their environment. While it is boasted that the Roman Empire lasted for 1,000 years, Indigenous nations had much greater longevity until their societies were destroyed.[62]

Civilized peoples looked down on tribal peoples, thinking they were controlled by nature rather than being in harmony with it. The Romans negotiated protection agreements with Indigenous Europeans, only to turn those arrangements into instruments of oppression. Meanwhile, in Rome, Indigenous Peoples were portrayed as stupid and backward.[63] The only time Natives merited attention was when they resisted and became "barbarians" in conflict with "civilization."

One needs to realize that worldwide Indigenous culture and ideology thrived well before modern civilization emerged. Archaeologists agree that *Homo sapiens* has been in existence for at least 200,000 years. Civilization began to flourish only 6,000 years ago, a mere 3 percent of that timespan. If a metre stick represents the span of humanity, civilization is represented by only the last three centimetres! Yet all the valuable human experience during the larger part of that timespan is not considered consequential or valuable. In fact, that period was Indigenous Eden, a time of harmonious relations between humans and the natural world.

All of this bias has marginalized and diminished Indigenous Peoples throughout world history. Now the "people without history" are beginning to have a voice and to explain their story.[64] While the relative stability of modern Europe is birthed from violent control of empires such as the Roman, there is rarely discussion of what that continent might have been like without that brutal legacy. Europeans have been able to construct magnificent universities and extensively trained scholars to promote their vision of civilization. They created formidable technologies and built militaries that have dominated the world. Many of these achievements are possible only because of the gains made by the plunder of Indigenous lands. As victims of colonization, Indigenous Peoples are among the most dispossessed, experience the most intractable problems, and have the fewest resources to advance and express their way of life.

Indigenous Eden once flourished in the Old World. Ideas of civilization spread slowly, with nascent communities in the Fertile Crescent in the Middle East. Humans began to realize that they were capable of exploiting natural resources—be they plant or animal, with little or no repercussion. It is a huge challenge to document the demise of Indigenous Eden in the Old World and is beyond the scope of one researcher to exhaustively study all the impacts due to the rise of civilization. However, it is possible to make a modest survey that can provide a glimpse.

The human complex brain is endowed with tremendous intelligence, prodigious memory, and insatiable curiosity and creativity. But does that mean that people are entitled to place themselves above the rest of Creation? Even the Bible stated that humans were to be stewards, helping to preserve God's garden. Or were these gifts to serve only ourselves, and our whims? Was this declaration of our superiority the original sin?

Rationalists argue that it is self-evident that people would want to protect themselves from threats and that there is a right to seek security. But when did natural creation become a threat? In Indigenous eyes, all parts of the natural world are gifts of the Creator. The animals willingly supply us with food, and the plants provide us with medicines. Certainly there were dangerous animals and plants, but they exist for reasons known to the Creator. People had to accept that and govern themselves accordingly. The ultimate sense of security came from the belief that the created world was benevolent and provided all the necessities required. The more people distanced themselves from nature, the more fearful humans became of it. This led to a breakdown of the sacred covenant to establish harmonious coexistence.

Some argue that Indigenous ecolizations would have become more complex and inevitably followed the same road as European societies. However, it is just as likely that, if European societies had continued to maintain a living link to the numinous rather than succumbing to materialism, modern civilization would not have ended up in today's degraded and vulnerable condition. In stating this, it has to be pointed out that spirituality is not the same as religion or theocracy. Those living in ancient societies maintained direct connection to the supernal and placed that above temporal interests. All of their relationships, especially with spirit, had to be constantly tended to and nourished. However, ancient Indigenous societies did have vulnerabilities. Once relationships became too broken to repair, such as through conquest and colonization, and once the sacred knowledge and ability to practise healing arts were lost, those societies lost their stability.

Evidence of the success of ecolizations was not in the building of great monuments and institutions, although these can be witnessed in Meso-America. Rather, it was the less obvious cultural and social achievements that resulted in stable, largely non-violent and non-aggressive cultures. The vibrancy of First Nations' belief systems has been eroded through historical contact with Europeans. Entire generations have been tragically severed from their spiritual heritage through racism, colonization, slavery, and residential schools. Unity can barely be maintained within communities that have disintegrated and become divided over power and money. Despite academics' musing about the need to revitalize ancient beliefs, real change begins only when families and communities begin to rejuvenate. Respect for, and support of, spiritual mentors will be critical. Unfortunately, too many people consider the supernal seriously only when they are in a state of crisis. Such a worldwide calamity is looming, so the time is right for reconciliation.

Today, Elders realize that the time has arrived to address the loss of sacredness in these deeply secular times. A Haudenosaunee prophecy predicts that it will take seven generations—we are now in the seventh generation—for the teachings to return and give Indigenous people an opportunity to turn things around. Elder Phil Lane questioned why Indigenous Peoples always seem to suffer the most. It is because, he said, they are making the sacrifice in order that the original human heritage not be lost. Is it possible that there can there be a renaissance? Can ancient meanings of spirituality be rediscovered and be relevant in the modern world? Can the concepts that everything has awareness, is interconnected and, therefore, deserves to be respected ever restore the environment of Eden?

Elder and academic John Mohawk ponders the dilemma of civilization.

> So there was something that happened in approximately 5000 BCE that caused people to consider the possibility of domesticating plants and animals. These people were settled in a place and they could no longer migrate to another place because that other place was already occupied. Here starts the kind of story we need to think about. There is a predilection in our species, you could call it our primate instincts, that has groups of us forever aggressively looking at the possibility of expanding and taking over and plundering others. From the beginning until now the whole civilization hasn't very successfully addressed this shortcoming.[65]

Ancient ways of peoples had been virtually eradicated with the rise of civilization in the Middle East and Europe. The war of civilization against ancient Indigenous cultures, another form of crusade, accelerated as European explorers reached the New World in 1492. When explorers such as Christopher Columbus came into contact with Indigenous Peoples of the Americas, they marvelled at the pristine environment, health, robustness, cheerfulness, hospitality, and generosity of their hosts. But they brought all of their biases against the "non-civilized" with them.

CHAPTER 4

FINAL CONQUEST OF EDEN

O ld World civilizations had begun to embrace the human-centred values that distanced them from ancient Indigenous ways of intimate connection to nature. Civilization is now regarded as "the stage of human social development and organization that is considered most advanced."[1] Unfortunately, the contemporary concept of civilization refuses to recognize the validity of any form of social organization that is not human focused. This is part of the reason why Europeans who arrived on the shores of the Americas were so quick to dismiss the value of the existing order. They judged Indigenous societies in which the transcendental was seen to supersede human judgment as being faulty. I employ the word *ecolization*[2] to emphasize that Indigenous societies are fundamentally different in nature from the current conception of "civilization."

The New World discovered in 1492 was an untarnished bastion of ancient Indigenous Eden—and there was nothing new about it. There is little doubt that the discovery and subsequent exploitation of the New World had tremendous impact on Old World prosperity in terms of providing powerful new resources. However, contact was devastating for ecolizations. Colonization of the New World centred on the Spanish and Portuguese quest for gold, silver, and other resources beginning in the 1500s. The greed and selfishness displayed by these behaviours demonstrated Wetiko characteristics. The amount of silver and gold circulating in the New World increased eightfold by the 1600s, making mass production of currency feasible and facilitating expansion of global trade.[3] A revolution in commerce occurred in the form of monetary institutions such as the Bank of Amsterdam (1609) and Bank of England (1694). Stock markets developed to finance the needs of colonial mercantile enterprises, including the Hudson's Bay Company and East India Company.[4]

Momentous Collision

Contact between First Nations of Turtle Island and Europeans of the Old World was probably the most dramatic collision of two diametrically opposed ideologies to ever occur in world history. Negative impacts from colonizer priorities and approaches almost annihilated the Original Peoples. From an Indigenous point of view, the story is one of broken spiritual, human, and environmental relationships and utter devastation of their world.

Much new insight about First Nations history has emerged based on Elders' revelations. They confirm that the most fundamental aspect of traditional life—the supernal and its influences on daily life—were discounted by European explorers and historians who understood little of its significance. Today, Indigenous scholars are attempting to redress the dismissal of Indigenous belief systems by reconstructing history based on Indigenous knowledge. New research methodologies such as ethnohistory, which adds oral history and cultural concepts to traditional methodologies, have emerged. But even these are not sufficient to fully take into account the foundational role of Indigenous beliefs.

The past cannot be properly interpreted unless the historian fully understands the ideology and motivations of historical actors. In the case of First Nations history, the further one goes back in time, the fewer historians and anthropologists understand Indigenous perspectives. From the lens of European self-adulation, tribal peoples were considered backward. Europeans contended that heathens had no credible belief in God or rational thought. What better proof could there be, they argued, than the absence of churches and government buildings? Indigenous ceremonies were considered mere superstition, especially when they involved invocation of the supernatural. Indeed, Christianity viewed them to be practices of the devil. At best, First Nations were "noble savages," brave and stoic but tragically lacking true character.[5]

The truth is that ecolizations, utilizing their sacred knowledge and practices, had created near-ideal societies in terms of providing meaning, equality, and well-being. Supernal consultation continued to guide Indigenous actions after European contact and during critical periods, such as when making treaty. First Nations believed that the foreigners who came to their shores would understand the importance of spirituality.

European aggression and arrogance was in full display at the moment of European contact with the Americas. Just as civilized peoples attacked nature, so did they attack Aboriginal Peoples who existed virtually seamlessly within their habitat. The Doctrine of Discovery, validated by papal law, accorded complete dominion over territory to the first Christian nation to "discover" it. The legal concept of *terra nullius* held that Indigenous lands were not "effectively occupied"; therefore, the people, land, resources, flora, and fauna could all fall under the authority of the "discoverers."[6] The Roman Catholic Church contended that Indigenous Peoples were under the influence of the devil and debated whether they were even human. Colonizers battled one another for supremacy, but diseases such as smallpox emanating from unsanitary European centres eliminated most of the problem of any Indigenous presence.[7]

"Discovering" Indigenous America

Columbus's drive to seek a westerly route to the riches of the Orient was largely the result of the fall of Constantinople to Islamic forces. Having been cut off the overland routes to the riches of China, Columbus's Enterprise of the Indies was essentially a business venture.[8] Educated individuals knew that the world was not flat but was a sphere. Few had the resources or motivation to embark on such a risky exploit, although Norse and Basque seafarers had already visited the northeast coast of what is today Canada.

Needing Church approval for exploration, Columbus appealed to the religious sensibilities of Spanish monarchs, Ferdinand and Isabella. He promised to convert heathens to Catholicism and bring back gold that would assist in covering the rising costs of warfare against the Muslim world. Columbus's services would not come cheap: He demanded and received promises that he would keep 10 percent of all wealth accumulated and receive the title of Admiral of the Ocean Sea, a position that gave him sway over new territories.[9]

The Vatican authorized Columbus to "capture, vanquish, and subdue all Saracens, pagans, and other enemies of Christ, to put them into perpetual slavery and take away all of their possessions and property." That was followed by another document called the *Inter Caetera* bull of 1493, which called for the "subjugation of all barbarous nations . . ." These documents formed the basis for Native conversion and their ulterior motives of exploitation and dispossession.[10]

In August 1492, Columbus embarked with three ships manned by eighty-seven men. Aided by favourable winds, the expedition reached the Bahama Islands in the New World in about six weeks. Along the way, Columbus miscalculated his position, staved off crew discontent, and cheated a crew member out of the prize for first sighting of land. Columbus's first accounts of interactions with the Arawak peoples are far different from later accounts.

> To win their friendship and realizing that there was a people to be converted to our Holy Faith by love and friendship and not by force, I gave some of them red caps, glass beads, and many other little things. This pleased them very much and they became very friendly. They later swam out to the ship's boats in which we were seated, and brought us parrots and balls of cotton and spears and many other things, which they exchanged for the glass beads and hawk's bells. . . .
>
> They do not bear arms, and do not know them, for I showed them a sword, they took it by the edge and cut themselves out

of ignorance. They have no iron. Their spears are made of cane. . . . They would make fine servants, and they are intelligent, for I saw that they repeated everything said to them. I believe they could easily be made Christians, for they appeared to have no idols. God willing, when I make my departure I will bring back half a dozen back to their Majesties so that they can learn to speak. . . .

I saw two or three villages, and their people came down to the beach calling to us and offering thanks to God. Some brought us water, others food, and still others jumped into the sea and swam out to us. We thought they were asking if we came from the heavens. One old man got into the boat, and the others, both men and women cried 'Come and see the men who have come from heaven, and bring them food and water.' Many men and women came, each bringing a gift and offering thanks to God. . . . These people are totally unskilled in arms, as your Majesties will learn from seven whom I captured and taken aboard, to learn our language and to take them to Spain. But, should your Majesties command it, all the inhabitants could be taken away to Castile, or made slaves on the island. With fifty men we could subjugate them all and make them do whatever we want.[11]

Columbus equated what he saw to the Garden of Eden: "I think the earthly Paradise lies here, which no one can enter but by God's permission. . . . to explore these lands I have newly discovered, and in which I fervently believe the Garden of Eden lies."[12] Then he quickly sized up these hospitable strangers and plotted how he could subjugate them.

Gonzalo Fernandez de Oveido, official historian for the Spanish conquest of the Caribbean, had a dim view of Native Medicine Persons who claimed to communicate with the spirit world: "They worship the Devil in diverse forms and images . . . inside there was an old Indian . . . whose evil image was standing there, and it is to be thought that the Devil entered into him and spoke through him as though his minister and told them the day on which it would rain and other messages from Nature . . . they did not undertake or carry out anything that might be important without considering the Devil's opinion."[13]

Going further afield to explore the pristine islands he named Hispaniola, Columbus took note of the inhabitant's gold trinkets. His priority quickly turned from religious conversion to an obsession with obtaining gold. In the end, not a single Arawak converted to Christianity. But Columbus did create the illusion that the land reeked of gold. "Hispaniola is a miracle. Mountains and hills, plains and pastures are both fertile and beautiful . . . the harbors are unbelievably good and there are many wide rivers of which the majority contain gold. . . . There are many spices, and great mines of gold and other metals."[14]

After returning to Spain then coming back on a second trip, Columbus was surprised to find that the men he had left at Fort Navidad to search for gold had all been slain. During his absence they had rampaged over the island, torturing and killing the inhabitants who had failed to lead them to gold and molesting and enslaving girls. The inhabitants had risen up and destroyed the fort.

This only hardened Columbus's resolve. Every Arawak male and female over the age of fourteen was required to produce a hawk's bell of gold dust every three months. Whoever failed to deliver was killed by having their hands amputated. This policy led to mass panic among the Natives, who fled to the mountains. There they were tracked down by hunting dogs and executed with swords and guns. In ultimate desperation, the Arawaks committed mass suicide. Up to a half million of the Indigenous population perished within three years of Spanish arrival.[15]

Word of Columbus's atrocities filtered back to Spain. Judged as excessive even by their standards, the Spanish monarchy relieved Columbus of his governorship powers in 1500. Up until his last days, Columbus insisted that he had acted honourably and was entitled to all of the riches promised to him. Though Columbus never actually landed on the mainland of continental America, his foothold in the Caribbean provided the springboard for the next unfortunate chapter in European subjugation of the New World.

Destroying the Sacrificers

Gregory Cajete elaborates on the sense of darkness that descended on the Aztecs after the banishment of the God of Knowledge, Quetzalcoatl, and the fatalism that motivated Aztec human sacrifice.

In Aztec mythology an epoch denotes the cosmic cycle of creation and dissolution, or of birth, growth, development, maturity, old age, and death. This metaphor is reflective of the 'fatalistic' perspective said to characterize Aztec prophetic poetry, a perspective that would play a pivotal role in their demise. The Aztec imagined Hernán Cortés as a reincarnated Quetzalcoatl, their great cultural hero whose return had been prophesized.

Quetzalcoatl, Lord of the Dawn, continually battles with his sacred twin Tezcatlipoca, Dark Lord of the North. The story of Quetzalcoatl, the hero, is one of transcendence and deep change, an embodiment of eternal creation and dissolution. Quetzalcoatl was to return near the beginning of the Fifth Sun, the epoch of the calendar time that began in 843 AD. It is said that priests of the Quetzalcoatl cult awaited his coming for the two "heavens" or two cycles of 52 years.

As a child Quetzalcoatl came to know and commune with living and spiritual beings, including the little spirits of nature known as tlaloques, who taught him the ways of the living Earth. As he grew, he performed many divine deeds, teaching his people the ways of divine laws and arts, building great cities, and creating a context for compassionate living and relationship to the Earth.

Alas, it is told that he was tricked into drinking hikuli, the milk of peyotl used in the ritual of human sacrifice by the jealous followers of Tezcatlipoca, thus forever compromising his position as ruler of his people. In this way the followers of Tezcatlipoca gained control of the minds and hearts of the people and drove Quetzalcoatl into exile. The new order then became one of pursuit of power and glory through war and human sacrifice.[16]

When the Spanish arrived in Central Mexico, Moctezuma, leader of the Aztecs, was well versed in visions and prophecies that strangers would arrive in strange vessels. According to Aztec prophecy, their exiled god of knowledge, Quetzacoatl was expected to renew the Aztec cosmos around the time Hernán Cortés made his fateful landfall.[17] The widespread awareness of this prophecy explains the excitement of the Taino who, upon earlier encountering Columbus, ran about exhorting their people to "Come and see the men from the heavens."

Further inland, Spanish conquistadors led by Hernán Cortés encountered the Aztecs, whose reputation was known mainly because of their practice of human sacrifice. For fifteen years Cortés had worked as an administrator on Hispaniola, where he helped mediate disputes and gained insight into the weakness of the Indigenous inhabitants. In 1518, he was selected to make an exploratory expedition to the continental mainland. Setting off with six hundred soldiers in eleven ships along with horses, Cortés transformed his mission into one of conquest. He exploited local resentment towards the Aztecs, who had raided surrounding tribes for sacrificial victims. He took advantage of the overwhelming superiority that metal armaments, horses, and aggressive tactics afforded the Spanish.

Soldier Bernal Diaz de Castillo said his motives for joining Cortés were "to serve God and His Majesty [King of Spain], to give light to those who were in darkness, and to grow rich, as all men desire to do." Cortés, a crafty politician, created an alliance with the Tlaxcalans, who were often raided for sacrificial subjects, and their 20,000 fighters. With the advantage of guns, swords, and horses, Cortés reached the Aztec capital, Tenochtitlan, and approached it on the pretext of negotiation.[18]

Cortés, who arrived with an Indigenous interpreter, was greeted with gifts because the Aztecs believed he could be the returning god Quetzalcoatl. His true intentions of conquest soon became clear when he brazenly took Moctezuma captive in his own city. Spanish authorities, upset that Cortés had launched a conquest rather than exploratory contacts, sent a force to arrest him but Cortés easily routed them. Disillusioned that Cortés could not be the returning Quetzalcoatl, Moctezuma and his advisors tried to persuade Cortés to leave.

After putting down the Spanish arresting force, Cortés returned to Tenochtitlan and found those he had left behind to guard Moctezuma had abused the local population and had been slaughtered. With Spanish weaponry, including head-to-foot metal armour, crossbows, and intimidating horses giving them virtual invincibility, Cortés easily regained control. Sharp metal swords could amputate, eviscerate, or decapitate with one blow. Cortés noted that Aztec fighting was ritualistic and did not employ deceptive tactics such as ambush. Armed with wooden and stone weapons, the defenders were slaughtered by the hundreds.

Moctezuma became dispensable and was executed. Realizing their revered leader was killed, the Aztecs ferociously turned on the Spanish. As the conquistadors fled the city, many perished as they fell into water and drowned under the weight of their loot. Cortés regrouped with his Tlaxcalan allies to retake the city, but by the time he returned in 1521, the Aztec population had been virtually wiped out by a smallpox epidemic.[19]

The Regrets of Las Casas

Not every Spaniard condoned the Catholic Church's treatment of Indigenous Peoples. Bartolomé de las Casas had moved to Hispanolia as a child and witnessed attacks and slave raids against the Caribs and other Native Peoples. By 1510 he became the first priest ordained in the New World. Questioning by what right the Indians, who were otherwise peaceful, could be treated with such cruelty, he realized that the true Spanish motive was extraction of gold and amassing wealth. He praised the virtues of Indigenous ecolizations:

> All people of these Indies are human, so far as is possible by the natural and human way and without light of faith—had their republics, places, towns, and cities most abundant and well provided for, and did not lack anything to live politically and socially, and attain and enjoy civil happiness. . . . And they equalled many nations of this world that are renowned and considered civilized, and they surpassed many others, and to none they were inferior . . . they surpassed also the English

and the French and some of the people of our own Spain; and they were incomparably superior to countless others in having good customs and lacking many evil ones.[20]

Convinced that Spanish actions in the New World were illegal, Las Casas journeyed to Spain to speak to King Ferdinand. To appease him, King Ferdinand bestowed the title Protector of the Indians, a position that carried little enforcement power. Spanish colonizers were in no mood to give up their riches or slaves, and Las Casas quickly became an outcast after returning to Hispaniola. His subsequent efforts to establish protective communities for Indigenous Peoples failed. In 1522 he retreated to isolation in a monastery and wrote his *History of the Indies*. Debates about the violent treatment of Indigenous Peoples led to the issuance in 1537 of papal bull *Sublimus Dei* that recognized that they were indeed human. Despite this edict, the enslavement of Indigenous people had become too profitable to stop.[21]

While the papal edict made a concession to the humanity of Indigenous Peoples, others such as Juan de Sepulveda, argued that the conquest of Indigenous lands could be justified on the basis of Aristotle's assertion of Indigenous inferiority. They were naturally sinners and had created deficient societies. Regardless of the words in *Sublimus Dei*, the Crown, the Church and the wealthy class all benefitted too greatly from the exploitation of the Americas for it to be otherwise. The Vatican's stance of taking over Indigenous lands on the basis of superiority of culture and religion set the precedent for international law.

Striking Gold

To the south in what is now Peru, Spanish conquistadors, adventurers looking to loot riches from alien lands, came across the territory of the Inca. The Inca's territory was among the largest in the world, stretching over 5,500 kilometres. The domain had not been acquired through force and conquest. A core population of 40,000 administered a vast region encompassing ten million inhabitants. That so few Incas ruled over so many subjects without overt coercion is testament to their spiritual leadership. Reverence towards the natural world was reflected in the Inca capital Cuzco, which was designed in the shape of the sacred Jaguar, and in the sacred site Machu Pichu, which was laid out in the shape of a bird. Magnificent ceremonies conveyed the Inca sense of spiritual authority and influence.

In 1532, Francisco Pizarro and 180 Spanish mercenaries arrived in the area by ship. He was aware of the easy success Cortés found in Mexico and intended to replicate that feat in his unabashed quest for gold and riches. Spanish authorities supported Pizarro, granting him a portion of all wealth produced for the monarchy. However, gold was sacred to the Inca and not a commodity of exchange. It was considered to be the sweat of the sun and was used in ornamentation and buildings.

Like Aztec leader Moctezuma, the Inca leader Atahualpa initially welcomed the strangers and agreed to a meeting. Once inside Cuzco, Pizarro studied how the city was laid out and infiltrated it with 260 soldiers, horses, cannons, and Native allies. Facing vastly superior and deadly weaponry, 7,000 Inca warriors fell without a single Spanish casualty. Like Cortés's treatment of Moctezuma, Pizarro took Atahualpa captive. Using strategies from Old World campaigns, the conquistadors exploited political divisions within the Inca realm and used torture and executions to establish control of the population. In times of conflict, the Inca treated their vanquished with respect; they were puzzled by the Spanish, who exhibited treachery, hypocrisy, and cruelty in the name of their God. The Inca could not imagine such brutality and did not recognize the danger they were in—they were lambs going to the slaughter.[22] In a bid to convince the Spanish to leave, the Inca agreed to give Pizarro a six- by five-metre room filled to a man's height with gold. Despite fulfilling this condition, Pizarro executed the Inca leader. Inca resistance continued to be quelled, but epidemics eventually carried away what was left of their population.[23]

The Quechua, successors of the Inca, ended up being literally worked to death in mines to satisfy the insatiable Spanish appetite for gold and silver. Spanish churches and buildings in Peru are built upon the foundation of temples to obliterate the memory of the Inca and to transpose Spanish culture upon the inhabitants. Pax Romana had arrived in the New World.

Infiltrating Turtle Island

When Indigenous Peoples encountered strangers on the eastern seaboard of what we call North America, they assumed that the newcomers shared their worldview and welcomed them peacefully. Indigenous Peoples continued their tradition of peacefully welcoming newcomers even as European contact extended deeper into North America. Under the cultural imperative to create positive relations, First Nations followed Protocols such as offering gifts and even intermarriage, creating kin-like relationships to draw newcomers into the circle of the community.[24] Such actions were not taken only for economic or military advantage, as many historians contend, but honoured the sacred Law of Relationships. When Englishmen first arrived, the original inhabitants initiated positive relationships through hospitality and intermarriage. A famous example, though one that is over romanticized and inaccurate, is that of Matoaka (who later took the name Pocahontas), the daughter of Chief Powhatan, purportedly offered in marriage to Englishman John Rolfe. Other examples in New France are Chief Membertou's friendship with Samuel de Champlain in Acadia and the Huron alliance with the French along the St. Lawrence River.[25]

As competition for lands and resources increased with growing settlement, conflicts occurred over misunderstandings about property. For Indigenous Peoples, land belonged to the Creator, not humans. This was incompatible with the English concept of private property. It did not take long for Europeans to launch a full-blown effort to destroy or drive Indigenous Peoples out of the New England colonies and appropriate their land.

The French had become adept at incorporating Amerindian Protocols such as Pipe Ceremonies and gift-giving into their diplomacy, enabling them to strategically build many alliances. However, they soon discovered that the minds of the Natives were not simply a tabula rasa upon which a new set of beliefs could be imposed.

Later, when the Jesuits realized that Indian religious beliefs went much deeper than they had supposed, their militant aspect came to the fore. They met objections with a directness incompatible with Indian conceptions of courtesy, seeking to catch out questioners in contradictions and openly ridiculing their traditional religious practices. They frequently enlisted the aid of European science and technology, impressing the Indians with mechanical gadgets and demythologizing their world by predicting eclipses. They quickly recognized the shamans as their most formidable opponents, vacillating between denouncing them as servants of Satan and attempting to convict them of simple chicanery. In such contests they sometimes failed to carry their audiences; when Le Jeune [a missionary] attempted to expose a Montagnais shaman in 1634, he merely exposed himself to public ridicule.[26]

Conflict over land arose not only between colonists and Indigenous people but also between competing European imperialists. Agriculture-based New England grew much more quickly than New France, whose economy was based in the fur trade. Inevitably, the two Christian nations could not coexist peacefully. A series of skirmishes broke out between 1754 and 1763, primarily in the Ohio Valley area. The French exploited Indigenous knowledge of the terrain and guerilla tactics to keep the British at bay for most of the time. Eventually, the powerful Iroquois Confederacy sided with the numerically superior English, allowing the latter to prevail at the Battle of the Plains of Abraham in 1759 and bringing to an end French suzerainty in the New World.[27]

Throughout the conquest of North America, First Nations were used as pawns and then betrayed as European powers battled for supremacy over North America's resources. By respecting Indigenous Protocols for friendship and trade, the French had secured many Indigenous alliances, including with the Huron and Anishinaabe. When their patron, France, lost their North American possessions, Amerindian allies in the Ohio Valley were apprehensive about what the new order might bring. As the New England colonists grew in numbers, they no longer needed to maintain close relationships with First Peoples to survive, causing them to more aggressively take over Indigenous land. Discontent of the former allies of the French came to a boil under Pontiac, who led a major and damaging uprising against the British in the Great Lakes region in 1761. Indigenous tribes perceived the British as the less trustworthy because of their usurpation of Indigenous land. The British had created enemies across the region—Indigenous nations whom they had driven out of New England, the French who were still smarting from their wounds, and their own colonists who were discontented over unfair taxation. The British desperately needed allies. Their first step would be to mend relations with Indigenous Nations.[28]

The British realized from firsthand experience that First Nations still posed a military threat. Now their own colonists were threatening rebellion over dissatisfaction with high taxes and dictatorial control, forcing officials to fight for their survival on many fronts. The Crown needed to take swift action to begin securing Indigenous allegiances in order to avoid being totally evicted from North America. British diplomat Sir William Johnson convened a series of meetings in the Ohio Valley to address Indigenous concerns and deal with their grievances. In those meetings he heard about the resentment created by colonists encroaching on and taking Indigenous lands by force.

The Royal Proclamation of 1763 recognized that "great frauds and abuses" had been perpetrated against the Indians to the detriment of His Majesty's interests. It quickly emerged from Johnson's consultations that protection of land was highest on the list of Indigenous priorities. Thus, the Proclamation declared Indian Territory to be off limits from settlement unless the British Crown first resolved Indigenous interests by way of treaty negotiation. The Proclamation recognized and protected the Indian Territories of the Indian Nations, mostly in the Ohio Valley, but also elsewhere that colonists had not settled, from encroachment.[29]

History gives the impression that the Proclamation must have been a benevolent gesture on the part of the British monarch. However, First Nations that participated actually dictated the only terms under which they would agree to British cooperation. They still held the upper hand and under no circumstances would they accept terms that they had never been consulted on. Additionally, the personal power of the monarch, who essentially took the advice of his advisors, was illusory, making his role in the process minor. Moreover, the British and First Nations had competing interests. Shawnee chief Tecumseh emerged as the leader of a coalition of Indigenous Nations who envisioned a sovereign Indian Nation existing independently alongside the British—a vision the British could tolerate if it served as a buffer zone. The Royal Proclamation of 1763, while purporting to defend Indigenous lands and interests was problematic. Legal phrases used in later treaties like "extinguish and surrender forever title to the British sovereign" were never fully discussed or understood and would have been met with immediate rejection by Indigenous leaders.[30] Both sides signed treaties under poorly understood terms—the British deliberately misled Indigenous leaders, who mistakenly trusted that their allies were dealing honestly. But the Proclamation served British purposes.

With First Nations' allegiance secured under the Proclamation, the British turned to quelling French dissatisfaction by recognizing their language and cultural rights under the *Quebec Act* of 1774. This groundwork was accomplished only two years before the American Revolution broke out. When the American Revolution erupted in 1776, First Nations played crucial roles in defending Montreal and Quebec from American attacks. British Loyalists fled to territories north of the Great Lakes previously controlled by the French and their Indian allies, in what would later become Canada. In the War of 1812 (also called Tecumseh's War), which would finally settle the boundary between Canada and the United States, Tecumseh and his alliance fought heroically to defend British territory in Canada against the American threat. He made the ultimate sacrifice after being deserted on the field at Moraviantown by cowardly British commander Henry Proctor.[31] The brilliant leadership of Tecumseh decided several battles and enabled the British to survive and thrive in Canada.

But these conflicts left First Nations a spent military force in eastern North America after 1814. The British sporadically signed a number of small and generally inadequate treaties that allowed settlement in their new Canadian colonies. It was widely believed that Indigenous Peoples would "melt like the snow before the sun" in the face of superior civilization.[32]

Indigenous Persistence

First Nations' efforts to protect their interests and preserve their culture are reflected in the negotiation of Numbered Treaties in what is now western Canada. Elders explain the principle philosophy behind their treaty negotiations as developing positive, kinship-like relations with the newcomers. The negotiations would create a partnership in which the two peoples would live together, side by side, as siblings. First Nations approached treaties with an attitude of profound respect, holding ceremonies and seeking Manitow's sanction. They understood that treaty required the parties to consult regularly and that both be involved in decision making.[33]

Certain words and phrases in the First Nations' languages contain concepts of how First Nations would live together and build relations among themselves and with others, such as the Crown and her subjects. In Cree, these concepts include Askeew Pim Atchi howin (making a living off the land); Wah kooh toowin (laws of familial relationships and the respective duties and responsibilities); and Wi Taski Win (living on the land in harmony).[34]

Showing profound ignorance about the perspectives and intents of First Nations, the chief negotiator of Canada's Numbered Treaties, Alexander Morris, concludes his report on the negotiations: "And now I close. Let us have Christianity and civilization to leaven the mass of heathenism and paganism among the Indian tribes; let us have a wise and paternal Government faithfully carrying out the provisions of out treaties, and doing its utmost to elevate the Indian population, who have been cast upon our care, and we will have peace, progress and concord among them in the North-West . . ."[35]

Despite having entered into sacred agreements with the British Crown, First Nations faced continued duplicity from the Canadian government, which had been entrusted to administer treaty benefits. Government authorities used Social Darwinist beliefs[36] of the late nineteenth century to blame Indigenous beliefs and practices for backwardness and lack of progress. According to Social Darwinism, some cultures, like creatures, evolved to become stronger and more able to dominate weaker ones. Canadian official policy to discourage, undermine, and eradicate Indian culture and ceremonies in the guise of civilization was given a name that shows the policy's true intent: detribalization. Participation in ceremonies became punishable through the courts: An 1884 amendment to the 1880 *Indian Act* penalized participation in the Sundance as well as the Potlatch, with up to six months' imprisonment.

While First Nations leaders endeavoured to abide by the treaties, several bands became caught up in the armed Métis-led Resistance of 1885. Repressive policies levelled towards First Nations after the Resistance included confinement to reserves and removal of children to residential schools, where they were intensively brainwashed. On the reserves, Indian agents, who had total judicial and administrative control, colluded with priests and teachers to disrupt ceremonies, confiscate ceremonial objects, and jail recalcitrant leaders. These measures were blatant violations of Treaties.

The *Indian Act* was designed to weaken the protected status of Indians and divest them of their reserve lands. Under assimilation policy, Aboriginal Peoples were to become a mere memory. The prognosis for Indian survival was not good as the Indigenous population plummeted to its nadir in 1910 amid talk of its imminent demise.[37]

Brainwashing Indigenous Youth

First Nations were initially open towards missionaries, welcoming them to live and teach in their communities.[38] This was an example of positive relations based on spiritual values. However, by the late 1880s, First Nations' admiration of the clergy deteriorated after several denominations began to operate residential schools and aggressively convert Indigenous children to Christianity, enforcing federal government policies of rapid assimilation (see Figure 4).

The Canadian government, seeking absolute control over the lives of First Nations, resolved to quickly rid itself of its "Indian problem." It determined that the most effective strategy was to focus on the most vulnerable and impressionable—the children. Prime Minister and Superintendent General of Indian Affairs John A. Macdonald was aware of Social Darwinist philosophy and gave strong support for the creation of Indian residential schools.

Figure 4: The transformation of Thomas Moore (Keesig), Regina Indian Industrial School, c. 1892.[39] Photos R-A8223-1 (before) and R-A8223-2 (after) appear courtesy of the Provincial Archives of Saskatchewan.

When the school is on the reserve, the child lives with its parents, who are savages, and though he may learn to read and write, his habits and training and mode of thought are Indian. He is simply a savage who can read and write. It has been strongly impressed upon myself, as head of the Department [of Indian Affairs], that Indian children should be withdrawn as much as possible from the parental influence, and the only way to do that would be to put them in central training industrial schools where they will acquire the habits and modes of thought of white men.[40]

Carlisle Indian Industrial School in the United States, one of the models studied when residential schools in Canada were proposed, had the motto "Kill the Indian, and Save the Man."[41] In other words, Indian children were expected to give up their respect and reverence for nature and learn how to attack and exploit it just like the White Man. This went against all Indigenous moral values and instincts, but, to government authorities, it was only proper that Indians embrace mainstream prosperity, greed, ambition, and power. This puts in another saying of the time in a different perspective—that Indigenous Peoples were "the White Man's burden." In actuality, the White Man was instead the Indigenous Peoples' burden."

Austerely robed Catholic clergy imposed their frightening views of God, heaven, and hell on their charges. Walking into the classroom, pupils were met with Lacombe's Ladder (Figure 5), a large chart created for residential schools.[42] It showed two paths: on one, converts strode happily and confidently towards heaven; on the other, sinister-looking Indians dressed in traditional clothing meandered down a road leading to hell, an inferno staffed by devils.

Pupils prayed incessantly—upon waking; before and after breakfast, dinner, and supper; before and after class time; mouthing a group rosary in the evening; and, finally, the bedtime prayer. Mass was held every Sunday and on other special days. The priests related a totally foreign account of the world and how it came to be. Pupils were informed that God created the world in seven days, capping it off with His finest work—the formation of man. Humans had the run of the world—so long as they obeyed His Ten Commandments.

Children had a hard time adjusting to the constant round of prayers and routines of class, chores, and structured recreation. For those who stepped out of line, punishment inevitably ensued. Before bedtime, everybody knelt by their beds to mouth a quick prayer before diving into bed. The unhappiest kids looked for the first opportunity to escape, and every once in a while word spread that "so and so" had run away. The escapee was inevitably captured and returned to close watch, detention, and more punishment. Children taken away from their parents by age six could be kept away from their parents on a year-round basis until age sixteen.[43] The result was cultural holocaust. When the "graduate" showed up at one's parent's home, the parents failed to recognize them, wondering, "Who is this person?" Parent and child could not speak the same language or recall shared experiences and values. It was disastrous for family and community relationships.

Survivor Eva McKay recounted: "In residential school, we were not allowed to talk our language and we learned from books about ourselves, and young children believed what they were saying about us. An Indian reading about herself or himself, from material

Figure 5: Lacombe's Ladder (detail). *Provincial Archives of Alberta PR2002.0256.0001*

which was written by a white person. Kids thought that this might be true, maybe my grandparents were heathens. We believed it. So we came out having different ideas and a different outlook on what we were about."[44]

Another survivor remembered:

> In the school there was a lot of physical violence. A lot of people got homesick and they decided they wanted to run away and the search teams would go out and the guy would be brought back. And they used to have this big common day room and all the small boys, the intermediate boys and senior boys were seated right around this entire thing. And the principal of the school at that time would come in, in the middle of the room. He had about a half-inch thick strap, about four inches wide and about two feet long. And he'd make the guy kneel down. He'd tell the guy to lean his head forward, he would put the guy's head in a leg lock and he would take the guy's arms and hold them behind his back and he would strap him in front of everyone to make a spectacle of him and an example for the rest of the people, to deter any running away because we were homesick, because we wanted to go home.[45]

Approximately 150,000 Indigenous students were forced into Indian Residential Schools from 1883 when the original four were constructed until 1997 when the last one was closed on Saskatchewan's Gordon First Nation. Intended as aggressive assimilation, the schools operated like reformatories where discipline and prayer were intended to elevate character. Government authorities believed that the declining population of supposedly inferior Indigenous Peoples meant that they were destined to vanish anyway. This is why meagre resources were invested in building infrastructure, qualified personnel, proper nutrition, and student well-being. Responsibility for the schools was fobbed off to Christian churches, primarily Roman Catholic but also Anglican and Presbyterian.

The schools' litany of problems was kept carefully hidden from public eyes. Even when information did escape, such as physician Dr. Peter Bryce's 1922 report, "The Story of a National Crime: An

Appeal for Justice to the Indians of Canada," the public tended to just shrug its shoulders. After raising his concerns about the mistreatment of Indigenous children, Bryce was fired by the Department of Indian Affairs.[46]

Accounts finally began to emerge in the 1990s when Phil Fontaine, Chief of the Assembly of First Nations, brought his experiences as a residential school survivor to the national spotlight. These included separation from family and community; sexual abuse; lack of cultural, social, and parenting skills; and a general sense of anomie that damaged the lives of survivors and their families. The legacy of residential schools also included rampant alcohol abuse, domestic violence, and suicide. Such dysfunctions led to children being adopted out to non-Indigenous families in what is called the "Sixties Scoop."[47] With so many other ills, including the government's assimilation policy, dismantling Indian reserve land bases, and lack of support for on-reserve development, First Nations communities were in an unprecedented state of turmoil.

The reality of residential schools is that they severed relationships with family, community, culture, past, and identity. It was a slow, but potent form of cultural genocide. Among the litany of ills identified by the Truth and Reconciliation Commission of Canada is spiritual abuse, the erasure of the Indigenous spiritual worldview.[48]

One of the most insidious effects of residential schools was the attack on Indigenous beliefs through demonizing them and breaking the continuity of knowledge and practice of ceremonies that had been passed down through generations. In 2008, the Government of Canada proffered a formal apology for the residential school system and established the Truth and Reconciliation Commission. Among the commission's Calls to Action is the call for "Respecting Indigenous Peoples' right to self-determination in spiritual matters, including the right to practise, develop, and teach their own spiritual and religious traditions, customs, and ceremonies."[49]

Demonizing Indigenous Spirituality

The demonization of Indigenous spirituality is a prominent theme in the history of contact. The Church instituted harsh measures to control evil and sin as they wrongly projected those onto Aboriginal Peoples. Indigenous cosmology viewed the spirit world as a positive force that reduced conflict between humans and with nature by employing healing ceremonies. There was minimal experience of stealing, murder, lying (as it was understood that the spirit world witnessed one's thoughts), etc. compared to modern non-Indigenous societies. Religions that endeavour to control moral shortcomings through human-made rules are never as effective as spiritual accountability as practised by First Peoples. This idea of saving souls for Christianity was actually an instrument for destabilizing Indigenous cultures, making it easier to legitimize usurpation of lands and resources.

Ecolizations did not lend well to the materialist agendas of wealth accumulation, projection of power, conquest, and creation of permanent boundaries. Indigenous Peoples were susceptible to both the breakdown of mutual respect and loss of practices of supernal healing. Ecolizations would lose their spiritual integrity if they abandoned their traditions and adopted the tactics of the colonizers. The Original Peoples were in a no-win situation: If they refused to conform to Abrahamic mores and expectations, they were dismissed as unprogressive, backward, and uncivilized. Ceremonies were outlawed and closeness to the land weakened. Indigenous healers carried their practices surreptitiously. In place of overtly practised healing ceremonies, the ideas of personal power, money, and faith in God were promoted as ways to ensure a successful life.

Immoral Laws

Europeans arrived in the Indigenous Americas with the assumption that they were superior cultures who had a right to claim those territories as their own. The constitutions of Canada, the United States, and other colonialist nations assume that their legal principles are superior to Indigenous codes of behaviours. The "White Man's law" are mostly concerned about property—its division, protection, and redistribution. Unlike Indigenous laws, such a legal system undermines positive human relationships, as well as those with the natural world. Cree lawyer and author Harold Johnson notes:

My ancestors, who prayed for me seven generations ago, never expected that your family would assume control over where I could or could not live, when and how much I hunted, how I prayed, and even who I am related to. No one expected that you would claim all medicines as your own and pass laws against any that were not to your liking. My ancestors who prayed for me never expected that I would have to ask your family's permission to get our food, to cut a tree for firewood, to build a home, to get married, to educate my children, to travel, or to live in the same community as my relatives. . . . We did not adopt an artificial entity; our law does not recognize them. We adopted the Queen and the children: real people, people with spirits, people capable of experiencing and showing kindness and pity. Artificial entities such as the state cannot learn to live in balance. They are incapable of experiencing sorrow, and hence kindness and pity. The state cannot experience. It has no life to learn from, no heart to look to for understanding. When the state is invoked by real people, these people deny what life and experience have taught them. They deny kindness and pity, and withhold the bounty and benevolence of the Queen Mother.[50]

Johnson argues passionately about the damage done to Indigenous culture because of European conceptions of property.

Behind the shelter of the law, enormous injustices are committed not only against my family but against the poor of every family, who are forced to sell their labour as resource extractors of one sort or another. Under our law, everyone has a right to the bounty of the earth: to the food she provides, to the medicines, to shelter, to clothing. All our physical needs are provided for, and the resources are there for everyone. Artificial entities such as Imperial Oil cannot have a greater right than humans to the resources of the earth. This is a territory rich in resources, abundant with timber, water, minerals, medicine, fruit, vegetables, wildlife, and fertile soil for cultivation. Everything we need for a good life is here. It is only because of the laws of property, and the fact that property can be held by artificial entities that create shortages for profit, that people in this territory go hungry, or do not own their own homes.[51]

The Global Experience: Africa

After the conquest of the Americas, there still remained pockets of Indigenous Eden in Africa, South East Asia, and Australasia. African tribal belief systems include an all-powerful Creator, among the Maasai called Enkai, the Kikuyu Ngai, creator and giver of all things, who bestowed blessings or punishments. Existence of spirits, veneration of the deceased, and use of traditional medicines are prevalent. Spirits act as intermediaries between humans and the transcendent. In ceremonies aided by drumming, one connects with life force called ashe or nyama. The supernal can be connected with through divination. Virtue is seen through behaviours, including respect, responsibility, generosity, honesty, and courage. There is belief in the cyclical nature of the world.[52]

Jacob Olupona, Professor of Indigenous African Religions at Harvard Divinity School, notes that Islam (mainly in northern Africa) and Christianity (mainly in the south of the continent) have arisen over the past century at the expense of Indigenous belief systems. In 1900, Christians constituted about 5 percent of the population and Muslims about 15 percent; traditional spirituality made up the remaining 80 percent of Africa's population of 120 million. Today, Christians number around 600 million (50 percent), Muslims around 500 million (40 percent), and adherents of the original Indigenous faiths are now only about 100 million, less than 10 percent of Africa's population, surviving mainly in the central region of the continent.

The fall of Indigenous Africa began with the Muslim conquest of the Magreb from 647 to 709 CE. European colonial expansion between 1881 and 1914 set the stage for toppling the remainder. Although the majority of Africans have tribal roots, most now identify as members of dominant state religions. Olupona notes, however, that Indigenous adherents tend to be syncretic, nominally adopting Christianity or Islam while still practising many aspects of their traditional belief. He adds that religion is not the best term to use as Indigenous Africans see spirituality as part of a holistic way of life.

> This is not to say that Indigenous African spirituality represents a form of theocracy or religious totalitarianism. . . . It doesn't have a creed, like some forms of Christianity or Islam. . . . African spirituality has always been able to adapt to change and allow itself to absorb the wisdom and views of other religions, much more than, for example, Christianity and Islam. While Islam and Christianity tend to be overly resistant to adopting traditional African religious ideas or practices, Indigenous African religions have always accommodated other beliefs.
>
> African spirituality is truly holistic. For example sickness in the Indigenous African worldview is not only an imbalance of the body, but also an imbalance in one's social life, which can be linked to a breakdown in one's kinship and family relations or even to one's relationship with one's ancestors. The role of ancestors in the African cosmology has always been significant. Ancestors can offer advice and bestow good fortune and honour to their living dependents. . . . A belief in the ancestors also testifies to the inclusive nature of traditional African spirituality by positing that deceased progenitors still play a role in the lives of their living descendents.[53]

Dr. Olupona warns of the consequences of loss of Indigenous belief systems.

> We would lose a worldview that has collectively sustained, enriched, and given meaning to a continent and numerous other societies for centuries through its epistemology, metaphysics, history and practices. For instance, if we were to lose Indigenous African religions in Africa, then diviners would disappear, and if diviners disappeared, we would not only lose an important spiritual specialist for many Africans, but also an

institution that for centuries has been the repository of African history, wisdom and knowledge. . . . Africans increasingly identify themselves as either Muslim or Christian, thus denying their unique African worldview that has always viewed everything as unified and connected to the land, the place of one's clan, lineage, and where people were cosmically birthed. Foreign religions simply don't have that same connection to the African continent.[54]

Disappearing Indigenous Asia

Asia contains almost three-quarters of the world's remaining Indigenous population. Like other parts of the Old World, history is extremely complicated and events are buried in the mists of the past. Many of these Aboriginal Peoples who came under the control of colonizers refuse to sell out the integrity of their cultures and continue to retain respect for the natural environment.

India maintains a list of Scheduled Tribes, historically disadvantaged people who are now recognized in the constitution. The Dalits, or Adivasis, are the original tribal peoples of India, currently numbering about 68 million. Successive waves of Brahmin and Muslim invasion always ended with the Original Peoples being taken advantage of and exploited. In 2015, I visited Acharya Nagarjuna University near Vijiawada to attend a conference on world Indigenous culture and literature. The students were primarily Dalits, commonly known as Untouchables, the lowest of the castes. In the past, the intentional touching by a Dalit of a person of higher caste could result in being put to death. Today, the government supports educating the Dalits.[55]

At the university, tribal dancers adorned with massive horn headpieces beat drums to greet conference guests. This is their custom for welcoming visitors. From students' presentations on their history and literature, attendees learned how the Dalits stoically accepted their lot, their toil forming the backbone of India's economy. Despite their lowly status, Christian missionaries who worked among the Dalits perceived them to be down-to-earth and honest in contrast to the vanity and aloofness of the higher castes. The proliferation of feathers, bone, and leather in India's national museum's exhibits on Original Peoples is testimony to their closeness to the land. Like Indigenous Peoples in North America, the Dalits' close ties to the land helped them learn how to preserve and protect it. The government official presiding over the conference commented on the severe pollution problem in India and admitted that the country needs to learn from Indigenous relationships with the environment if India is going to solve the problem.

China's 1.3 billion people are virtually all Indigenous as they are the original occupants of that land. Approximately 9 percent, such as the inhabitants of Inner Mongolia, are classified as national minorities by the majority Han government. The Chinese government has implemented an enlightened policy of recognizing prior rights of national minorities in their territories. These include culture, language, and resource rights, even where they are outnumbered by the majority Han. Chinese reverence for the natural world is ingrained in their medicinal practices and cuisine, and they maintain connection with the spirits of their ancestors.[56]

The Case of Indonesia

Indonesia, considered to be the world's most populous Islamic country, is an instructive case. Islamic traders first came to the area in the fourteenth century. Today, 87 percent of the country's inhabitants are declared to be followers of the Islamic religion, although the country has a predominately Indigenous population. But being Indigenous means close cultural connection to land, stewardship of nature, and adherence to ancient ideology and values.

Indonesia is a bewildering array of up to 18,000 islands stretching over nearly 5300 kilometres. Melanesian hunter-gatherers are said to be the first modern humans to occupy Indonesia, migrating from southeast Asia 40,000 years ago. Another wave arrived from the island of Taiwan around 6,000 years ago. The primary modern descendants of these peoples are the Javanese, who number approximately 100 million, or 40 percent of Indonesia's population. Other groups have migrated over the centuries, bringing with them the same philosophy of closeness to nature that marks them as Indigenous.[57]

It is difficult to get a clear picture of the state of Indigenous Peoples in Indonesia. Of the country's 250 million people, 95 percent are described as Indigenous by government. However, officials do not use the strict United Nations definition of Indigenous Peoples as those originally rooted in the land. Because of centuries during which Malays, Tamils, Arabs, and other groups settled in Indonesia, authorities have come to view them all as being Indigenous. The Javanese, who are the major Aboriginal group, constitute nearly half of Indonesia's population. As Indigenous Peoples, the Javanese accepted and created relationships with the various waves of traders and settlers. The Javanese, who now identify as Muslim, practise a syncretic religion called Abangan Islam that incorporates elements of their traditional practices. Indigenous Peoples have difficulties in getting their rights recognized. Apart from acknowledgement of their status and culture, tribal peoples are also pressuring the Indonesian government to recognize their rights to almost 13 million hectares of land.[58]

In recent centuries, Indonesia became the destination of traders and colonialists who brought with them a different mindset about relationship to the land. Buddhist monks from China appeared in 671 CE, bringing religious and organizational influences. In other areas, Hindu holy men, traders, and settlers appeared. In both cases, trade and intermarriage led to alliances with local chiefdoms. These foreigners sought not to destroy, but to influence local spiritual practices through friendly relations.

Islamic traders began arriving in the fourteenth century. An account of an early Islamic settlement noted: "He [local sultan] is constantly engaged in warring for the Faith and in raiding expeditions, but is withal a humble-hearted man, who walks on foot to Friday prayers. His subjects also take pleasure in warring for the Faith and voluntarily accompany him on his expeditions. They have the upper hand on all of the infidels in their vicinity."[59] However, the key strategy of Islam was to entice Indigenous communities to convert in order to gain favourable access to trade goods.

Following the arrival of Islam in Indonesia, the Dutch appeared in 1498. Vasco de Gama was not only an accomplished seafarer, but also an adventurer keen to cash in on European discoveries as had happened in other parts of the world. Copious amounts of profits were made from spices, enough motivation for de Gama to set up colonies. Acting as pirates, the Portuguese entered into Indigenous communities, raiding and pillaging. Through superior weaponry and divide-and-conquer tactics, the Dutch East India Company took de facto control of Indonesia.[60] They managed to maintain their grip by employing heavy-handed responses to uprisings. Their hold on power did not end until 1942, precipitated by the end of the Second World War and the machinations of an Indonesian Muslim nationalist named Sukarno. A cadre of Islamic intellectuals and politicians led the movement to conceive the modern state of Indonesia, which was not initially envisioned as an Islamic nation. Sukarno's successor, Suharto, was also Muslim, and by 2004, Islamic parties became the dominant political force.

A recent report on "The Situation of Human Rights of Indigenous Peoples in Indonesia" notes that, while Indonesia is a signatory to the United Nations *Declaration on the Rights of Indigenous Peoples*, their government argues that the concept of Indigenous Peoples extends to all Indonesians, with the exception of ethnic Chinese. All Indonesians are to have the same rights. The government has rejected calls by specific groups identifying themselves as "original Indigenous inhabitants." This has implications for government recognition of Indigenous spirituality and the ability to practise it.

> Indigenous peoples continue to face restrictions to exercise their Indigenous religion and belief as laws and practice remain discriminatory against persons and families following Indigenous religion and belief. Though freedom of religion and equality are guaranteed as one of the fundamental human rights in the Indonesian constitution, Indigenous peoples have been forced by law to identify with one of the officially recognized religions (the others being Protestant, Catholic, Buddhist or Hindu) as otherwise they face great difficulties to obtain citizenship ID and register civil status.[61]

Reports from the Orang Rimba tribe in Indonesia reveal an aggressive campaign to convert the tribe to Islam. Their region has seen some of the world's most rapid deforestation since the government granted economic incentives for development in the 1980s. Half of Sumatra's forests have been slashed and burned, replaced by palm oil and rubber trees. One village leader observes: "If you came before you would have seen our forest. It was pristine with huge trees. It's all gone. It happened in the last few years. The palm plantations came in and then the forest started to burn." An Elder said: "What we want is for them to stop taking away our forest. We don't want houses like the outsiders. I am at peace and happy in the forest. I am a person of the jungle."[62]

On the other hand, the Indonesian government argues that it is doing good things for the Orang Rimba: "Before Islam they just believed in spirits, gods and goddesses, not the Supreme god Allah. When someone died, they didn't even bury the dead. They just would leave the body in the forest. Now their life has meaning and direction. For now we are focussing on the children. It's easier to convert them, their mind isn't filled with other things. With the older ones it's harder."[63]

The story coming from the community differs: "After a while we wanted to send our children to school, but the teacher wanted to see the birth certificate. And for that you have to have a state religion that the government recognizes. So we had a tribal meeting and discussed what religion we should choose, and decided to choose Islam. . . . It was a very heavy and difficult decision, but we feel like we have no choice if we want to move forward, so our children can have the same opportunities as the outsiders."[64]

The Orang Rimba express concern: "We have no space to live. We are always told we are nomadic people with no religion, no culture. Our religion is not respected. The government is always insisting that we convert and live in houses and in one place. We can't do that. Our way of life is not like that. . . . We have been around before the new religions arrived, but now it's like they rule us and want to clean us from this country. We have to fight back."[65]

The government spokesperson is adamant: "On the identity card they have to state what religion they have. There are those that have become Muslims, some who have become Christians. So now they are beginning to know God." Meanwhile, in a local hut children are heard reciting, "There is no god but Allah. I will protect Islam till I die."[66]

A similar account arises of children recruited for education from the province of West Papua. With the offer of free schooling, several boys were brought to a mosque in Jakarta. Once there, the boys were given Islamic vestments and made to recite the Shahadah, the prayer of conversion. They were given Muslim names and told that using their previous identities was forbidden. Education focused on reciting the Qur'an: "If we didn't read the Qur'an and pray at certain times, we were locked up and then we were burnt." They had no means of communicating with their families. When some tried to run away, they were caught and beaten. They were informed that when they returned to their communities they were to Islamicize the others. The Indonesian minister of economic affairs, commenting on thousands of children brought down this path, praised the effort stating that "it is one of our ways to obtain a ticket to heaven."[67]

This pattern follows the template of colonization by Christians in which the population initially welcomed outsiders and were willing to learn about others' beliefs. However, the newcomers proved intolerant of Indigenous belief systems. Children were removed and brainwashed in residential schools. This is spiritual imperialism, imposing a supposedly superior religion on peoples who already practised a pure form of spirituality.

Verse 2:256 of the Qur'an states: "There is no compulsion in religion." However, this applies only to the "peoples of the book"—Jews and Christians, and not to "pagans." While there is tolerance for peoples of the book, there is much less shown towards polytheistic Indigenous Peoples. Pragmatic exemptions have been made for Zoroastrians and Hindus, however.[68]

Australasia

Aboriginal presence in Australia extends to very ancient times, as far back as 50,000 years. It is estimated there were about a half million Aborigines at the time of European contact in 1788. They were semi-nomadic hunter gatherers with a rich tradition of relating to the spirit world. Their Dreamtime tradition describes Ancestors being placed upon the land and building relationships with the flora and fauna. Traditional healers worked with spirit entities that interacted with living beings. Epidemics that broke out upon contact decimated Aborigine populations by as much as 90 percent. In places such as New South Wales, Australian authorities carried out campaigns of extermination. Indigenous people face challenges with recognition of their rights, including denial of land rights on the basis of the legal concept of *terra nullius*. Aborigine children were forcibly removed from families to hasten assimilation. Although there is growing recognition of their rights, Aboriginal Australians have yet to receive full recognition in the country's constitution.[69]

Many of the Pacific islands were populated by Polynesians around 1200 CE. In New Zealand, Maoris constitute about 15 percent of the population. Under British policy, arrangements for coexistence are based on the Treaty of Waitangi entered into in 1840. Despite occasional conflicts, the treaty has provided a framework for relatively peaceful coexistence. By having seven out of 120 seats in the New Zealand Parliament, Maoris are able to continue pressing for fulfillment of their Treaty Rights.[70]

A critical reason for the expansion of modern civilization and its suppression and persecution of Indigenous ideologies is based upon belief about our relationship with the natural world. Ecolizations did not conceive that people were the central purpose of Creation. But, over time, humanity came to envision itself as exceptional, and deities increasingly incorporated human form. Rather than continue ancient ceremonial practices of direct interaction with spirit, people themselves assumed the role of interlocutors of divine experience.

CHAPTER 5
RELIGION OVERTAKES THE WORLD

Spirituality and Religion

Elders respect all beliefs, as they consider them to emanate from Manitow. However, they are becoming increasingly aware that there are significant distinctions between traditional spiritual practices and mainstream religions. Mosôm Danny frequently pointed out that we do not follow religion as defined in the Western world.

> We do not have a religion, but rather a way of living that includes prayer, worship. The Indian way is not a religion but a way of understanding the spiritual world. The teacher is the spirit, who comes to us through thoughts and the actions of others. It is a close relationship with the Creator in all aspects of our lives. Ceremonies allow for meditation. Aboriginal spirituality is open to anyone who is interested.[1]

A dictionary definition of spirituality states that it is "a sense of connection to something bigger than ourselves, and it typically involves a search for meaning in life." In contrast, religion is described as "the belief in a god or in a group of gods; an organized system of beliefs, ceremonies, and rules used to worship a god or a group of gods; an interest, a belief, or an activity that is very important to a person or group." It is also defined as "a set of beliefs concerning the cause, nature, and purpose of the universe, especially when considered as the creation of a superhuman agency or agencies, usually involving devotional and ritual observances, and often containing a moral code governing the conduct of human affairs."[2] Scholars are clear that the creation and interpretation of religions is influenced by human thought and, therefore, is unique to a specific time and place.

One may ask the question: which came first—spirituality or religion? It is certain that, prior to the emergence of modern religions, Indigenous cosmology existed. Informed observers have to admit that all faiths had their original roots in ancient systems. To put it another way, Indigenous worldview is the "mother of all belief systems." Aboriginal ontology is the "original instruction," but religions have lost aspects of its holism over time. The Western world has come to live in a state of denial of the transcendent with rates of atheism as high as 30 percent.[3]

In Indigenous philosophy, supernal experience occurs within the individual. As a human, one is born with a specific purpose or mission that is embedded deep within our consciousness. It is with this in mind that the Cree and Saulteaux used ceremonies, vision quests, and meditation to understand how to fulfill their purpose. A great deal of latitude was granted to the individual in pursuing one's goal as long as they remained within spiritual norms. Elders offered guidance; however, they did not coerce or interfere. How did ancient peoples come to realize these principles since they didn't have manuals? The answer is simple—they interrogated the ethereal world using Protocols and ceremonies. With a sincere, honest, and fervent approach, it would be unusual for an individual to not receive an answer in the form of a dream, vision, or omen. Indeed, a person was not deemed to be fully human until one had experienced supernatural revelation.[4]

Religion as Relativistic

Relativism is "knowledge [that] is relative to the limited nature of mind and the conditions of knowing; a view that ethical truths depend on the individuals and groups holding them."[5] In other words, there is no absolute truth other than that which happens to be one's point of view. "In religious studies, research of 'the sacred' should not be treated as a priori, or assumed . . . it is a classificatory term or a classification that refers to a distinctive set of ways humans relate, or respond, to a set of objects that have been demarcated by them as inherently meaningful, powerful and/or agencies or vehicles of superhuman life. . . . In the study of religion two primary approaches are often employed: the historical-descriptive presentation of religious data, and the systematic analysis and classification of religious data."[6]

Popes, including John Paul II, have expressed concern about relativism: "Once the idea of a universal truth about the good, knowable by human reason, is lost, inevitably the notion of conscience also changes. Conscience is no longer considered in its primordial reality as an act of a person's intelligence, the function of which is to apply the universal knowledge of good in a specific situation and thus to express a judgment about the right conduct to be chosen here and now. Instead, there is a tendency to grant to the individual conscience the prerogative of independently determining the criteria of good and evil."[7]

Relativism did not exist in traditional beliefs, where the transcendent was the ultimate authority. Indigenous Peoples in various cultures had innumerable names for Manitow and âtayôhkanak but recognizing supernal authority in all matters created a common basis for belief and practice. Indigenous Peoples understood that Manitow gave different ceremonies to different groups. However, the commonalities were always understood and Protocols and practices were often interchanged. The introduction of Christian denominations caused divisiveness that had not previously existed.

Sacred learning is more than what is simply obtained from book learning. The spiritual journey is personal and not a slavish adherence to a rigid system. Experience is a difficult process of gaining self-knowledge and discipline to become a better person. Some

Elders have observed that Christianity has been intolerant of Indigenous ceremonies and wondered why this is the case. If the Church is so certain it has the correct belief, why is it not more welcoming rather than feeling threatened by Indigenous cosmology?

As described earlier, the entire basis of Indigenous belief is that the etheric realm beyond the physical is real. In contrast, the material has the undeniable sense of reality as perceived through our physical senses. It was the intention of Manitow that upon birth a veil is drawn over one's etheric memory. Life can be likened to going to a movie and becoming so totally engrossed in the cinematic action that one forgets one's daily routine. In that sense, we are on a stage and are watching the worldly drama into which we are born. We are spiritual actors in a physical drama. Shakespeare's expression "all the world's a stage, and all the men and women merely players" is very apt.[8] But while we are conscious during the production, we tend to forget why we became involved in the show in the first place. We mistake the stage for real existence and forget about our true origins. Mosôm Danny cautioned that one will struggle, not only to achieve one's purpose for living but also to reconnect with our actual home. It will take several lifetimes to acquire the relationship lessons that will eventually enable us to supersede this worldly learning environment.[9]

The problem with religions is that they are byproducts of civilization. With the rationalist, secular, and materialist outlook, the idea of a direct relationship to the numinous has been expunged. Churches give the supernal little more than lip service. The link to our spiritual side becomes increasingly weak. In Indigenous ecolizations, these mystics were adept at ceremonial practice, and found means to pierce the ethereal veil. This is how they could "miraculously" locate game and lost people and communicate with animal and plant âtayôhkanak.[10]

To Elders, sacred truths are self-evident and do not need to be proven. They can debate the finer points of what their dreams, visions, and meditations mean amongst themselves. But the fundamental requirement to follow the Good Path remains unquestioned. In traditional beliefs, there was no concept of devil or hell.[11] There was only bad judgment or ill-considered choices that took one off the Good Path, Red Road, or Sweetgrass Way. The ways in which one remained on the Good Path was by following the Law of Relationships and the Seven Virtues. Spirituality provided a sense of certainty that there was a higher power that rendered clear instructions about one's purpose for existence, proper behaviours, and what to do when things went wrong. These instructions were understood and did not have to be written down.

Miracles are defined as unexplainable events that produce wonderful results. Few today believe that miracles can actually occur. One reason is because such phenomena are rarely, if ever, witnessed anymore. A chapter in *The Knowledge Seeker: Embracing Indigenous Spirituality* is devoted to accounts of miraculous events as witnessed by reputable non-Indigenous sources. There is another way to explain miracles by looking at events today.

Today, we have numerous unexplainable events of the non-miraculous kind. Recently, a gunman in Las Vegas took up position in a high-rise hotel, killing dozens and wounding hundreds at an outdoor concert. Authorities never discovered a motive.[12] Virtually every week there is news about some horrific shooting or massacre for which no one is able to provide an explanation. Perhaps it is mental illness, they conclude. The public says, "I can't believe this happened. What will be next?" Such events are the mirror opposite of miracles. A world where social and environmental conditions are in a downward spiral spawns the conditions for such abominations. Conversely, following the Good Path makes it more likely that miracles will be witnessed.

Changing Face of the Creator

J.H. Brennan is one of those rare scholars who has examined the phenomena and perception of spirit throughout human history. His book, *Whisperers: The Secret History of the Spirit World,* charts its evolution up to modern times. He notes that, over time, the image of the Creator increasingly assumes a human resemblance.

Brennan maintains that the gods maintained a direct and close relationship with humans early in their existence, but this connection waned over time. Initially, the relationship with the supernatural was one where humans were dedicated followers of the deities, unwilling to engage in any behaviour that was not supernally condoned. Brennan argues that this remained the case up until the time of early civilizations. Unfortunately, he does not include perceptions among Indigenous Peoples of the Americas that the Creator continues to be a benevolent provider of gifts.[13]

Brennan observes that spirit deities were initially perceived as benign and were seen as evil only after some time had passed. For example, Judaism declared that "all the gods of the heathens are devils" and, therefore, must become subservient to Jehovah. Such an admonishment was part of the re-visioning of their god as an exclusive deity and their monotheistic god's displacement of any other form of sacred relationship with nature. Indigenous Peoples, while recognizing the spiritual essence in all things, never denied the supremacy of Manitow. Their faithfulness to the Creator helped them to maintain a consistent relationship with the rest of Creation. On the other hand, the new religions created a multitude of gods who were partial only to their followers.[14]

Sumeria (3200 to 500 BCE), in Mesopotamia, is regarded as the "cradle of civilization." As individuals began to have vested interests in land for agriculture, communal groups had to develop more sophisticated forms of organization to contend with encroachment and competition by individuals. Statues of deities began incorporating animal and human forms. These gods sometimes "spoke" through the statues. The Sumerian gods became disturbed by the behaviour of humanity: "The people became numerous. The gods were depressed by their uproar. The deity Enlil heard their noise. He exclaimed to the great gods: The noise of mankind has become burdensome."[15] The advice of the deities then came less frequently. A Mesopotamian monarch lamented: "My god has forsaken me and disappeared, my goddess has failed me and keeps at a distance, the good angel who walked beside me has departed."[16] Archaeological studies of Sumeria and Mesopotamia reveal that a series of conflicts emerged in what were the first recorded wars, an indication that the new religions were not able to maintain overall harmony.

Egyptian civilization (3150 to 30 BCE) was preoccupied with their deities, and their ability to connect with them through dreams and to petition for help in the afterlife. The ability of the pharaoh and priests to connect through rituals involving nature was critical. Egyptian deities appeared in part-human and part-animal or bird form. The supreme deity Ra, the sun god, was a later innovation and appeared as a human body with the head of a falcon wearing a head-dress of the Sun. Set, the god of storms and misfortune, took human form with the head of a dog. Isis, the goddess of magic, appeared as a woman with wings, and Osiris, the deity of agriculture, adopted a fully human form. God was personified in the pharaoh. Priests cast out evil and played roles in healing the living and intervening with the afterlife.[17]

Among the Greeks, oracles were relied upon to maintain supernal contact. Delphi was a major divination centre where the quality of one's decision-making would be referred to the Oracle to decipher whether the gods condoned it. The deities could intervene in human affairs—for example, when going into battle. In the epic Greek poem of history, the *Iliad*, one deity warns Achilles not to enter the fight lest he be killed. In another situation, Achilles is instructed not to take revenge against King Agamemnon. The gods could inspire individual soldiers to perform acts of heroism.[18] As Greek thought and philosophy evolved, it elevated the meaning of human existence and led to a more individualistic approach to temporal and spiritual matters. Greek gods appeared in human form and the focus of philosophy turned towards the development and perfection of the body and mind.

Roman gods Jupiter, chief deity and god of the sky; Mars, god of war; Mercury, messenger of the gods; and others appeared in human form. Roman gods took great interest in the daily affairs of their corporeal underlings. These deities were often in conflict with one another, and, correspondingly, Roman civilization was a heavily militarized one, and Mars was one of the most important gods. Romans were fatalistic and obsessed with omens such as lightning and thunder, meteorites, or the behaviour of birds and other animals. The emperor, self-styled as a god, could order the deaths of slaves, rivals, and even family members with impunity.[19]

Abrahamic Religions and Human Centrality

Greek and Roman civilizations, with their burgeoning urban centres and increasing power based upon exploitation of neighbours, were distancing themselves from ancient Indigenous ethics. Philosophies such as the belief in "natural slavery" normalized the process of enslaving tribal peoples. For example, the Hebrews were victims of exploitation during captivity in Babylon (597 to 538 BCE).[20]

Out of the Hebrew experience emerged the Abrahamic covenant. The teachings were to serve as a guide for future generations. According to Jewish scriptures, Abraham, the first Hebrew patriarch, received the promise of a special relationship between God and His chosen people. When Yahweh (Jehovah) led the Jews away from Egyptian slavery around 1400 BCE, Moses received the message of divine authority in the form of the Ten Commandments. In presenting the Commandments, Jehovah said: "I am the Lord thy God, which have brought thee out of Egypt, the house of bondage. Thou shalt have no other gods before me . . . for I the Lord thy God am a jealous God."[21] Brennan notes that the first commandment is actually not a declaration of strict monotheism, as it does not deny the existence of other gods. Rather, it simply states that they are not to be given as much respect. Unlike Christianity and Islam, however, Judaism did not practise proselytization.

The first five books of the Old Testament are known as the Torah meaning "instruction" or "law."[22] One of the Bible's central tenets is the idea of domination over nature.

> Then God said, 'Let us make man in our image, in our likeness; and let them rule over the fish of the sea and over the birds of the air and over the livestock and over all the earth, and over all the creatures that move along the ground.' God created man in His own image, in the image of God He created him; male and female He created them, and blessed them, and said to them: 'Be fruitful and increase in number, and fill the earth, *and subdue it* [emphasis added]. Rule over the fish of the sea and over the birds of the air and over every living thing that moves on the earth.'[23]

The prophets who penned the Old Testament understood that there were consequences to abandoning the ethics of Indigenous Eden. Adam and Eve, the "first" human beings, could enjoy Eden as long as they tended the Tree of Life. God warned humans that they could taste of all of the wonders of the created world except for one: "The Lord commandeth the man: You are free to eat from any tree in the garden, but you must not eat from the tree of the knowledge of good and evil, for when you do eat of it you will surely die."[24] This is a powerful archetype. The authors of the Old Testament foresaw that eating of the tree of the knowledge of good and evil, and believing that they could determine their own destiny without help from God, would embark humanity on a new path and usher them out of the Garden of Eden.

> For God knows that in the day you eat from it your eyes will be opened, and you will be like God, knowing good and evil. When the woman saw that the tree was good for food, and that it was a delight to the eyes, and that the tree was desirable to make one wise, she took from its fruit and ate and she gave also to her husband with her, and he ate. Then the eyes of both of them were opened, and they knew that they were naked; and they sewed fig leaves together and made themselves loin coverings.[25]

This was the original sin in the Old Testament, the state into which humanity fell after choosing to leave Indigenous Eden. Adam and Eve represent those humans who chose the human-centredness of civilization over the values of Indigenous Eden.[26] Biblical scholars agree that although often portrayed as a transmission from God, these scriptures were written over the course of centuries by numerous authors who were comfortable making the bold statement that "God made man in His own image."

In the Old Testament, humanity gains the protection of God through a New Covenant. However, adherents must submit to and obey God's rules as conveyed to Moses in the form of the Ten Commandments.

And God spoke all these words: "I am the Lord your God, who brought you out of Egypt, out of the land of slavery. You shall have no other gods before me. You shall not make for yourself an image in the form of anything in heaven above or on the earth beneath or in the waters below. You shall not bow down to them or worship them; for I, the Lord your God, am a jealous God, punishing the children for the sin of the parents to the third and fourth generation of those who hate me, but showing love to a thousand generations of those who love me and keep my commandments. You shall not misuse the name of the Lord your God, for the Lord will not hold anyone guiltless who misuses his name.

Remember the Sabbath day by keeping it holy. Six days you shall labor and do all your work, but the seventh day is a sabbath to the Lord your God. On it you shall not do any work, neither you, nor your son or daughter, nor your male or female servant, nor your animals, nor any foreigner residing in your towns. For in six days the Lord made the heavens and the earth, the sea, and all that is in them, but he rested on the seventh day. Therefore the Lord blessed the Sabbath day and made it holy.

Honor your father and your mother, so that you may live long in the land the Lord your God is giving you. You shall not murder. You shall not commit adultery. You shall not steal. You shall not give false testimony against your neighbor. You shall not covet your neighbor's house. You shall not covet your neighbor's wife, or his male or female servant, his ox or donkey, or anything that belongs to your neighbor."[27]

The New Testament is based upon the idea of a renewed covenant in which Christ, as Messiah, fulfills the prophecies of the Torah and ushers in the potential of atonement for humanity's sins. It opens up a new phase where salvation also becomes available to non-Jewish Gentiles. The tireless proselytizing of the Apostle Paul, decades after Jesus Christ's death, led to Christian conversions in Greece, Asia Minor, the Middle East, and North Africa. From an Indigenous perspective, the New Testament can be seen as an effort to salvage some elements of original spirituality. Where the Old

Testament focused on fear, control, and retribution, Christianity seeks healing through forgiveness and love. But in the Indigenous approach, salvation is not promised by a saviour, but is only possible as a result of personal spiritual struggle.

The Book of Revelation, the last chapter of the New Testament, foretold the consequences of the decision to leave the Garden of Eden and failure to heed the commandments. The repercussions take the form of multiple disasters that will befall humanity.

> And then many will fall away and betray one another and hate one another. And many false prophets will arise and lead many astray. And because lawlessness will be increased, the love of many will grow cold. (Matthew 24:10–12)[28]

> But understand this, that in the last days there will come times of difficulty. For people will be lovers of self, lovers of money, proud, arrogant, abusive, disobedient to their parents, ungrateful, unholy, heartless, unappeasable, slanderous, without self-control, brutal, not loving good, treacherous, reckless, swollen with conceit, lovers of pleasure rather than lovers of God, having the appearance of godliness, but denying its power. Avoid such people. (Second Timothy 3:1–5)[29]

> There will be great earthquakes, and in various places famines and pestilences. And there will be terrors and great signs from heaven. (Luke 21:11)[30]

It is apparent that the Abrahamic religions, having strayed down the path of human-centred ideology, had been creating demons of their own making. Once humans began to redefine human spirituality as a reflection of its own image, humanity became more responsible for policing its own moral behaviours as with the Ten Commandments.[31] No longer was accountability directly to the transcendent through dreams, visions, ceremonies, and healing. Right and wrong were measurable only through the Bible, and churches meted out punishments to keep their flocks in line. Religious authorities would project this hellish worldview onto hapless Indigenous cultures.

Roman Catholicism

Early Christians were highly committed to the transcendent and had no particular interest in power or wealth. They tended to keep a low profile to avoid persecution by the Romans. Everything changed after Roman Emperor Constantine attributed his victory at the Battle of Milvian Bridge to a vision of Christ. He ordered that persecution of Christians cease. On his deathbed he converted to Christianity, providing the example that eventually led to the Roman Catholic Church becoming Rome's official religion. The idea of redemption from sin held personal appeal to Romans who had indulged in horrendous atrocities.

In 325 CE, Constantine convened the First Council of Nicaea in order to clarify the Church's belief system. Not all Christian leaders were enthusiastic about Catholicism becoming the religion of the state that had persecuted them. Their skepticism was not misplaced: Constantine's true passion was empire building, and the role of the new popes would slowly become more political than spiritual, fundamentally changing the nature of Christianity. The Council of Constantinople in 553 CE disavowed notions promoted by Church scholar Origen of the pre-existence of souls and their transmigration through reincarnation. A more fundamental reason for decreeing that humans only live once appears to have been Emperor Justinian's desire to regulate the spiritual life of his subjects.

The Catholic Church did not condone any form of communication with the etheric: "Beloved, believe not every spirit, but try the spirits whether they are of God; because many false prophets are gone out into the world." Another passage reads: "Regard not them that have familiar spirits, neither seek after wizards, to be defiled by them: I am the Lord your God. . . . Thou shalt not suffer a witch to live."[32] Only under authority of the Church could communication with the supernal and miracles occur.

A 1320 CE papal bull authorized an inquisition into all those who "made magic" and "worshipped or made pacts with the devil." Trials led to thousands being accused of sorcery, many of whom were burned at the stake. Needless to say, anyone of a mystic bent who performed rituals was quickly forced to practise underground.

Activities that had found acceptance since ancient times fell into the realm of secret societies.[33]

In *The Pagan Christ*, Tom Harpur notes that early Christian theology, as developed under the sway of the Roman Empire, took a literalist approach.

> In the third and fourth centuries C.E., the Christian Church made a fatal error. Either deliberately, in a competitive bid to win over the greatest numbers of the largely unfettered masses, or through willful ignorance of the true, inner sense of the profound spiritual wisdom it had inherited from so many ancient sources, the Church took to a literalist, popularized, historical approach to sublime truth. What was preserved in the amber of allegory, it misrepresented as plodding fact. The transcendent meaning of glorious myths and symbols was reduced to the farrago of miraculous or irrelevant, or quite unbelievable 'events.' The great truth that the Christ was to come in man, that the Christ principle was potentially in every one of us, was changed to the exclusivist teaching that the Christ had come as a man. No other could match him, or even come close.... The implications were enormous.[34]

Harpur's point is that the human being called Jesus Christ recognized in historical records should not be confused with the archetypes he represents. Harpur notes what happened to the pagans, a name originally used by Romans to describe barbarians but now directed towards citizens who disagreed with the new Catholicism and questioned Church officials. When challenged by its pagan critics about the real sources of its gospels, dogmas, and rites adopted wholesale, the Roman Catholic Church reacted with fierce hostility. It hunted down anyone, whether Christian or not, who bore witness to the old truths, closing pagan philosophical schools, burning thousands of books, and excommunicating anyone who dared to question the new orthodox line.[35]

Harpur maintains that the only authentic way of teaching spirituality is through mythology and archetypes. These transcend the vagaries of human interpretation and are an effective means of comprehending the deeper significance of life.

> What is amazing is the universality and similarity of these ancient myths, though they are found in widely disparate cultures and date from the very mists of antiquity. Whether Chaldean, Sumerian, Persian or Egyptian—or indeed, as we shall see, from Central Africa or the Americas—they seem to have come from a single highly advanced source of intellectual understanding. It's almost as though long ago, there was one virtually cosmic religion that eventually and gradually deteriorated over eons.[36]

Harpur offers the example of how ancient myths are incorporated in Christ's story.

> [In] the Osiris/Dionysus myth, the 'hero' is the savior of man, God incarnate, born of a virgin in a cave on December 25; he has a star appear at his birth, is visited by the magi from the East, and turns water into wine at a wedding; he heals the sick, casts out demons, and performs miracles; he is transfigured before his disciples, rides a donkey into a special city, is betrayed for thirty pieces of silver, and celebrates a communal meal with bread and wine; he is put to death on a cross, descends into hell, and is resurrected on the third day; he dies to redeem the world's sins; he ascends into heaven and is seated beside God as a divine judge.[37]

Harpur's interpretation of Egyptian mythology is controversial. However, he makes a valid point about the employment of archetypes in religion. He argues that the Ancients understood that nature was a powerful analogue of the transcendent: "ancient wisdom recognized infinitely better than modern the essential kinship of the two. The lack of a deep connection between sacred values and the natural world today contrasts sharply with what we have foolishly called 'primitive' religions around the world, and accounts in no small measure for the dryness and overly cerebral nature of much of traditional Christian worship."[38]

The Bible certainly suggested intolerance for unauthorized spirit communication: "Regard not them that have familiar spirits, neither seek after wizards, to be defiled by them. . . . I am the Lord your God. And the soul that turneth after such as have familiar spirits, and after wizards, to go whoring after them, I will even set my face against that soul, and will cut him off from among his people. And he made his son pass through the fire, and observed times, and used enchantments, and dealt with familiar spirits and wizards: he wrought much wickedness in the sight of the Lord, to provoke him to anger."[39]

Harpur goes on to observe that "the Church's deplorable record of persecutions, wars and other atrocities would have never taken place. Uncounted millions would have been encouraged to nurture and bring to fruition their own moral and spiritual Christhood, instead of always passively waiting for a perfect savior from outside to do the job for them. That, of course, would not have suited ecclesiastical authorities bent on maintaining control of both bodies and souls."[40] If followers failed to fulfill their special covenant with Him, God threatened to "intervene and overthrow these forces of evil in a cataclysmic show of force, that he would destroy all that opposed him, including all of the kingdoms that were causing his people to suffer."[41]

In 476 CE, German tribes overthrew Romulus Augustus, the last of the Roman emperors, ushering in a period today described as the Dark Ages. It did not take long for the German and French, inheritors of Roman hegemony, the Holy Roman Empire, to resume their bias against Indigenous practices. The Catholic Inquisitions of the 1300s were authorized to "investigate all those who used images or sacred objects to make magic and those who worshipped or made pacts with demons." By 1350, over a thousand French citizens were tried for sorcery and over half were burned at the stake.[42]

Such "dangerous" practices included "the possibility of invoking the whole hierarchy of angels and demons, each with their own names and attributes. The rituals for such spirit-raising varied, but usually involved such procedures as drawing chalk circles on the ground, pronouncing incantations, observing ritual conditions of fasting and prayer, and employing such apparatus as holy water, candles, swords, wands and metal lamina. There is no doubt whatsoever that these rituals were extensively practised, both by contemporary intellectuals and by less educated would-be magicians."[43]

Reformation

Power struggles escalated after the discovery of the New World in 1492. As arbiter of disputes, the pope apportioned the spoils of the New World between the Kingdoms of Portugal and Spain, with most going to Spanish interests. The sordid sub-story of Spanish conquest of the New World was the search for gold on the pretext of saving souls. A few, such as Bartolomé de las Casas, objected, resulting in the pope issuing the papal bull *Sublimus Dei* in 1537 and declaring that the inhabitants of the New World were not, in fact, subhuman minions of the devil.

The riches of the New World magnified the insatiable appetite of the Holy Roman Empire. Church leadership became so corrupt that simple followers of the faith saw that its behaviour was at great variance with the words of Christ. In 1517, Martin Luther, a professor at the University of Wittenberg, finally took a stand. He posted his list of ninety-five Theses (abuses) by the Church on the door of Castle Church in Wittenberg, Germany. The abuses included the selling of indulgences to gain spiritual salvation. The newly invented printing press enabled Luther's objections to be rapidly disseminated.

The Protestant Reformation was founded upon Luther's effort to rediscover true Christianity.[44] Political machinations and international intrigue by the Church grew so severe that, in 1881, anticlerical groups threatened to harm the pope in order to make Church leadership take their concerns seriously. The Church finally got the message, disavowing any further involvement in politics. Church encyclicals turned their attention to more appropriate matters such as helping the poor and defending the rights of workers.

Questioning the Faith

Much of Jewish ritual is based upon sacrifice, an aspect taken up by Christianity. In the Christian tradition, Jesus, the Lamb of God, is sacrificed through his crucifixion to atone for the sins of humanity. Easter, the occasion of Christ's resurrection, is, therefore, the most sacred day for Christians and participating in the Holy Communion, symbolic of Christ's offering, is an important ritual. Not all Christians believe in the interpretation of the Catholic Church, however. Gnostics see the story of Christ as more about a spiritual mystery than about a physical event.

Gretta Vosper, an ordained United Church minister, challenges religious orthodoxy in her book *With or Without God*. She notes that archaeological and historical research proves that mythology has been incorporated into the liturgy over the centuries. Much of the Church's canon was formulated after Roman Emperor Constantine adopted Christianity as the empire's official religion. In the process of regularizing the creed, Constantine imposed certain interpretations—for example, eliminating the concept of human reincarnation in favour of Christ's resurrection. Hope for spiritual redemption now relies upon the condition that all the rules of the Church are followed. Those who disagree are excommunicated or condemned to eternal damnation.

Vosper observes that the Bible is a human-created document: "We started by creating the concept of God. Then we created the concept of Christ. . . . We created our doctrine and dogma, our traditions, and our holy stories. We created church," she continues. Vosper acknowledges the difficulty among preachers of conscience to broach these discrepancies when faced by a resistant flock.[45]

Christian doctrines came to carry the weight of legal authority. It was the excesses of this theological system, for example the regulation of international affairs, which eventually led to political wars that were backed by religion. In other words, the Church was meddling too much in politics. Under the Reformation, the state would no longer have a role in dictating religious beliefs, which should then be a private matter only. This led to concepts of freedom of religion and separation of state and religion.[46]

Christians who are concerned about the veracity of liturgy find it problematic that there are contradictions built into what is considered to be an infallible Bible. Vosper encourages the church to "speak a language that is open to intellectual exploration, spiritual quest, and whatever experiences of the divine are brought to them."[47] She also candidly notes that Christianity blithely glides over excesses of its past, "the heinous ecclesiastical activities of the Dark Ages, the witch trials, the Inquisition, the brutal child-rearing practices, the missionary zeal that annihilated whole cultures, the deep anti-Semitism that culminated in blind-eyes turned towards Nazi Germany."[48]

The redemption offered by Christ's sacrifice not only absolves practising Christians from sin, but also guarantees them eternal life. Christianity places more emphasis on faith than on difficult spiritual struggle. As long as Catholics adhere to the faith and follow its rituals, sins other than the most egregious can be overlooked as long as one receives the final sacraments.[49] This is a concept difficult for Indigenous adherents to grasp, as nothing can replace the individual's inner struggle. Spiritual progress is fundamentally rooted within oneself. This is where the imprint needs to be made: It is only through personal realization that maturity and transcendence can be achieved. The disciplines of fasting, sacrificing, sharing, and seeking dreams and visions are beneficial for everyone. There is no easy way to progress along the Good Path.

It took until the post–World War II era for the Catholic Church to acknowledge that non-Christian religions are equally as valid. The Vatican II Council of the 1960s recognized that other faiths can provide salvation.[50] It took even longer for the Church to accept that Indigenous culture and spirituality is not only worthy of its notice but also contributes to the totality of world faiths. While Elders embrace this hard-won sense of acceptance, many recognize that the Church will never be capable of going far enough to incorporate true Indigenous practices and will settle for mere symbolic gestures only.

Relationship to Indigenous Peoples

When comparing belief systems, it is incorrect to describe Abrahamic religions as monotheistic and then to dismiss Indigenous religions as polytheistic. As with Abrahamic religions, all tribal peoples recognized one Supreme Being, although they called the Creator by different names. Thus, Indigenous Peoples were, in fact, monotheistic. But Manitow was too mysterious to be reduced to human form. However, they also communicated in ceremonies with spirits such as âtayôhkanak which oversaw the various manifestations of animals and plants. These spirits were not worshipped as deities but were seen as helpers gifted by the Creator to assist people to learn how to function in the world. Abrahamic monotheism denied the presence of spirit in all things and handed a monopoly to a single god.

The God of the Old Testament threatened humans when they disobeyed. In contrast, the benevolent Manitow showered humans with his gifts of Creation and was more tolerant of human foibles. I have heard Elders say that while Christians attend their churches in fear of God, participants in ceremonies chuckle at the humour revealed in stories of Creation. Why does the duck waddle? It's because Wîsahkecâhk had kicked it in the shins. Manitow has a sense of humour and so should humans as they enjoy harmonious relationships.

Baron de Lahontan, a military officer in New France, saw through the priests' misrepresentation of Native beliefs when they argued that conversion to Christianity was necessary.

I have read a thousand Ridiculous Stories writ by our Clergymen, who maintain that the Savages have conferences with [the devil]. And not only to consult him, but pay him a sort of homage. Now all these advances are ridiculous; for in earnest, the Devil never appeared to these Americans. . . . In fine, after using all possible means for a perfect knowledge [sic] of this matter; I conclude that these Ecclesiastics did not understand the true importance of the great word Matchi Manitow (which signifies an Evil Spirit, Matchi being the word for evil and Manitow for Spirit). For by the devil they understand such things as are offensive to 'em, which in our language comes near to the signification of Misfortune, Fate, Unfavourable Destiny, etc. So that in speaking of the Devil they do not mean that Evil Spirit that in Europe is represented under the figure of a Man, with a long Tail and great Horns and Claws.[51]

An anonymous Elder points out differences in approach between Abrahamic religions and Indigenous approaches to spirituality.

The thing too, well, with Christianity you have to have Clergy, who are appointed or self-appointed into the clergy appoints other clergy and they oversee the spiritual needs of the people. Well with the Native people everything just about, it's built in. They, the people, appoint their leaders who pick the singers for the ceremonies and the singers of the songs. Everything is amongst the people and they don't have clergies that will declare this day as a holy day and you must act and behave in this way, must be someplace special that the clergy presides over. Now, so that's one of the big differences, it is without force, no that isn't quite the right word I was looking for, coercion, that sort of thing. Well, with Christianity you do have coercion if you don't believe certain things you, if you want to change the church doctrines you can be excommunicated.[52]

Ojibway preacher Reverend Doyle Turner speaks about the need for Christians and Indigenous Elders to understand one another.

It is of utmost importance as native people to have a solid spiritual/theological base to stand on as we begin to come to a place of healing and peace within the Christian/Traditional maze created for us. There is a great gap of misunderstanding and intolerance between the Christian and religious traditions of our collective peoples, and it is a source of much local conflict that causes factioning. A healing needs to occur between these factions to enable us to articulate a coherent religious philosophy or theology to the youth or the next generations of our communities. We can begin to move toward a place and time of healing by writing, gathering and publishing the religious thought, history and story of the Indigenous peoples.[53]

There is no question that Christianity has been the primary bene-ficiary in acquiring lands and resources as its ideology spread across the world. Sated by consumption of Indigenous lands and coloni-zation of the people, Christianity now presents itself as a moderat-ing force that promotes human rights and tolerance. Europeans and Americans have taken the lead in establishing norms of humanism that are the international standard for behaviours sanctioned by the United Nations. However, there are significant reasons why such a model will not resolve humanity's underlying anomie.

One reason is the magnitude of reconciliation that is required to truly rectify the injustices of the past. More fundamental from an Indigenous perspective, however, is the nature of the humanist approach. Humanism emphasizes the agency of human beings and favours rationalism and empiricism over supernaturalism or super-stition.[54] This thinking has its roots in Enlightenment values, which promoted the notion that all virtue could be achieved through rea-son alone. In other words, it is a strictly secular approach to welfare that emphasizes physical well-being but dismisses any notion of the transcendent. The philosophy of reason has not prevented a mul-titude of atrocities and abuses from occurring. This is because it is not a holistic cosmology that acknowledges the spiritual connection of all beings. From an Indigenous perspective it is a paradigm that lacks moral authority.

Researcher J.H. Brennan concludes that eliminating the mysti-cal from our consciousness shuts off an important facet of our lived experience.

Many of the old psychic marvels have been devalued, and with them the ease and wonder with which our ancestors met a spiritual creation. We live as if the material world was all there is. We armor ourselves with skepticism. But if this armoring sometimes protects us from mistakes, it also locks us in a men-tal prison. We are no longer open-minded enough to wonder if the world is really like that. If anybody challenges our beliefs,

we write them off as 'unrealistic,' stupid or incurably roman-
tic. Yet the evidence that has arisen—the evidence of history,
the evidence of experience and observation, the evidence of
modern physics—positively demands that we consider a new
paradigm. It may be unfamiliar and uncomfortable, but that
is the price paid for progress. The new paradigm suggests
humans are more than they realize.[55]

Individuals have lost personal agency because they have become
dependent on mediators in religion. First Nations were never divided
by intervenors. "And that's the difference again, we are much closer
to the Creator than the White people, because He has created for us
to live, and we are all related, even our dog out here. After we pray,
we say, 'To all our relatives' in our language, in Dakota, when we
end our prayers. It also means the spirit relatives too, everything that
God has made, I am addressing them too."[56] Elder Wilfred Tootoosis recounts: "One Elder once told me that White people had the
same power as the Native people years and years ago but they lost
it, it was taken away from them and that's what is going to happen to
the Indian people if they don't live right. There will be no more faith
healing of the sick people if we don't live right. We are going to lose it
like the others have already lost it."[57]

Academic Paula Gunn Allen writes: "One of the problems with
the Western world, in all of its aspects today, right now in white folk's
time, is that we don't understand spirits. We don't understand that
right here standing with us are multiple worlds coexisting, cohabit-
ing, and occupying the same space with us."[58] Activist John Trudell
describes the distinction succinctly: "There's a difference between
spiritual and religious. Religious is about submission and obedience
and authoritarianism. Spiritual is about taking responsibility."[59]

The Rise of Islam

Rome was successful in spreading Roman Catholicism across the
empire, including the Middle East. It established a new capital in
Constantinople (modern Istanbul) and built churches in places like
Turkey, Egypt, and Syria. The expansion of Christianity would be

halted by the rise of the emerging religion of Islam. According to Islamic belief, the first Muslim prophet was Adam, the first man expelled from the Garden of Eden. All subsequent prophets of the Old Testament, while commonly thought of as Jewish, are viewed as prophets who culminate with Muhammad and the Qur'an. Muhammad revealed that he was visited by the archangel Gabriel in 610 CE. The Mosque at Mecca commemorates the vision in which the prophet conferred with Adam, Abraham, Jesus, Joseph, and Moses before being transported to heaven.[60] The first call for obedience to Allah's will was directed at Adam.[61]

Abraham became discontent over veneration of nature idols. He proclaimed that God was above and beyond nature.[62] Islam traces its lineage directly to Abraham through his eldest son Ishmael, conceived with a servant girl. Christ is viewed as being only another prophet. Judaism and Christianity, while their peoples are of the book, are seen as incomplete religions that are superceded by Islam. Indigenous Peoples, who are not peoples of the book, are inaccurately portrayed as polytheists who are wayward disbelievers. Because they were not monotheists, pagans were required to either accept Islam or be killed, whereas Jews and Christians had the option to pay a tax.[63]

Muhammad, who was a merchant, is a deeply charismatic and revered prophet. He did not consider himself to be an avatar or god but simply a human messenger. Many saw his creed as a pragmatic form of living—fostering strong family and community ties. Since its inception, Islam has been as much a social and political institution as a religion. The Prophet's inspiration behind Islam is reminiscent of the Hebrews who created the original Abrahamic religion. Declaring one God was a means of providing direction and unity to Arab tribes. As Judaism is exclusive to Jews, Islam is exclusive to Muslims.

The words of the Qur'an as transmitted to Muhammad are seen as the direct revelation of Allah's intent. Some adherents memorize the Qur'an word for word.[64] Allah instructs that all humanity must be brought together in religious unity under Islam, which itself means submission. Adherence is manifested through the Five Pillars of Islam: declaration of faith (Shahadah), prayer five times a day (Salat), fasting during the holy month of Ramadan, charity (Zakat), and pilgrimage to Mecca (Hajj).[65] Rituals are external indicators of faith, as opposed to Indigenous ceremonies that involve direct inter-action with Grandparent Spirits, âtayôhkanak, and Ancestors. Simi-lar to the tenor of the Judaic Tanak, severe punishment can be meted out to Muslims who stray from God's will.

Islam faces internal differences such as those between the Sunni and Shia branches: a division that began when adherents disagreed over succession to Muhammad and whether the Prophet's concepts of morality and justice were respected. The Shia believe they observe the deeper meanings of the Qur'an.[66] Sufis, a more mystical brand of Islam, consists of a minority who decry militarism and harsh jus-tice. They prefer to cultivate meditation and self-denial to eliminate selfishness and other base desires.[67] Today Islam is expressed in a variety of ways, from ultra-conservative to reformist. In some cases, religious extremism has emerged. Elder Phil Lane made the obser-vation that fanaticism thrives when religious fervour is not balanced by intellect.[68]

Other Major Religions

Non-Abrahamic religions do not fully ascribe to the precept that cre-ation exists exclusively for human purposes. Although highly insti-tutionalized, they maintain semblances to Indigenous spirituality in their dictums about human behaviour and their relationship to the cosmos. According to Buddha (c. 563 to 483 BCE), there are four fun-damental truths of life—suffering, arising, cessation, and the right way. The eight-fold path includes virtues such as devotion, mindful-ness, compassion, truthfulness, peacefulness, meditation, honour, and being helpful. Observers of Buddhism admire its emphasis on peace and tolerance.[69] Buddhism resembles Indigenous spirituality in that individuals are largely responsible for their behaviours. How-ever, in seeing suffering as inevitable, Buddhism has a more pessi-mistic outlook. It values distancing one from worldly distractions to gain spiritual insight. For Indigenous Peoples, engaging in rela-tionships with all aspects of life in a balanced manner is considered essential.

Hinduism has a long tradition dating back to around 1500 BCE. It has no particular founder or prophet and did not advocate the conversion of others. There are a variety of authoritative texts, the oldest being the Vedas, that include philosophical and ritual guidance. Hinduism sees itself not so much as a religion but more as a way of life. It sees the sacred in all things. Hinduism includes several paths of seeking, such as devotion, physical disciple, learning, and visionary experience.

The Hindu faith has a deeply ingrained belief in the supernatural. Brahmin priests could summon spirits, communicate for purposes of divination, or drive out unwanted disincarnate entities. Priests undertook extensive interest in supernatural forces. One Sanskrit saying goes: "Everything that exists is in the power of the Gods and the Gods are in the power of magical conjurations."[70] Brahmins have been known to put on public displays of their abilities, including growing seedlings into full plants in a very brief space of time, a feat reminiscent of Native American Medicine Persons.[71] This suggests roots in the Indigenous cultures of India that predated Hinduism. Other practices resemble Indigenous ceremonies, such as the use of incense in place of tobacco in rituals, meditation, and demonstrations of sacred gifts.[72]

As with Indigenous beliefs, Hinduism has no particular prophet or parchment that officially creates its spiritual system. While there are specialists in rituals, such as the Brahmins, Hindus enjoy a high degree of independence in pursuing their spiritual paths. The focus on individual development and sacred way of life parallels Indigenous approaches. Their traditional value system did not glorify materialism and encourage capitalism. They did not invade foreign countries for the purposes of colonization, although the caste system created internal division by treating the Dalits as untouchable. However, India's dense population shows that there is imbalance with the natural world.

In Hinduism, world events occur in cycles. The world has gone through the earliest cycle of relative peace and happiness, a second cycle of confusion, and is in the third cycle—degeneration of human behaviours. The final stage is world destruction. However, individuals can liberate themselves from these cycles with efforts and lessons that extend over several reincarnations. Reflection and peacefulness are highly valued as illustrated in the life of Mahatma Gandhi.

Gandhi rose above racism and espoused an approach to resolving conflict that did not have to include violence.

Both Buddhism and Hinduism arose from earlier Indigenous traditions. In India, there remain over 100 million Indigenous Peoples. Some, like the Naga, still live in synchronicity with nature. and retain connection to their Indigenous heritage and values. In larger societies, one begins to see increasing intervention of human individuals as interpreters of the spiritual. In other words, institutionalization sets in. Yet Buddhists and Hindus remain more of a spiritual than a materialistic people. Virtually all Chinese people can be understood as indigenous to the land. The eight percent of the population who are not part of the majority Han are identified as "national minorities"[73]

Elements of Indigenous cosmology persist, including recognizing spirits of nature and Ancestors. Shamanism is China's oldest belief system, as it was in Japan, Korea, Tibet, and elsewhere in the Far East. In the past, Chinese Shamans were known for ceremonies to maintain harmony between earth and heavens, including holding dances to bring rain. Their healers employed both herbal remedies and curing ceremonies. There is a powerful belief in honouring and maintaining relationships with ancestral spirits that persists into modern times. One's illness might be ascribed to neglecting those entities, and appropriate prayer and ritual, such as the burning of money, can remedy the neglect.[74]

Chinese mystics describe the field of potential that underlies all things as Wu Chi. Existence is originally a state of calm, but when it manifests into matter, it becomes subject to constant change. This constitutes the essential nature of dualism. The state of calm is yin and the state of change is yang, concepts that form the basis of the divinatory *I Ching* or *Book of Changes*. Carl Jung, who used the *I Ching* in his personal life, became convinced that responses to queries included a psychic aspect that went beyond the mere subconscious: "metaphysic phenomena could be explained better by the hypothesis of spirits than by the qualities and peculiarities of the unconscious."[75]

China grappled early in its civilization with an enormous population, a phenomenon that puts pressure on harmonious relationships with nature. Warfare and violence can be found in the history of China; however, they did not direct that violence outwards to world conquest.

To China's north, the depredations and brutality of Mongol warlord Genghis Khan was an aberration to a people who were otherwise Indigenous. Genghis Khan, born in 1227, was the founder of one of the world's largest empires. He grew up in an environment where tribal rivalries, raids, and conspiracies were common. After vanquishing Mongol rivals, Khan turned his ambitions west and fought bloody battles to extend his empire. At Urgench, in Afghanistan, his men slaughtered one million people in one of the world's worst massacres. Forays into northern China resulted in the death or displacement of millions. His successors continued pillaging and killing as far west as Baghdad and Poland in Europe. Up to 20 million perished as a result of his military campaigns.[76] However, his wars were not religiously inspired. The primary motives for Mongol expansion appear to have been revenge, glory, and booty. Of his exploits, Khan said, "I committed many acts of cruelty and had an incalculable number of men killed, never knowing whether what I did was right."[77]

Excepting Khan, the Chinese and Mongols do not meet the definition of a Wetiko civilization because the core of their ideology had not lost its respect for the natural world or of a broader sense of spirituality. Regardless of abuses, the potential for spiritual balance and restorative healing was present. Wetiko religions are clearly discernable by their fruit: aggression, conquest of territories across the globe, exploitation of others' resources, forcible conversion, and their version of Pax Romana.

Spirituality in General Decline

Human relationships with the ethereal are in general decline, a sort of increasing obliviousness. From speaking directly and intimately to humans, spirit becomes more remote and less responsive to humans' plight. Its decline corresponds with increasing human-centredness and pride. This results in anomie about what spiritual reality is, and even whether there is such a thing. From an Indigenous perspective, there is no question that the incorporeal world is real. The issue is that through attitudes and behaviour, modern humans have become unable to recognize that reality. Anyone who claims to have direct contact with spirits is declared a fraud, mentally unstable, or delusional. Secular thinking leads to lost understandings of the ways the heavens are a force with tangible impacts on the quality of human existence. This does not mean that everyone in modern societies has lost their intuitive sense of the numinous. It is something that persists from ancient human heritage. However, constant exposure to irreverent systems will eventually erode what little is left of that intuitiveness.

Waking consciousness is highly unreliable. Magicians and others skilled at deceiving people demonstrate how easily our perceptions can be tricked. Our memory is so wobbly that it is difficult to recall what happened the day before, let alone a week, month, or year ago. One thinks one perceives so much yet is unable to detect what is going on in the mind of the person next to us. Knowing that such information exists, why is it not possible to access it directly? Highly developed spiritual senses once made such things possible among Indigenous Peoples.

In Indigenous ecolizations, humans were humble and thankful for the gifts of Creation. They recognized that spirituality is only one aspect of knowing, but it is the most important, as it is a higher form of wisdom and is foundational to establishing sound knowledge systems. However, over time, people began to interject their own image onto deities. As humans increasingly became mediators of the sacred through religion, they not only distanced themselves from direct commune with the ethereal but were also compelled to take more responsibility for their own moral shortcomings by creating human-made laws and moral codes.

Renaissance of Indigenous Spirituality

Canadian census results suggest that Indigenous spiritual practices are experiencing a resurgence. In the 1991 census, nearly 2.5 percent of respondents identified Indigenous spirituality when asked about their religious affiliation. By 2001, that number had

ECOLIZATION (INDIGENOUS)

CIVILIZATION (NON-INDIGENOUS)

Figure 6: 1492—Spiritual and Ideological Divide. *Map by Freepik*

risen to 4.5 percent, a nearly 200 percent increase. In contrast, iden-
tification with mainstream religions including Catholicism and
Protestantism had dropped.[78] An independent study in forty-two
Indigenous-controlled schools revealed that two-thirds of youth had
participated in ceremonies and that half preferred Indigenous worldviews to other forms of belief.[79]

The resurgence of ceremonies is having a positive effect on communities and, especially, on the lives of Indigenous youth. Studies suggest that rates of substance abuse and suicide are declining
among populations where Indigenous faith is strong. This should
suggest to policy makers that supporting a return to spiritual ways
will bring positive developments for all.[80]

Ecolization

In Figure 6, the Indigenous ecolization, which flourished for about
200,000 years prior to the rise of civilization, is indicated in black.
The inhabitants of Indigenous Eden placed high priority on spiritual

values and recognized the inherent worth of all created things. They understood that the Creator placed them on Earth to live harmoniously and to be stewards of nature. Their world was marked by healthy and stable relationships with both the natural environment and with one another. The result of these non-exploitative relationships with nature is abundance of food and resources, a healthy environment, and harmony between groups. Indigenous Eden was not perfect and people made mistakes. However, because the underlying values included the potential to rectify misdeeds, the potential to restore healthy relationships always remained.

First Peoples feared the force of human greed that in Cree is called Wetiko. These cultures went to great lengths to ensure this force was kept at bay. Those who exhibited selfish behaviours placed their own interests above those of the community and the rest of Creation. If they would not change, their communities banished or, if necessary, killed them. The people realized that Wetiko would destroy the sacredness of societies if left unchecked.

Civilization

Civilization occurred in the areas of the world in which human-centred ideology was on the ascendant. The idea of human-centred Creation arose in the Middle East approximately 6,000 years ago. Increasingly, human figures were incorporated into portrayals of deities, suggesting society's abandonment of spiritual humility. Greek philosophers questioned the role of humanity and extolled self-aggrandizing values of human intelligence and beauty. Wetiko civilization spread aggressively across Europe with Roman conquests of tribal peoples who they labelled barbarians. Man's special relationship with God, who was now cast in man's image, was formalized in the Abrahamic religions of Judaism, Christianity, and Islam. Elevating human responsibility instead of utilizing spiritual accountability results in more religious conflict.

Civilizations have marked Wetiko tendencies to exploit the natural environment and seek greater power and wealth at the expense of the weaker. Symptoms include prolonged armed and territorial aggression. By 1492, Christian and Islamic powers, empowered by the wealth they could gain and emboldened by the apparent weakness of Indigenous Peoples, began to conquer and acquire territories around the world. Global expansion led to massive growth of military technology, manufacturing, transportation, resource exploitation, and conflict. These developments catapulted Wetiko influence around the globe. At present, virtually every nation needs to pursue Wetiko-like policies of acquiring wealth and projecting power in order to survive.

More comparisons between ecolizations and civilizations are included in Appendix 1.

CHAPTER 6

KNOWLEDGE, SACRED AND PROFANE

Questioning Humankind's Place in the World

P hilosophy, which originates from Greek word *philo*, "love of wisdom," is a pursuit of questions regarding issues such as existence, nature of mind, and morals. In particular, metaphysics looks at the nature of reality and knowledge. Socrates (470 to 399 BCE) claimed that he did not necessarily possess knowledge but was principally a pursuer of wisdom. But fundamental to him and his successors, Plato (424 to 347 BCE) and Aristotle (384 to 322 BCE), was the focus on humanity itself, and questions about how people could achieve fulfillment.[1] Plato was a great proponent of the need to use reason as opposed to superstition or supernatural thinking. Aristotle carried this insight further by emphasizing that the common person simply has to use their own judgment to distinguish between good and evil. Abandoning divine direction amounted to the biblical eating of the fruit of the Tree of Knowledge of Good and Evil.

While Greek philosophers maintained that plants and animals had some sort of soul, by virtue of their intellect, humans were positioned above the rest of Creation. When they separated man from the rest of created beings, they set in motion man's departure from countless millennia of Indigenous belief. From the Aboriginal perspective, being reliant upon nature meant that such a declaration of independence makes no sense.

The increasing preoccupation with man's self-image and distancing from nature is a pattern that progresses from Egyptian to Greek and Roman cultures. The departure from Indigenous values also manifested itself in religious form. Biblical theologians going back to Abraham (around 2000 BCE) declared that humans are the central focus of Creation. Indigenous Peoples, who were not part of this vision, came to be portrayed as uninformed, uncivilized, weak, and inferior. As centuries of civilization unfolded, European thinkers increasingly touted human arts, wealth, military conquest, and territorial expansion as signs of their superiority.

Indigenous spirituality was portrayed as illusionary and an impediment to human progress, something that had no place in civilization.

In any primitive society it is impossible to consider the arts apart from religion, or religion apart from social morality. Man's sharpening self-consciousness gave him a sense of isolation from the rest of life, and almost all of his activities other than those necessary to keep him alive were directed to establishing a harmonious, satisfying and effective relationship with the external world. Perhaps no contribution made by prehistoric man to his successors is more important than the body of magico-religious attitudes, beliefs and custom that grew up as part of this mental traffic with the universe ... then looking outwards, he saw comparable souls or spirits present in all things, animate and inanimate, and possessing a terrible power over man himself. .... Then at the opposite extreme from his unconscious mind, man's young untried intellect made valiant efforts to order and rationalize all his imaginative projections *and so devised stories concerning the origin of spirits* [emphasis added], gods and men and their relationship with one another that became a part of the body of belief.[2]

As children of the Enlightenment, anthropologists were not equipped to appreciate and understand the principles of ancient, let alone contemporary, Indigenous spirituality. After all, they were trained to deny the validity of anything that could not be grasped by the mind and witnessed physically. With their rationalist intellectual bent, the focus was on parsing every minute discrepancy of cultural information. If one Indigenous group revered one spirit and another group a different one, there is no possible consistency in beliefs, they concluded. They "missed the forest for the trees."

Rise of Rationalism and Expunging of Spirituality

The face of philosophy has shifted over the centuries, beginning with the Greeks' questioning their role in the world around them, to the medieval period during which virtually all of European inquiry was based on biblical interpretation, and, finally, to modern reasoning. Contemporary philosophy is firmly based upon the idea of rationality in all areas. It requires that any form of knowledge must undergo a thorough process of investigation, discussion, and verification. The acquisition of knowledge involves reasoning based upon observation of evidence and the assumption that human intelligence alone is capable of resolving all questions. Rational thinking forces one to conclude that there is no reliable proof of a supernatural reality.

Christianity made the mistake of contesting the findings of scientists such as Galileo, who confirmed that the planets revolve around the sun. Instead of accepting such knowledge as a gift of knowledge from the Creator, the Church discredited Galileo, subjecting him to the Inquisition and forcing him to recant. The scientist had challenged the medieval order and lent further credibility to scientific methods.[3] In the process, spirituality declined and secularism was invigorated. Another proponent of eradicating supernatural thinking from religion and ordinary discourse was Immanuel Kant (1742 to 1804), author of *Religion and Rational Theology*, who stated that

The final touchstone of the reliability of judgment is to be sought in reason alone. . . . So far as morality is based upon the conception of the human being as one who is free but also, just because of that, binds himself through his reason to unconditional laws, it is in need of neither the idea of another being above him in order that he recognize his duty, nor, that he observe it, of an incentive other than the law itself. . . . for whatever does not originate from himself and his own freedom provides no remedy for a lack in his morality. Hence on its own behalf morality in no way needs religion *but is rather self-fulfilling by virtue of pure practical reason* [emphasis added].[4]

Over against biblical theology, however, there stands on the side of the sciences a philosophical theology which is a property held in trust by another faculty. This theology must have complete freedom to expand as far as its science reaches, provided that it stays within the boundaries of mere reason and makes indeed use of history, languages, the books of all the peoples, even the Bible, in order to confirm and explain its propositions.[5]

The Age of Reason

The Renaissance, between the fourteenth and seventeenth centuries, was based upon the philosophy of humanism and glorification of arts and literatures. The focus was exulting man's image and accomplishments. One theory for its emergence was the ravages of the plagues that had caused millions of deaths and the ineffectualness of religion's response. The Enlightenment paved the way for its progeny—the Age of Reason. The elite and their artisans wanted people to think more about how they could appreciate their current life. Scientific discoveries in astronomy, mathematics, geography, physics, and physiology were applauded. Finally came the idea of progress that, by its own wit and ingenuity, humanity could build an increasingly ideal and perfect world.

Seventeenth-century thinkers such as René Descartes and John Locke furthered the argument that human reason rather than theological interpretation could furnish the answers to human problems. Locke proposed that protecting individual rights, respect for equality, and representative government were not only rational, but also effective means of governance. Freedom and equality existed before civilization, he contended, and is, therefore, natural law.[6]

On the other hand, fellow philosopher John Hobbes is seen as deeply skeptical about the inherent morality of humans.

In the 'natural condition of mankind,' humans are equal, despite minor differences in strength and mental acuity. Hobbes's notion of equality is peculiar in that it refers to the equal ability to kill or conquer one another, but quite consistent with his notion of power. This equality, Hobbes says, naturally leads to conflict among individuals for three reasons: competition, distrust, and glory. In the first case, if two individuals desire a scarce commodity, they will compete for the commodity and necessarily become enemies. In their efforts to acquire desired objects, each person tries to 'destroy or subdue' the other. On account of the constant fear produced in the state of nature, Hobbes believes, it is reasonable to distrust others and use preemptive strikes against one's enemies. Hobbes also considers humans to be naturally vainglorious and so seek to dominate others and demand their respect. The natural condition of mankind, according to Hobbes, is a state of war in which life is 'solitary, poor, nasty, brutish, and short' because individuals are in a 'war of all against all.'[7]

Philosophers John Locke and Jacques Rousseau pointed to Native Americans as a model for the practice of natural freedom, where order was present despite a high degree of individual freedom.[8] Locke agreed that some concept of the transcendent had to be preserved, otherwise moral corruption and anarchy would result: every individual "could have no law but his will, no end but himself. He would be a god onto himself, and the satisfaction of his will the sole measure and end of his own actions."[9] Rousseau lamented about how science was steadily divorcing humanity from its connections to nature. Yet, he did not recognize the virtues already practised in Indigenous ecolizations, let alone the rights of non-human entities. European intellectuals demonstrate little insight into Indigenous cosmology.

These thinkers did not understand the extent to which ancient social order was based upon the sacred compact that required a great deal of energy to maintain. Such relationships also extended to the natural world. Critics of the Enlightenment warned that some of its propositions were simplistic and naïve and could lead to materialism and corruption. Nevertheless, the Enlightenment became a powerful engine of human progress.

Scientific discoveries and accompanying technological developments influenced thinking about economics and property. Adam Smith's *Wealth of Nations* touted free enterprise that created wealth, which, he argued, benefitted society. These developments rapidly expanded human domination of nature. Meanwhile Indigenous Peoples, deemed to be lacking in religion and science, were seen as increasingly backward and irrelevant. None of the "enlightened" bothered to ask Indigenous sages about the wisdom of these "civilized" developments.

Philosophy textbooks with names including *On the Nature and Existence of God*[10] and *Existence: Essays in Ontology*[11] are suggestive of the origin and purpose of humanity but do not include a single reference to spirit or spirituality. Western philosophy has entirely purged itself of any argumentation based on the numinous. Instead the insinuation is that man and his rational mind is paramount. Philosopher and scientist René Descartes' famous line "I think therefore I am" further positioned the human mind above all else.[12]

One of the fundamental flaws of embracing rationalism and human reason alone is that thought thrives in a world of dualism and relativism. In rationalist thinking, each side of intellectual debate inevitably negates the other. Values and beliefs of different sides are often strikingly different and fervently held. Anything that can be advocated in rational argument can also be contradicted, often only for the purpose of being oppositional. In such a scenario, there is always a winner and a loser. There is no absolute or transcendent authority that acts as an ultimate arbiter and unifier.

Humans are given an unprecedented gift of intellect and self-awareness. However, intellect without spiritual grounding is a dangerous and damaging tool when misused. It is an error to think that the only way humans can thrive on Earth is through controlling all forms of life. The Creator's gifts are more than adequate for essential human needs.

Rationalists mistake Indigenous references to spirit as faulty and fictitious portrayals of reality. For example, they will say the White Buffalo, which represents the sacred, is nothing more than a genetic mutation. However, the point is not about the mutation, but about the archetype that stands behind that symbol and which gives it meaning. In many ways, mythology is more potent than physical reality. Humans prefer to remember the significance behind events more than the specific details. Others claim that Native Peoples were slow to develop science because of their superstitions. However, Indigenous Peoples were perfectly capable of observation and analysis. The difference was that they were unwilling to manipulate nature if it was deemed unwise or there was no pressing need. These "sciences" would have eventually been developed over the long term and were being developed in areas such as agriculture, astronomy, and architecture. Those were all developed in conjunction with interrogation of the transcendent and consideration of the well-being of future generations. Indigenous Peoples are just as capable of using rational thought as any other group. However, they understand that rational thought needs to be guided by spirituality.

Universities of Civilization

The University of Bologna, founded in 1088, was the earliest in medieval Christian Europe. The Latin word *universitas* referred to a community of scholars. At Bologna there were concerns about defending the interests of the weak against empire and Church. There was a desire to promote humanism as engendered in the rediscovered writings of Aristotle, which surprisingly had been preserved through the efforts of Arab scholars. Believing that independent inquiry could provide solutions to enduring problems, early universities focused on areas such as rhetoric, logic, arithmetic, and the arts. Scholars were allowed to self-regulate their studies and were offered protection from interference by outside political interests, including those of the Church. Thinkers who had tremendous influence on public thinking include Galileo at the University of Pisa and Martin Luther at the University of Wittenberg.

The focus on Aristotelian knowledge gave primacy to human reason as a basis for understanding the natural world. Insight could emanate through inspiration of the human mind. Unfortunately, the value of insight by consulting Ancestor and spirit sources that served Indigenous people so well was gradually discounted. Advances in scientific theory leading to tangible results emboldened proponents of rationality who began to believe that one's intellect was the key to unravelling all of the mysteries of Creation. The Enlightenment and victory of intellectualism paved the way for what are touted as the greatest advances in science and technology. Rationalism provided a readily accessible method of manipulating the physical world. Tangible rewards could be had without the need to dabble in the murky waters of mysticism. Practitioners of witchcraft and sorcery were considered frauds and viewed as a threat to established religion and society as a whole.

Historians like to portray all human institutions as if they originated with human-centred values. The Aztecs of Meso-America, the Chinese, and the Hindus of the Indus Valley did not embrace the philosophy that humankind had a God-given right to override nature. The Aztec, Mayan, and Incan civilizations continued to venerate natural spirits and their urban centres were constructed with extreme sensitivity to the environment. The Chinese retained great respect for the forces of nature, reflected in their deep-seated tradition of acknowledging the disincarnate. In the Indus Valley, despite later invasions by Aryans and Muslims, many aspects of the ancient Harrapan culture persisted in the mysticism of Hinduism and yoga, including veneration of deities of nature.[13]

Wetiko historians point to any transgression by ecolizations to prove they were "just like us." All societies make mistakes. The Aztec abandoned bravery and became fearful and distrustful of nature when they saw convulsions such as eclipses, volcanoes, and earthquakes. As a result, they carried human sacrifice to the extreme. Eventually, they would have figured out how such processes of nature worked and overcome their fear. The Haudenosaunee, who had become embroiled in violence, reformed their practices when they created the Great Law of Peace that mandates that discussion must replace violence. Indigenous ecolizations that remained faithful to spirituality always succeeded in overcoming Wetiko.[14]

The definition of knowledge is "facts, information, and skills acquired by a person through experience or education; the theoretical or practical understanding of a subject."[15] This definition does not appear to accommodate spiritual experience, although theoretically it could. Having a relationship with the transcendent is also experiential in nature and is a normal part of obtaining knowledge in the Indigenous world. To excel at such an endeavour involves effort similar to obtaining a doctoral degree or training for the Olympics.

The rationalist approach deviates from Indigenous values in two ways: it obviates the need for spiritual guidance and inspiration, and it promotes head thinking over heart thinking. Heart thinking prioritizes maintaining proper relations, whereas head thinking emphasizes objectification, categorization, and value judgement. This leads to divisive and oppositional thinking. For example, if Ruler A has an army of 1,000 soldiers, then it is logical that Ruler B should develop an army of 2,000 soldiers in response. Missing from the equation is any question of "Is this the right course of action?" or "Is there a better way of dealing with this relationship?"

Britain and other European nations created colonies across the world and built universities where they promote European rationalist ideologies. Universities are unwitting promoters of a colonialist agenda of promoting resource exploitation and domination. Scholar Leanne Simpson notes:

> Part of being Indigenous in the 21st century is that regardless of where or how we have grown up, we've all been bathed in a vat of cognitive imperialism, perpetuating the idea that Indigenous Peoples were not, and are not, thinking peoples— an insidious mechanism to promote neo-colonialism and obfuscate the historic atrocities of colonialism. In both subtle and overt ways, the current generation of Indigenous People has been repeatedly told that individually we are stupid and that collectively our nations were and are void of higher thought. This is reinforced when the academic industrial

complex—often propped up by Indian [now Indigenous] and Northern Affairs Canada (INAC)—promotes colonizing education to our children and youth as the solution to dispossession, poverty, violence, and a lack of self-determination over our lives. Cognitive imperialism also rears its head in every discipline every time a student is told that there is no literature or no thinking available on any given topic from Indigenous intellectual traditions.[16]

Dismissing Indigenous Knowledge

Modern university disciplines promote rationality, science, and technology as the solutions to contemporary society's challenges. Others realize that universities are in desperate need of a new paradigm. It will be extremely difficult to persuade some segments of academia about the value of Indigenous knowledge. Professor Frances Widdowson dismisses the worth of Indigenous spiritual knowledge, arguing that it is "implausible" and "radically at odds with established data" and uses evidence that is "spurious, grossly mishandled, or otherwise utterly unconvincing."[17]

She argues, "It is one thing to assert that Indigenous groups have these beliefs, and another to maintain that these beliefs are a 'way of knowing' that results in 'knowledge.' There are serious ethical problems with the latter, because it would mean promoting quack 'treatments' such as prayer, access to sacred knowledge to manipulate and exploit others."[18]

In her paper "Academic Freedom and Indigenization: Should the Dissemination of Pseudoscientific 'Ways of Knowing' be Protected?" Widdowson advocates banning the teaching of traditional knowledge based on the supposition that it constitutes "pseudo-science." This argument blithely ignores the fact that Indigenous wisdom is an ancient, long-surviving, and successful ideology. Widdowson concludes that such information promotes "ideas contrary to knowledge. . . . Deceiving others, even if it is rooted in good intentions, also cannot inspire trust. To deny this realization to Aboriginal people is a form of educational malpractice, preventing many individuals from becoming actual contributors to knowledge production, theoretical understanding and human progress."[19]

Researcher Albert Howard singles out Indigenous spirituality as being inconsistent with university learning.

I have said that ideas that are irrational and antiscientific constitute intellectual primitivism. I don't, in fact, subscribe to the prevalent stereotyping of native people as all thinking alike, as there is every possibility that some native people are free of spiritual beliefs. I know that many other people are mired in beliefs unsupported by evidence, and I characterize all spiritual, irrational and uncritical beliefs as primitive, regardless of the ethnicity of the believers, as they are emblematic of a distinctly earlier period. . . . a clamour of censorship represented the level of opposition to our contentions that spiritual beliefs, mythologies and the unquestioned views of Elders are backward elements in the educational system, reverting back to the dark ages, that attempting to incorporate such features into rational programs is an assault on academic studies, and that the initiative will entrench the low educational levels suffered by Aboriginal students, while imposing a burden on non-native students. More alarmingly, critical thought will be eliminated, because the application of it will expose the fallacy of Indigenous and Traditional Métis 'Knowledge.'[20]

Indigenous knowledge has historically been portrayed as primitive and superstitious and inconsistent with secular rational thinking. Unfortunately, Indigenous Peoples have never owned universities with immense financial resources to promulgate their points of view. To counter the prevailing argument about primitivism, it is vital that Elders and scholars find ways to revitalize and reinterpret their knowledge systems for today's needs. It will be challenging in our current academic climate, but there are ways for each of the major disciplines to Indigenize their approach to education and research.

Philosophy, which addresses issues such as the reason for existence, moral and ethical behaviour, and quest for knowledge, is simply too rationalistic to evaluate Indigenous Knowledge. Philosophy must recognize that the transcendent is real and is a higher form of intelligence. This goes beyond the concepts of ethics and morals as they are defined by thought alone. Philosophy needs to appreciate that spirituality does not mean the abandonment of reason. In fact, spirituality enhances and dignifies knowledge. Elders place high importance on the development of intellect while realizing that it can only be accomplished properly within a context of genuine reverence.

Political science deals with partisan thought, behaviour, and systems of governance. Governments are concerned with the distribution of power and resources and approach this in different ways, for example, deciding whether they are democracies or dictatorships. Political science is a creature of civilization. The political process becomes an endless struggle for power and wealth between individuals or groups each having different ideologies and priorities. Both the left and right wings of politics suffer from the same problematic roots of rationalism and its perpetual potential for divisiveness. Absent is the idea that a higher power can be the ultimate arbiter of human affairs. Theocracies place the priorities of their religion over those of others in the name of their authority, but because of their investment in civilization, they do not function in the same manner as ecolizations. Governments give little attention to the non-humans that Indigenous Peoples consider to be their kin. Whenever environmental impacts are studied, it is mainly to assess the potential for resource exploitation. Regulations for conservation of flora or fauna recognize the utilitarian rather than spiritual value of created beings.

History as a field began with Herodotus around 500 BCE and is a recent development in terms of human deliberation.[21] Indigenous Peoples recollected their history orally to preserve their identity and sense of place. Negative occurrences were dealt with through healing so society could move forward without continuing to bear scars. Historians have had difficulty interpreting tribal history because there is such a paucity of understanding of the nature of Indigenous worldviews. From the Indigenous perspective, one could suspect that the reason why history began to be recorded was to keep track of all of civilization's sins.

Economics is another distinctive tool of the civilization project. The discipline of economics is concerned with maximizing the production, consumption, and distribution of wealth. In the Canadian context, economic activity is based upon capitalist and globalist models. Original Peoples in the Americas did not employ money or banking systems that distorted the intrinsic value of commodity exchange. Moreover, banking inflates the actual value of economic activity. In other words, non-Indigenous economics were geared to maximize rapid exploitation, expansion, and enrichment—generally of elites. Capitalism permits a very limited number of individuals to amass incredible wealth and power at the expense of others. Indigenous ecolizations did have commodity systems that enabled trans-continental commerce without distorting economic value.

Economics needs to realize that the fundamental purpose of material exchange is for survival. Market-based economies cater to human demands by ravaging other life forms and extracting earthly resources. It is improper to treat non-human consciousnesses as a commodity. One should realize that placing value only in money exchange removes the potential for human spiritual growth. This system damages positive relationships and carries immense potential for abuse. Money empowers greed, the personification of Wetiko that our peoples so deeply dread.

The discipline of geography does not recognize that the land's value is more than just property and a resource to exploit. It should recognize that Earth is a macrocosm of living elements that all need to be respected in their own right and recognized as the foundation for human well-being. Rather than measuring and quantifying everything, the emphasis needs to be placed on recognizing the sacred nature of Creation. Measurement and quantification should occur only if there is a spiritually valid need to do so.

Fine arts has historically been concerned with aesthetics and beauty and, more recently, with meaning. It needs to distance itself from works intended only to glorify human self-image, pride, and achievements. Traditional cultures used art to portray spiritual qualities that they deemed important, including elements inspired by nature. The other important role of art was for healing. Humanity does not need more reinforcement of its current self-absorption and arrogance.

A definition of science states: "the intellectual and practical activity encompassing the systematic study of the structure and behaviours of the physical and natural world through observation and experiment." The scientific method is defined as: "a method of procedure that has characterized natural science since the 17th century, consisting in systematic observation, measurement, and experiment, and the formulation, testing, and modification of hypotheses."[22] There is no room for spirituality in these definitions. The apparent success of science in manipulating the material world has given it an aura of legitimacy and invincibility.

One can master chemistry textbooks full of formulas. It appears at first glance that Indigenous knowledge has nothing to contribute. Yet, too many chemicals are produced that are destroying the environment, not to mention poisoning people. Pharmaceuticals of dubious use are being pumped out primarily to produce profit. If there was Indigenous chemistry, production of chemicals that destroy the environment and kill people would not be allowed. Chemistry infused with an Indigenous perspective and a sacred dimension would ponder whether seven generations would benefit prior to producing drugs.

Although the ethereal is not measurable by scientific instruments and is not taught in university courses, it is a valid component of knowledge because the consequences of ignoring it are real. Science conducted in a spiritual way would not produce weapons of mass destruction or technologies that remove humanity from connection to the natural world. It is a higher form of intelligence and wisdom that transcends rationality and materialism. This is why ancient societies were not only productive but also healthy and stable.[23]

Balancing Spirit and Mind

A mind disconnected from spirituality can become like a boat lost in turbulent waters or, worse, like a rabid dog, dangerous and out of control. This can exacerbate the excesses of individualism in contemporary culture. People are literally becoming alienated through the loss of respect for the transcendent and lack of sense of purpose in life. Free will is a paradox—humans can exercise free will, but it can lead to exaltation or self-destruction. Now, when the influence and force of spirit is very weak, we are left with mere rationalist insight. Micmac Elder Albert Ward points out: "The mind is different. It is different because your mind is, we could say, it is black magic. If you let your mind do all kinds of things for you and your mind takes over your body and your heart is not telling you anything and it's just using your mind."[24]

Academic John Mohawk recalls how little respect was accorded to the wisdom of his peoples' knowledge.

> Indians were strongly urged to believe that their people had no knowledge, that they couldn't think clearly, that they were savages, and so on. My experience is that the reverse is true. Today they have no knowledge and they've embraced a system of faith: faith that the grocery store is good food, faith that the doctor says he knows what to do for you. You have a faith, but you're not encouraged to do what you need to do to avoid getting sick, and you're not encouraged to do what you need to do to stay healthy. . . . They have been pounding a message into our brains that future utopian societies can be built upon a foundation of technology and a foundation of engineering and that's going to build a wonderful future world. At the same moment, what's been happening is that the biological foundation of our world is being eroded by exactly those people who stood to profit from that ideology.[25]

Hawaiian Indigenous activist Nalami Minton talks about the need to return to spiritual fundamentals in our quest for answers on how to survive.

> As cosmic peoples, the Indigenous peoples of the earth realize that the problems of genocide and planetocide that have been generated over the last couple thousand years need to be healed from a profound level, from a cosmic and spiritual level. It's good to hear the voices of our ancestors to remind

us how to live. In the ancient languages of our traditions, we believe that our people love the land so much that when we 'die' or transition, we merely enter another dimension . . . . So we can always call upon our ancestors, who are always with us for their guidance, wisdom and help.[26]

In a similar vein, Indigenous science philosopher Gregory Cajete observes how modern thinking has contributed to shabby treatment of the environment.

During the Age of Enlightenment, Western culture broke with the ancient human 'participation mystique' as a basis for its relationship with nature and substituted a relationship based purely on objective scientific/rationalist thought, which viewed the universe from a purely materialistic standpoint. Nature became a mass of 'dead' matter ripe for manipulation and material gain. Animals became 'dumb' and Indigenous peoples became 'savage primitives.' All had to be controlled and developed for their own, and Western society's good.[27]

Chicano ecologist Dennis Martinez illustrates how our attitudes affect how we treat the habitat.

There is no Indian word for wilderness. There are words that correspond to 'wild'—that which we don't control. Wilderness implies a lack of relationship, even though it means in its earliest meaning 'self-willed.' We don't manage nature, we work with nature. But we don't control nature. . . . We are co-creators with the plants and animals; and unlike Islam, Judaism and Christianity, God did not create the earth and then rest on the seventh day. Every day is Creation. Every day is Earth Day and ceremonies of world renewal are carried on every year by Indigenous Peoples worldwide.[28]

A New Paradigm

The Enlightenment and its knowledge systems, such as those promoted by universities—political science, economics, engineering, etc., have been the driving influence on global development and social ethos over the past few centuries. Scientific discoveries have often been conceived for profit motives as well as by the need to innovate in times of war. In terms of the span of human presence, the paradigm of nationalism is but a tiny fraction. What occurred in the Americas after contact was a huge unleashing of Wetiko in the New World. Society is now dominated by materialism, greed, social breakdown, rampant crime, environmental degradation, and species destruction that can be ascribed to Wetiko culture. One sage remarked: "We used to look up at the sky and wonder at our place in the stars. Now we just look down and worry about our place in the dirt."[29]

Elders are our philosophers. However, they have not had the benefit of centuries of scholarship by thousands of academics in multitudinous universities through which they could advocate their philosophy. This is one reason why Indigenous thought is so little understood or appreciated. The Old Ones have always been willing to discuss issues in a respectful and sacred manner. They spend hours debating fine points of knowledge until consensus is reached. On the other hand, their wisdom has been blatantly ridiculed, persecuted, and co-opted over centuries. Elders do not reject all modern intellectual and technological advances made by virtue of rationalism and reason. They accept intellect as a unique and essential feature of human being-ness. Their concern arises when the intellectual function becomes divorced from the supernal. Placed under the light of spirituality, it becomes clear that many contemporary knowledge and technology systems need to be revised or eliminated.

Indigenous Paradigm

An example of an area in which tribal knowledge can provide a new paradigm is in science. According to theorist Gregory Cajete:

Native science reflects a celebration of renewal. The ultimate aim is not explaining an objectified universe, but rather learning about and understanding responsibilities and relationships and celebrating those that humans establish with the world.[30]

. . .

This model challenges all concerned to take Indigenous science seriously as an ancient form of applied knowledge for sustaining communities and ensuring survival through time. It also challenges readers to accept Indigenous science as a tool and a body of knowledge that may be integrated with Western science in new and creative ways that sustain and ensure survival.[31]

The relative lack of environmental degradation and social discord is a tribute to the success of Indigenous methodology that included, among other things, ceremony and prayer. This wisdom stands in contrast to the results of "modern" science that is conducted within the context of modern materialist and exploitative knowledge systems. Much of it is pursued to expand human "welfare" and artificial and military technology, and, of course, for pecuniary gain. The outcomes, particularly over the past two hundred years, are bringing humanity to the brink of environmental and societal catastrophe.

Why is there is no role for spirituality in science? Some of the world's most renowned scientists think that there should be. Einstein's insights into general relativity, the nature of matter, and so on, did not come from experimentation but, rather, through intuition, a process akin to Indigenous thinking. He made reference to God in his musings. He had a conscience, regretting the role he played in making nuclear weapons possible. He acknowledged that far more goes on than what we know with just our five senses: "The belief in the existence of basic all-embracing laws in nature also rests on a sort of faith. All the same this faith has been largely justified so far by the success of scientific research. But, on the other hand, everyone who is seriously involved in the pursuit of science becomes convinced that a spirit is manifest in the laws of the universe—a spirit vastly superior to that of man, and one in the face of which we with our modest powers must feel humble."[32] Other scientists now theorize that consciousness is everywhere and pervasive throughout the universe. Conservation of information and energy implies that human consciousness is somehow transmuted after death.

Some ask how it is possible to make decisions outside the rational framework when one consults the ethereal. Skeptics think hearing voices in ceremonies is just hallucination. But what if one receives accurate information that is not otherwise rationally accessible? What if unimaginable phenomena such as miracles suddenly occur? Is it possible to resolve the ideological conflict between materialism and spirituality?

Indigenous philosophers have never advocated that the rational mind be ignored or left undeveloped. Indigenous people have always recognized that mind and intellect is a vital tool for learning and discernment. However, it must be guided by and defer to the sacrosanct. Otherwise people will stray well off the Good Path.

CHAPTER 7

THE BIG RUSH

Power and Inequality

The power of one person or group over another is rooted in inequality. Inequality began with the hoarding of plants and animals at the advent of agriculture. Rather than all having common access to the bounty of nature, parts of Creation were hived off for the benefit of certain groups. This gave the hoarders the advantage of not having to be constantly in balance with nature. Building up their own assets gave them a resource and power advantage over others. Originally, the Creator intended that all have equal access to the earthly gifts. Although groups had privileged and exclusive spiritual relationships within their territory, it was against Indigenous ethics to not share resources with visitors. Imbalance with nature eventually led to overexploitation and overpopulation.

There are multiple forms of hoarding. Money enables stockpiling and empowers the wealthy to control economic development. Nations amass technology and weapons as a means of exerting power over others. Monotheism creates exclusivity of religious authority. Monopolizing knowledge occurs at institutions where information to which all should have access is not well disseminated to the general public.

Perfect equality did not exist in Indigenous Eden. A natural system of inequality existed based upon spiritual accomplishment. Those who demonstrated the most command over spiritual virtues were respected more. Those who had more wisdom were naturally deferred to and followed. This form of hierarchy was based on deference to spirit and ethics of acting for the benefit of everyone and to preserve unity.

Money: The False God

In Indigenous culture, the concept of private property was virtually non-existent. Exclusive use of belongings revolved only around ceremonial objects and recognized spiritual obligations. Sharing or outright giving away of property was a key method of maintaining positive relationships, such as in the Potlatch practised on the west coast of North America. If anything, Indigenous ecolizations had sanctions against those who refused to share, especially when such sharing was deemed necessary. Violations against this precept could be severe. Listening to Elders discuss how traditional values in contemporary Indigenous communities have deteriorated, one of the main culprits identified is money. Its use brought about selfishness and jealousy and undermined traditional values of sharing.

The primary objective of capitalism is the generation of profits. It is not possible to have a spiritually fulfilling relationship with money. Currency is only a medium of exchange and not a goal in itself. Over the course of recent history, humanity has witnessed the dramatic expansion of materialism. Prosperity generated by wealth is regarded by world leaders as the panacea for all of humanity's ills. Currency is a perfect Wetiko tool. It is an artificial Creation, enables people to exchange commodities and amass wealth with mind-boggling speed, and is not accountable to nature. As an ultimate solution to human welfare, economic prosperity is a false god. Materialism advances human economic and material comforts but does little for integrity of the soul.

Will cash be a lasting solution when economic systems fail? Immense entrenched interests, including international conglomerates and banks, have huge stake in guarding the status quo. But, maintaining this structure comes at great cost. The economic machine has little interest in protecting the natural environment. Aspects of holism, including human relationships, are ignored. Basing decisions solely on finances can be destructive to social relations. As long as the primary focus of governments remains on secularism, materialism, and wealth, spiritualism will have little room to thrive.

Money is the crack cocaine of modern development. It provides a motivator for pursuing personal profit for its own sake and makes it much easier to conduct quick transactions and amass large amounts of wealth. Currency leveraged by banks inflates the value of the economy to the point that the entire enterprise resembles a ponzi scheme. Creating artificial wealth may create more jobs and income, but how much does it add to real societal value? More of what society wants is produced than what it truly needs. What replaces the glue that keeps societies united when the economic engine fails? When humans, in their hubris, believe that prosperity alone is the answer, it leads to self-deception and disrespect for the sacredness of life.

The 1820s Acceleration

The 1820s are significant in terms of understanding the momentum that brought the world to its current point. First, it is around this period that the global population of non-Indigenous peoples begins to outstrip those of Indigenous populations.[1] A second factor is that it is the first time that world population begins to exceed one and a half billion, the number that should not be surpassed if imbalance with the natural environment is to be avoided. Paul Erlich argues that number is appropriate given the level of consumption of modern advanced societies, expectations for resource abundance, minimizing conflict, avoiding damage to species, and respecting other cultures such as those of Indigenous Peoples.[2] The third consideration is the entrenchment of the ideology of the Enlightenment, or Age of Reason, in the thinking of Europe's leading institutions. Abandoning religiosity led to the fallacy that the humans alone are capable of solving all of the world's ills. Finally, rationalism and scientism led to the explosion of unfettered economic and technological developments that have created problems discussed in this book that have gotten out of control. In other words, astonishing change has happened over the last two hundred years, a mere flash in the pan in the panorama of the human drama. Fuelled by technology and globalization, civilization since the 1820s has been on steroids: a hyper-civilization. If this is a flash in the pan, perhaps it is an aberration and humanity will come back to its senses. On the other hand, it might be what finally destroys us all.

Secular economies of resource and capitalist exploitation exacerbated racism and colonization of Indigenous Peoples. The consequence of this action is short-term prosperity for the dominant society. However, the longer-term outcome is the deterioration of human relationships and destruction of the natural world.

The Canadian government, acting as the agent of the British Crown, violated the Law of Relationships repeatedly as it refused to honour the family-like relationships called for in treaties. Instead, it pursued an agenda of cultural destruction and assimilation. One can only imagine how things would have been different in Canada had First Nations' value systems been respected.[3] Indigenous communities today continue to reel from the erosion of their traditional values and environment.

Abandoning our Creator-given place in the world, we have turned to money and materialism for a sense of purpose, direction, and fulfillment. Commercialism and consumerism have become the new mantras: "We convert the buying and use of goods into rituals, that we seek our spiritual satisfaction, our ego satisfaction, in consumption. . . . We need things consumed, burned up, worn out, replaced, and discarded at an ever-increasing pace."[4] Such activities are portrayed to children as examples and role models to emulate. It is estimated that each child in America is exposed to 40,000 commercials each year. Does one really feel fulfilled and satisfied because of a new car or house?[5]

It is a problem when one sees everything as being about oneself, including the never-ending need for money and status. In reality, life should be more about giving than taking. Indigenous Peoples lived a less stressed life because they did not have a compulsion to overtake nature but lived with its rhythms. The focus of traditional cultures was developing close bonds with nature. This approach is jokingly called Indian time—doing things only when ready and necessary. But it has its serious side. This is the type of wisdom that would make survival possible for a million years—the average life span of mammalian species.

People have become seduced by the illusion of prosperity. We have come to believe that our artificially created world provides all we need when, in fact, the natural bases upon which our systems depend are crumbling. We cannot afford to "feed the greed" anymore. This is not to paint all non-Indigenous people as corrupt. They still retain in their genes the instincts of their Indigenous Ancestors; however, the longer they live in the world of avarice, the more they will lose their intuition.

Reign of Wetiko

Esteemed Indigenous academic Jack Forbes, whom the author had the privilege of meeting at the University of California at Davis, explored the implications of the concept of Wetiko (a Cree term also known as Windigo in Anishinaabe/Ojibway). Wetiko is a mythical creature of greed and selfishness that cannibalistically preys on humans and brings about disunity and destruction. Forbes wanted to explain the European destruction of Indigenous Peoples wherever contact occurred. Despite First Peoples' hospitality and helping the newcomers to survive, the encounter invariably ended up in the host's slaughter and destruction.

In the thesis of his book *Columbus and the Cannibals,* Forbes says: "I shall argue that Columbus was a wetiko, that he was mentally ill or insane, the carrier of a terribly contagious psychological disease, the wetiko psychosis.[6] The Native people on the other hand were sane people with a healthy state of mind, with sanity defined as having respect for other forms of life and other individuals."[7] Forbes notes that the first patterns of oppression and exploitation appeared in Mesopotamia and Egypt about 5,000 years ago. He contends that "the quest of many Europeans to totally penetrate, subdue and change the natural world must be viewed in part as a psychological phenomenon—that is, as a need fulfillment or compulsion which is non-rational or irrational in character."[8]

He makes the connection between oppression and colonialist religions.

> The expansion of Christianity and Islam are strikingly similar in their effects on local and indigenous cultures. Much of the 'local color' and richness of local cultures disappears when the majority is tipped in favor of a missionizing religion. . . . The result has been the loss of incredible richness and cultural variation among humans, and more importantly, the loss of freedom. . . . Males may also have to become more violent and dominating, as this behavior is often prized by the state and rewarded with upward mobility, honours, and higher status.[9]

The rise of Wetikoism occurred in stages: the beginning of the idea of human exceptionalism; the imbedding of human centeredness in religion; the boost provided by the conquest of the Americas; and, finally, the explosion of trade, technology, and colonialism that accompanied the Industrial Revolution. At first, this spiritual malaise existed in small areas of the Middle East. Later, it became part of state religions such as Roman Catholicism and Islam. Then power and wealth that flowed from raping the resources of the Americas fuelled the ability of colonizers to spread their economic and military might. Finally, Wetiko's influence spread to all corners of the world, with economics and military power being the essential foundations of nationhood. Non-Wetiko civilizations, such as the Chinese, Japanese, and Indian developed governments that imitated Wetiko powers in their pursuit of wealth and power as a response to European expansion and aggression.

Forbes states: "In many respects the twentieth century has been the most disappointing period in modern history. We have witnessed the failure of so-called 'western democracies' to solve their most pressing internal problems, the failure of Marxist-Leninism to come to grips with the issues of bureaucracy, authoritarianism and the self-interest of newly-empowered elites, the failure of technology, the failure of organized religion, and the failure of the most highly trained and 'educated' generations of human beings in all of history to do more than paper over the great problems facing the world."[10]

In *Dispelling Wetiko,* social commentator Paul Levy directly connects avarice with contemporary economics.

> Seen as a symbolic entity, the destructive force working through the global financial system, for example, is the revelation of the essential features of the wetiko disease displayed graphically and schematically in its architecture, operations and overall design, such that anyone with a trained eye can discern the telltale signs and spore prints of this maleficent psychopathology getting down to business. The global economy (which can appropriately be referred to as 'wetikonomy') displays the fear and scarcity-based, linear logic of wetiko disease as it reduces everything to the bottom line of dollars and cents. Only concerned with the immediate gratification of short-term profits to feed its never-ending hunger for more money, the wetikonomy destroys the genuine wealth of the whole system, considering people, communities and the environment to be nothing more than collateral damage.[11]

Levy squarely connects the rise of greed to the modern conception of civilization.

> It is not a coincidence that the development of wetiko corresponds to the rise of what Europeans choose to call civilization. The unsustainable nature of industrial civilization is based on, and increasingly requires, violence to maintain itself. Genuine civilization, in essence, means not killing people. . . . Modern society suffers from the overly one-sided dominance of the rational, intellectual mind, a one-sidedness that seemingly disconnects us from nature, from empathy, and from ourselves. Due to its disassociation from the whole, wetiko is a disturber of the peace of humanity and the natural world, a sickness which spawns aggression and is capable of inciting violence among living beings.[12]

Forbes sees the propensity for avarice as self-propagating.

The Wetiko world creates an intensive propaganda system designed to perpetuate the values of such a system. . . . The Hollywood movie industry frequently exults the 'two-bit' hustler as well as card-sharks, racketeers, gangsters, 'hit-men,' violent secret agents, violent cops, and so on. Movies may occasionally oppose such behavior, but usually after making it clear that money and the 'good things in life' are frequently to be found in close association with crime, crooked business deals, big-time politics, Las Vegas gambling, and so on.[13]

Lakota holy man Lame Deer commented: "If this earth should ever be destroyed, it will be by desire, by the lust of pleasure and self-gratification, by the greed for the green frog skin [money] by people who are mindful only of their own self, forgetting about the wants of others.[14]

Levy describes the nature of Wetiko "as if a psychic parasite has taken over our brain and tricked us, its host, into thinking we are feeding and empowering ourselves while we are actually nourishing the parasite."[15] Avarice is a transcendent and potent force that exists in a non-local field and originates beyond space and time, he contends.

Forbes concludes that this mass psychosis continues to thrive because society has failed to recognize it. Europeans who came to the Americas subconsciously and unwittingly brought Wetiko with them, as it was all they knew: "The Wetiko psychosis and the problems it creates have inspired many resistance movements and efforts at reform or revolution. Unfortunately, most of those efforts have failed because they [society] have never diagnosed the Wetiko as an insane person whose disease is extremely contagious."[16] Indigenous Peoples had to resist the unprecedented onslaught of the spectre of greed: "It was a sad day when these outcasts set foot on the Land of the Free. Unfortunately, they brought all their fears with them and without an awareness of their trespassing laid claim to virgin land that was not theirs."[17]

The infectiousness of greed self-perpetuates as one interacts with it: "One of the tragic characteristics of the wetiko psychosis is that it spreads partly by resistance to it. That is, those who try to fight wetikos sometimes, in order to survive, adopt wetiko values. Thus when they 'win' they also lose." In other words, if one battles the monster of avarice using its methods, one ends up becoming a Wetiko oneself.[18] Those trying to maintain the integrity of Indigeneity can be the most vulnerable: "The people who usually suffer the most are honest, 'simple' democratic people of the world, the non-materialistic, the freedom-loving, and the truly spiritual."[19]

It is been extremely painful both physically and psychologically for Native Peoples to go from having everything to having nothing. Indigenous People need to find a way to move on from lamenting loss to focusing on recovery and healing.

> Now, if we were to use those privileges that they will allow us to have then it would also mean that we would be, have become a part of them, which means that we would become accomplices. So if we don't like what they are doing, if we think that they are thieves, villains, then we are joining them, we would also become that too. And we would be thieves of our own resources. . . . Then they say, 'Well, you get all these benefits free education, free medicare, and all these other things, and getting welfare,' but again we are still the victims and if we understand that we are okay. Even if we are going to be receivers, all these other benefits to us, we are still, we still consider ourselves the victims. But when we join them then we are helping to, we are helping these to take away, we have been asking only for little bits of stuff, education, welfare, that's only small stuff. . . . When we move over to their side, then we are in possession of all that loot that has been stolen from us, or our forefathers, then we would be put in a position of stealing from our own parents and grandparents.[20]

Yet the fate of Indigenous Peoples has historically been blamed on their supposed shortcomings: "The poor natives of California had neither the strength nor the intelligence to unite in any formidable numbers; hence when now and then one of them plucked up the courage to defend his wife and little ones, or to retaliate on one of the many outrages that were constantly being perpetrated upon them by white persons, sufficient excuse was offered for the miners and settlers to band and shoot down any Indians they met, old or young, innocent or guilty, friendly or hostile, until their appetite for blood was appeased."[21]

Avarice is the opposite of generosity and indicates a lack of respect for spirituality.

> Paulo Friere's methodology [in his book *Pedagogy of the Oppressed*]—helping people to understand the social-political world around them—is vital, and yet something is missing. The flavor is European and if it has a 'religious' element, it consists in a kind of humanism. Humanism represents, of course, an admirable philosophy within the framework of European materialism and agnosticism. On the other hand, a critical method limited to the arena of socio-political human behavior as perceived through materialism is one that will never solve the problem of wetikoism. Why? Because one must take 'critical awareness' beyond the limits of purely human situations in order to fully grasp the milieu in which humans actually have our existence . . . the basis for those efforts, if they are to be successful, must rest on the spiritual regeneration of each of us.[22]

Forbes examines the concept of spirituality as religion in its purest sense. Spirituality "is not prayer, it is not a church, it is not theistic, it is not atheistic, it has little to do with what white people call 'religion.' It is our every act. If we tromp on a bug, that is our religion; if we experiment on living animals, that is our religion; if we cheat at cards, that is our religion; if we dream of being famous, that is our religion; if we gossip maliciously, that is our religion; if we are rude and aggressive, that is our religion. All that we do and are is our religion."[23]

Delving further, Levy surmises that the archetype of Wetiko exists in the Bible. "In the biblical lore that has influenced Judeo-Christian civilization, the story of Adam and Eve's banishment from the Garden of Eden certainly seems like the timeless archetypal moment of wetiko entering into the human realm, as spoken in the language of mythology. Eating the fruit of the Tree of Knowledge—knowledge of good and evil, that is—resulted in the 'Fall' of our species." Levy continues hopefully: "This 'sin' was inspired by the snake—but if we see the snake as a disguised form of God, since God created all and everything, then the process of discriminating between good and evil was a necessary step for humanity."[24]

Greed is waging a war on human higher consciousness, and unfortunately this devious force is winning: "The Big Wetikos who control the levers of power, be they the super-wealthy CEOs of corporations, bank presidents, or leaders of nation states, are particularly dangerous because they frame and define the terms of our dialogue by choosing the metaphors which dominate the agreed-upon historical narrative.... Big Wetikos in positions of power craft the limits and parameters of our conversation and debate.[25]

Renowned Cree singer Buffy Sainte-Marie observes that humanity in its current state of evolution is immature but is in the process of "ripening."[26] She says, "The white carry the greed disease ... they need to be cured, but they usually don't mind their disease, or even recognize it, because it's all they know and their leaders encourage them in it, and many of them are beyond help."[27] In her song "The Priests of the Golden Bull" she laments of the greed of Wall Street and the false idol of the Golden Bull representing exploitation, plundering, and profiteering:[28]

> Who brought the bomb wrapped up in business cards
> And stained with steak?
> Who hires a maid to wash his money?
> Who keeps politicians on the take?
> Who puts outspoken third-worlders in jail
> Just to shut them down?
> Oh the lies vary from place to place but the truth is still the same,
> Even in this town
>
> Money junkies all over the world
> Trample us on their way to the bank
> They run in every race
> Windego

Wetiko civilizations are very distinct. In their worldview, human requirements take precedence above all else. The natural world is subordinated to the point where its exploitation is no longer immoral. Their governments justify the never-ending desire for resources, wealth, and power. Economic growth, technological development, and military systems become legitimized. However, the weakness of these civilizations lies in their artificiality. They survive in a bubble of human-made technology, kept alive by constant expansion and resource exploitation. Their citizens become increasingly divorced from the real world. As their nations expand to colonize Indigenous lands, they lose the sacred sense of connectedness.

Nations of the Abrahamic religions have led the aggressive exploitation of the natural world and domination of Indigenous Peoples. Hence, it is no surprise that Christianity and Islam, of all the world's religions, have been the ones that expanded across the globe. Both have harnessed their religion for political, military, and expansionist purposes.

It appears that our minds, which the Creator provided in order to enable humans to discern and live in material reality, are being systematically disconnected from nature. Governments spew fake news, propaganda, and outright lies. Promotion of artificial intelligence exacerbates the reach of human activities, which already have far outstripped human wisdom. Experts say that there will come a time when even the biggest governments will not be able to grasp how very advanced intelligence systems work. The Big Wetikos, the "one percent," will pull the strings of artificial intelligence until it outsmarts even them.

Plundering Resources

A new wave of global expansion was fuelled by the industrial revolution. Innovative ways to make textile production more efficient led to the invention of machines and factories. Techniques were developed for processing and producing metal. Steam locomotives and ships revolutionized transportation and extended markets around the globe. Rubber, originally discovered by the Indigenous Peoples of South America, found its way into tires, boots, and electrical wires among many other things.[29] Observing the Pennsylvania Indians use oil and tar to waterproof canoes led to the start of the American oil industry.[30] Americans were seeing the impacts of the Industrial Revolution by the early 1800s.

Urbanization and mechanization meant increased demand for goods and the need to pursue natural resources internationally. In the process, the Indigenous Peoples who occupied much of the resource-rich territories found themselves subjugated and often forced into becoming partners in the destruction of their natural environments.[31]

In *The Theory of Moral Sentiments* (1759) Adam Smith, the leading proponent of capitalism, admits that exploitation is fine if it adds to the enrichment of life.

> What is the end of avarice and ambition, of the pursuit of wealth, of power, and pre-eminence? Is it to supply the necessaries of nature? The wages of the meanest labourer can supply them . . . why should those who have been educated in the highest ranks of life, regard it as worse than death, to be reduced to live, even without labour, upon the same simple fare with him, to dwell under the same lowly roof, and to be clothed in the same humble attire? . . . It is the vanity, not the ease, or the pleasure, which interests us."[32]

Smith provides an honest assessment about how personal wealth is pleasing to the individual ego. The pursuit of luxury, now taken to its extreme in developed countries where people live by the axiom greed is good, is utterly removed from Indigenous ethics. Both capitalism and communism paint people solely as economically driven creatures being either producers or consumers. In ecolizations, the idea of exploiting the Creator's gifts and of disregarding the integrity of other created beings is unacceptable. The products of hunting and gathering were to support the community, not to enrich individuals. What is the worth of luxury if spiritual needs are not met? Personal enrichment feeds the greed that destroys relationships, and this needs to be avoided at all costs if social harmony is to be preserved.

The captains of industry, those who are most willing and able to lead the exploitation of the environment, cannibalize the gifts of Creation for economic development. The banking system takes deposits and inflates that amount by lending it in multiples more as loans. Governments blithely run up massive deficits based on the idea that economies are "too big to fail." At some point, one wonders if it is all just a huge Ponzi scheme. Is more money and ever-increasing wealth really essential for survival? Why does local development always wait on the availability of funding? Ultimately, people should be able to find ways to create what they need on their own. Why are people becoming increasingly reliant on "fake" foods that damage their health? This was not the case in Indigenous Eden, where stewardship of resources enabled flora and fauna to flourish. But economics deems it necessary to create dependencies in order to ensure cash flow. Such profiteering will be backed up at the point of a gun if necessary.

As principal architects and beneficiaries of industrialization, Europe and the United States have set the tone for the world's economic and political systems. However, the flaws in this grand enterprise are beginning to show. While there has been widespread prosperity, resources are dwindling and economic disparity is becoming increasingly stark. An Oxfam study found that the world's twenty-six richest individuals own as much wealth as 3.8 billion of the poorest people, half of the world's population.[33] To put it another way, the richest on average are 13,000 times wealthier than the poorest, and that gap continues to grow. Such incredible concentration of wealth is made possible by policies of materialism and rationalism that imply that economic prosperity is created by the wealthy. Moreover, politicians believe that those most capable of generating riches, be it through raw talent or invested inherited money, are those who can solve the world's problems.

According to the International Monetary Fund: "Widening income inequality is the defining challenge of our time." Pope Francis agrees with these pundits, stating: "inequality is the root of all evil."[34] Developing countries are experiencing pervasive inequities in access to education, health care, and finance. This disparity is exacerbated by globalization in which lower-paid labour becomes increasingly accessible, and the assets of the wealthy are sheltered in tax havens.

Scourge of Inequality

One of the first consequences of inequality is the breakdown of social relationships. Capitalism, the root of American prosperity, is effectively what is now causing the deterioration of the country along several fault lines. Symptoms include increasing poverty, higher unemployment, worsening crime and drug abuse, mental illness, and a breakdown in social trust and respect. With the shine of capitalism and free enterprise wearing off, people are suddenly realizing that countries that foster greater equality are creating more positive economic, social, and political outcomes. These include regions such as Scandinavia, where governments progressively tax the wealthy to redistribute largesse for common benefit. This enables education, health, and other social support systems to function well.

Citizens need to feel that their country's economic system is not only fair, but that it truly cares for their welfare and provides meaning and purpose for their lives. Traditional Indigenous ecolizations could provide an example, as they had all of those bases covered. They did not have a lot of advanced technology or gadgets, but individuals lived healthy and meaningful lives. Dread the thought that humans can actually live without computers and social media! Yet by all accounts, individuals who live in societies where there is a high degree of harmony and mutual support live purposeful and joyous lives. Finally, Indigenous Peoples were careful not to overturn the delicate balance between human populations and nature. Overpopulation generated by modern civilization is a great challenge, one that politicians are loath to address.

In the same breath, we must recognize that there is no such thing as utopian solutions or perfect equality. Even ecolizations did not have perfect equality, as individuals were recognized on the basis that some had greater gifts for hunting, mediating, or healing. However, the benefits of those gifts were shared for the greater good of the community, and status was recognized on that basis.

Causes of War

The word *war* derives from the German word *werran*, which means "to introduce confusion."[35] There are two theories on why war occurs. One says that the urge to engage in warfare is an inherent characteristic of human populations derived from its ancestral roots and animal heritage. The other is that wars begin when social and environmental stresses and challenges force groups to engage in conflict to ensure security or access to resources. Indigenous philosophers, of course, would have a concern with the first interpretation, as they believe that humans are capable of maintaining positive relationships. Ultimately, they realize, conflict is rooted in the second factor—the lack of sharing. War can be viewed as a byproduct of perceived inequality and social breakdown and manipulation of the weak by the strong for purported economic and political betterment. All of these are byproducts of Wetiko civilization.

With the dilemma of too many people and too few resources, there is a need to return to a healthier balance with the environment. The reason why populations have risen to their current levels is because of domination of nature made possible by exploitation, technological development, economic expansion, and the perception that larger numbers provide greater security.

Mainstream thinkers denigrate and demonize ancient peoples through the theory of evolution that suggests people developed from primates and inherited violence from the animal world. It is unfair and unreasonable to assume that prehistoric peoples were bloodthirsty savages. This interpretation is coloured by a lack of understanding of Indigenous philosophy and by projecting modern man's shortcomings onto a population unable to defend its own record. The emergence of wars coincides with the rise of city states in Mesopotamia approximately 5,000 years ago when Indigenous ideology was abandoned and societies created armies to assert themselves, not only over nature, but also to test their strength against one another.[36]

Was warfare occurring to the same extent among the peoples of the Indigenous Americas? The world "discovered" by Europeans in the late 1400s was the last remaining stronghold of what was an ancient universal culture based upon Indigenous mores. Skeptics of Indigenous exceptionalism like to argue that the advanced societies, in particular the Aztec, Mayans, and Incas, were on the road to civilization just as unfolded in the Old World. However, these Amerindian societies could not conceive of the notion of partitioning nature in the same way that borders were created and fought over in the Old World. Respect for the essence of all created things was still honoured in the Indigenous Americas. Conflicts both on the North American Plains and in Meso-America had more to do with spiritual imperatives such as cultivating the virtue of bravery or other spiritual quests rather than for territorial gain. Borders were fluid as people did not feel entitled to place ownership over autonomous natural environments. Instead, Protocols of a sacred and political nature were employed to preserve peace. If conflict broke out, resolutions would be pursued in ceremony, as it was the will of the Creator that harmony be restored.[37]

Current peace and harmony is an illusion because of relative prosperity, first from the rape of the resources in the Americas, then from the industrial revolution and technological revolution, and from the exploitation that accompanies globalization. Contemporary society exists in a form of Pax Romana in which the foundations of power and wealth need to be in place to ensure smooth functioning. Governments are in constant pursuit of economic expansion and jobs to maintain the illusion of stability. Police and military forces ensure that the government's power structure remains intact. In Indigenous societies, neither currencies nor police forces were priorities. But when economic expansion and its false sense of abundance and harmony fade in Wetiko civilizations, conflict will quickly rear its head. Resource and food crises are looming because of overpopulation and climate change. Short-term prosperity has been achieved by asserting human predominance but that will not lead to long-term stability. Unfortunately, the wisdom of ancient ways will become evident only after it is too late.

Globalization

Economic and political globalism is touted as another solution to humans' ills. It is not a wise approach because it removes people further from their connectedness to land and exacerbates the pressure on limited resources. After World War II, the United States under

President Eisenhower pursued a policy of developing a strong military, not only to protect the United States but also to enable it to influence world affairs. This strategy included government, private industry, and science. At the same time Eisenhower cautioned:

> The total influence—economic, political and even spiritual— is felt in every city, every state house, every office of the federal government. . . . Yet we must not fail to comprehend its grave implications. Our toil, resources and livelihood are all involved; so is the very structure of our society. In the councils of government, we must guard against the acquisition of unwarranted influence, whether sought or unsought, by the military-industrial complex. The potential for the disastrous rise of misplaced power exists, and will persist. We must never let the weight of this combination endanger our liberties or democratic forces.[38]

The military-industrial complex has become a major international economic and political juggernaut. The United States spends around one trillion dollars per year on maintaining its armed forces and developing new armaments. This constitutes nearly half of world military expenditures and America's outlay is higher than the next dozen largest powers combined. Americans prosper enormously through this web of industry that creates pressure for every country to acquire ever-deadlier weaponry. However, this buildup of arms further threatens an already fragile world. The maintenance of power and wealth comes at a high price.

Civilization's fraught relationship within itself and with the rest of Creation is becoming increasingly apparent. Will humanity recognize the peril that the cumulative effects of these developments present? Moral evolution has been badly outstripped by technological development. The only remaining question is whether remedial actions can be taken before it is too late. The loss of sacredness will endanger the world until people figure out how to return to their true heritage. The last two hundred years are one-tenth of 1 percent of human history—that sliver of time may destroy us. Hopi spiritualist Evehema warns:

We are now faced with great problems, not only here but throughout the land. Ancient cultures are being annihilated. Our peoples' lands are being taken from them. Why is this happening? It is happening because many have given up or manipulated their original spiritual teachings. The way of life that the Great Spirit has given to all people, whatever your Original Instructions, are not being honoured. It is because of this great sickness called greed, which infects every land and country.[39]

We're going to need water, the land is going to be so dry and nothing will grow and trees will be starting to dry up and that the time we will, everything will beginning to come to the end, and another thing that I seen in my vision is the civil war again, the people will fight. I see women and children running up the hill with the barbed wire fence and everything like that and get caught on that. I seen people are shot down get killed by guns everything.[40]

Curses of Civilization

Where miracles were possible in healing-focused Indigenous Eden, the opposite is characteristic of modern civilization. As problems go unaddressed, misfortunes and disasters mount.

On March 8, 2014, Malaysian Airlines Flight MH370 went off course and disappeared on a flight from Kuala Lumpur to Beijing. On board were twelve crew members and 227 passengers. Radio communications ceased after the Boeing 777 entered Vietnamese airspace. Confusion reigned. Neither Malaysian nor Vietnamese flight controllers knew the airplane's location. Reports by military radar and satellite communications revealed that MH370 had veered off course, proceeded west over the Andaman Sea then south into the Indian Ocean. It is estimated that the aircraft flew for almost eight hours until it ran out of fuel and crashed into the South Indian Ocean about 1600 miles west of Australia. The search for the aircraft became the most extensive and costly in aviation history and covered 1.8 million square miles. About thirty pieces of debris have since washed up in and around Madagascar.[41]

Investigators concluded that the airplane was functioning properly and that the errant flight path was because someone in the cockpit took unlawful control of the plane. But it is a mystery as to what the motive was. There was no evidence of terrorist involvement. Some suspect that pilot Zaharie Ahmad Shah may have been responsible. However, the final investigation report concludes that there could be no absolute certainty of the cause without evidence from the plane's black boxes. This left relatives of the victims, as well as an interested public across the globe, in frustration and anguish.

On September 25, 2017, Stephen Paddock rented a room on the thirty-second floor of the Mandalay Hotel overlooking the site of the Route 91 Harvest music festival in Las Vegas. With apparent ease he smuggled in an arsenal of twenty-four firearms, including AR-15 rifles equipped with bump stocks that allow the gun to fire bursts of ninety rounds in ten seconds. At 10:00 p.m. on October 1, Paddock broke the room's windows and sprayed 22,000 festival goers with bullets. Pandemonium broke out once attendees realized they were being attacked. Over the next ten minutes, people scrambled in all directions, uncertain of where exactly the rifle fire was coming from. Altogether, fifty-eight perished and 851 were injured by bullets or during the stampede to escape.

By the time police entered his room, Paddock had turned his weapon on himself. Investigators concluded that the assailant had meticulously planned the murderous event over a significant period of time. But they found no explanation or clear motive for why the sixty-four-year-old former accountant and real estate businessman would commit such a heinous crime.[42] The incident led to a renewed call for firearms control. But President Trump dismissed the idea saying, "He was a very sick man" and new laws won't stop someone like that.[43] It is true the shooter was a sick man but his sickness is a symptom of the society he lived in.

John Mohawk laments the myopia of modern society in understanding the damage it has inflicted.

> It's like the Original man, he was the last one to leave the Creator's side, and the White man was the first one to leave, he didn't even look back to the gifts he was given and look at

them now, he's lost all his gifts, he doesn't know who he is and he moves very fast. He gets all over the world and wants everything, he wants to control everything because he has lost all those gifts that the Creator had given him. But the Anishinabe was the last one to leave the Creator's side and many times he's turned around and looked at the Creator and the Creator had to coax him to go. That's how slow he's walked and that's how we are, like that Original Man. We walk very slow and examine what's there and we don't jump into things right away, as soon as we jump into things right away we try to go real fast and we fall flat on our face. The White man has to understand that and not to push us, he's always pushing, trying to make things happen right away. But with us, we have to examine, we have to move slowly."[44]

Elder Albert Ward notes what is really important is not material possessions but the quality of your relationships. "But when you are trying to get to your own people, and you find a lot of happiness, and you don't have to have a whole lot to be happy. That's another good thing about our culture. You don't have to have a bunch of other things. What's important is your Spirit. What's happened is you got what's in you and that's what makes you strong and happy. But you cannot buy anything like this, your own culture and your own love. You cannot buy that. You got to earn that."[45]

The pursuit of wealth and power brings short-term prosperity to people but has adverse effects on our animal and plant "relatives." The damage being inflicted on flora and fauna is dramatic and often fatal. Ignoring the plight of our nature "relatives" increases the potential for environmental catastrophe and could inevitably spell the end of everything that humanity has created.

CHAPTER 8
HARMING OUR RELATIVES

Adaptation and Survival

As late as the eighteenth century, Euro-American thinkers believed that the world God created was perfect. The natural Chain of Being could not be altered, as that would contravene God's perfection.[1] The discovery of mammoth and dinosaur fossils forced a change in that view, and with the penning of Charles Darwin's *On the Origin of Species*, the idea of species extinction gradually became accepted.

Darwin's theory of evolution portrayed interspecies relationships in terms of competition and dominance. This approach is flawed and has since been discredited. It is now understood that to survive as complex systems, organisms must cooperate both within species as well as with others. However, the theory of survival of the fittest left a unique stamp on thinking—that it is necessary for people to overcome nature as well as competitors to survive.

Awareness of how environmental issues can affect our host nikâwînân askiy (Mother Earth) is a recent development. The first meaningful literature and activism on environmentalism only began in the early 1960s. At that time, governments had no environmental reviews. However, concern over the impact of construction projects and industrial pollution on nature was growing.

In the 1960s, oil industry spokespersons regularly dismissed the idea of pollution, saying that nature was simply too enormous to ever be totally affected. Oil was used in negligible amounts prior to the Industrial Revolution. But the invention of the gasoline motor and its importance for military use created a revolution in energy demand. Petroleum has come to dominate nearly every part of our lives. It fuels vehicles, powers industry, provides plastics used in everyday goods, and becomes ingredients in pharmaceuticals, cosmetics, fertilizers, and pesticides. Countries use an astounding 30 billion barrels of oil annually and this resource has become the world's most valuable commodity. But petroleum is toxic to virtually all forms of life.

Witness the situation we are now in. Pollution is everywhere: in the air, in the soil, in the water, in creatures, and in our own bodies. How wrong the skeptics were! So great is the impact of oil consumption on the climate that a new geological epoch has been named—the Anthropocene. The impact of our activities is now being placed on the scale of major geological events such as large meteor strikes, major volcanic eruptions, and ice ages that resulted in previous mass extinctions.

Anthropocene

The Anthropocene is a presumed interval of geologic time distinguishable by the impact of human activities. Almost one-half of the Earth's surface has been modified by agriculture or urban development. Plutonium isotopes that remain in the soil from nuclear experiments in 1950 suggest that the epoch we live in began in the mid-twentieth century.[2]

Indigenous Peoples are dismayed over the negative interactions that have damaged our relationships with our plant and animal kin. Never in ancient law could this have been condoned. Some archaeologists attempt to prove that ancient peoples also overhunted and wasted resources. One would not deny that mistakes or poor judgment occurred. However, this does not delegitimize their philosophy that demands consistent respect for the spirits of animals and other created entities. It was understood that everything is connected in a web of interdependency and that damaging that harmony would bring about misfortune.

Skeptics point out that there exist dangerous animals and other perils in nature that can harm humans. In Indigenous thinking, this was not a reason to try to destroy or eliminate the source of such apparent threats. Rather, it signified that these dangers had to be respected and dealt with wisely, keeping in mind that everything has a reason to survive. Accounts that appear in the media of peaceful relationships nurtured between humans and wild animals such as wolves or tigers demonstrate what is possible.

The irony is that the technology people create to control and improve things almost always has negative consequences for the natural order. Fishing methods such as deep-sea trawling provide more food for expanding human populations but damage ocean floors, making it more difficult for marine life to thrive. As an unintended byproduct, plastics will soon outweigh sea-life as items such as bottles, packaging, and industrial waste accumulate in greater quantities. Plastics are notoriously slow to disintegrate, and when they do, micro-particles inflict further damage on marine life.[3] Natural structures such as the Great Coral Reef that provide the richest environments for marine life are deteriorating at an alarming rate. With such trends, the bulk of current seafood sources could disappear by 2050.[4]

Change and Extinction

Ecologists have identified rapid change as the factor that is the greatest threat to species survival. Today, such changes are most often the result of human activity. The main reason for habitat destruction is the population growth that alters the natural environment. Laws that attempt to protect endangered species have only limited effectiveness. Some industries see the presence of species as a nuisance to their business enterprises. Governments prioritize economic development over natural conservation. Whatever the cause, the rate of species extinction has shot a thousandfold. Altogether, about six hundred species have disappeared since the Industrial Revolution and over 3,000 species are currently listed as critically endangered. The prospect that 25 percent of the millions of species could be in some danger of eventual extinction due to human activity should be alarming.[5]

Critically endangered organisms include those at immanent risk of disappearing in coming years due to low numbers, a decline in fertility, overhunting, or destruction of remaining habitat. Some are close to humans in genetic markers such as the Cross River gorilla, mountain gorilla, western lowland gorilla, Sumatran orangutan, and brown spider monkey. Other endangered large land animals include the Sumatran elephant, Bactrian camel, Sumatran rhinoceros, black rhinoceros, Javan rhinoceros, northern white rhinoceros, West African lion, Malayan tiger, Siamese South China tiger, Amur leopard, Asiatic cheetah, North African cheetah, Arabian leopard, and Florida panther. Some, such as the Barbary lion, Pere David's deer, and Wyoming toad, no longer exist in the wild and are found only in zoos.[6]

Almost half of the world's free-roaming animals could become extinct outside of zoos by 2100. Species already extinct due to human activity include the Tasmanian tiger, Bali tiger, Caspian tiger, Javian tiger, western black rhinoceros, California grizzly bear, Carolina parakeet, Japanese sea lion, Labrador duck, passenger pigeon, New Zealand quail, Atellar's seacow, toolache wallaby, great auk, golden toad, and dodo bird. Nearly a thousand extinctions have occurred over the past 500 years.[7]

Whales at risk of extinction include the blue whale, bowhead whale, finback whale, gray whale, sperm whale, humpback whale, and North Atlantic right whale. Shockingly, the modern industrialized fishing industry has managed to harvest 90 percent of existing stocks in recent decades.[8]

Human Factors

The North American bison, once numbering over 60 million, came close to extinction. Tribes relied almost entirely on bison for food and other necessities. The motive for mass slaughter of these majestic creatures was to undercut Indigenous Peoples' independence and bring about their subjugation more quickly. The Plains grizzly and prairie wolf became extinct in the face of settlement. The grizzly bear, eastern timber wolf, and sea turtle are rapidly declining in numbers due to sport hunting and poaching.

Passenger pigeons, birds sacred to Indigenous Peoples, once numbered in the billions. They were relatively large birds over a foot in length. A flock was like a great cloud that could take days to pass. But they were easy to catch—using a large stick or throwing a stone could bring down several. There were novel uses such as targets for shooting practice, and tens of thousands of pigeons were killed at a time. Birds were cooked in creative ways. Feathers were used in mattresses. It was generally thought that passenger pigeons would never be eradicated. But by 1900 the only remaining birds were those stuffed and placed in museums.[9]

The accelerating rate of species extinctions due to rapid change puts tens of thousands of species in danger. The pattern is clear. Scientists estimate species could start disappearing at 10,000 times the normal rate. Dozens could go extinct every day![10] Almost 50 percent of the world's primate species, the group most like us that includes monkeys, lemurs, lorids, galagos, tarsiers, and apes, are at risk.[11] According to the World Wildlife Federation's Living Planet Index, of 4,000 species of vertebrates studied, the average loss of numbers is a shocking 60 percent since the 1970s.[12]

The effect of climate change on water supply is another threat. Some of the world's most water-scarce countries, such as Saudi Arabia, Bahrain, Jordan, Kuwait, and Australia, will suffer severe water shortage and become less habitable due to excessive heat.[13] As flora and fauna that support human life withers, little will be left for future generations. The average life span of mammalian species is one million years. Our human pride and unshakeable belief in our own cleverness leads us to think that we can survive anything. But with the breakneck speed of change that is now occurring, how much longer will humanity be able to endure?

Decline of Forests

Half of the world's forests have been eliminated since the dawn of civilization. "Land clearance has been a defining characteristic of civilizations—culture based around cities and agriculture—since they emerged around 8,000 years ago."[14] Such deforestation has had massive impacts on the environment, including an increase in atmospheric carbon, heating of local environments, and species loss. Europe has lost half of its forests. In the Mediterranean Basin, where there were once forests, only rocky hills remain. Environmental activist Lierre Keith notes: "Agriculture, hierarchy, deforestation, topsoil loss, militarism, and imperialism became an intensifying feedback loop that ended with the collapse of the bioregion [Mediterranean Basin] that will most likely not recover."[15]

Today, tree cover amounting to about the size of New Zealand is lost annually due to factors such as agriculture, logging, urbanization, industry, and forest fires. Increasing air temperatures aggravate fire susceptibility. Loss of tropical forests in places such as Brazil and Indonesia threatens critical habitat for nearly half of the world's animal and plant species. Indonesian fires in 2015 caused up to 100,000 premature human deaths.[16]

The world's most important ecosystem is the Amazon, which produces about one-fifth of the world's oxygen supply. At the time of European contact in the mid-sixteenth century, over ten million Indigenous people lived in the area of Brazil and scientists have discovered that they played an important role in creating the Amazon. Amazon soil is low in fertility; however, like their neighbours the Inca, Amazonian tribes were talented in their ability to foster plant growth. Over thousands of years, they cultivated and tended the Amazon, enabling it to become a lush forest.[17] Today, only about 900,000 Indigenous people, or less that one half a percent of Brazil's population, remain in the Amazon. However, 13 percent of the country's land is set aside for them, an amount that developers feel is too much.

Burning the Amazon rainforest has resulted in the loss of a fifth of its tree cover, and the rate of deforestation has increased dramatically under President Jair Bolsonaro's policy of creating more agricultural and ranching land. Biologists fear that other changing conditions, including increasing temperatures, lower rainfall, and the decreasing ability of the soil to regenerate growth, will result in the rainforest's ultimate disappearance. Bolsonaro has fiercely rejected foreign criticism, accusing Europe of having a colonial mindset. This position blithely ignores the fact that most Brazilians are originally Europeans who arrived over five centuries ago and who have done little to change their attitude towards exploiting nature. Bolsonaro claims that the changes he is making will even benefit Indigenous people: "You want Indigenous people to carry on like prehistoric men with no access to technology, science, information and the wonders of modernity. Indigenous people want to work, they want to produce and they can't. They live isolated in their areas like cavemen."[18]

A similar story can be told about natural grasslands around the world. They have been converted to wheat, corn, and other crops that support civilization in its current form. Where crops grow, herbicides and pesticides are used against "weeds" that are usually native plants, rodents, and insects. Genetically modified organisms bring greater profits at the expense of other vegetal life that is eliminated through chemicals like Roundup. Food production systems deemed crucial to modern life are also destroying much of the planet's biological diversity.

Recent research indicates that 40 percent of insect species are declining and many could become extinct within decades. Groups most endangered include butterflies, moths, bees, and beetles. Threats arise from habitat change; draining wetlands; use of insecticides, herbicides, and fungicides; and climate change. The impacts of insect decline will be severe, as they pollinate plants, clean water systems, and provide food for other creatures. They are the foundation for many biological systems that humans rely on for survival.[19]

Global Warming Threat

Most people, especially the elderly, have noted change in the weather patterns during their lifetime. The evidence is already upon us, including temperature extremes, melting glaciers and ice caps, larger hurricanes, and more severe fires. The great concern is that once temperature rises 1.5 degrees Celsius beyond pre-industrial levels (using 1850 as a baseline), feedback loops will greatly magnify climate deterioration.

Once that occurs, reversing or stabilizing temperature rise will be impossible. Over the next few centuries, Greenland and Antarctica's ice will melt, adding an additional seventy feet to ocean levels. A billion people in hundreds of cities around the globe, including London, New York, and Tokyo, will be devastated by flooding, contaminated water, and power shortages by 2050.[20]

The first major international agreement to address global warming is the United Nations Framework Convention on Climate Change agreed upon in Rio de Janeiro in 1992. Building upon that foundation, the 1997 Kyoto Protocol set limits for greenhouse gas emissions to be met by 2012. That target was later postponed to 2020. The Intergovernmental Panel on Climate Change warns that temperatures could rise as high as six degrees warmer than pre-industrial levels by the year 2100. That rise will be catastrophic in terms of ever more extreme weather events, crop destruction, loss of forests through fire, and disappearance of numerous species that will be unable to adapt. Armed conflict and disease will increase. In order to address this challenge, countries will have to reduce their current fuel consumption by 50 percent by 2030 and 100 percent by 2050.[21]

Some feel that the current state of government inaction means it is already too late to keep temperatures 1.5 degrees below pre-industrial levels; they argue that it is likely that temperatures will rise two degrees by 2040. This problem is exacerbated by the withdrawal by the United States, the world's largest per capita emissions producer, from the Paris Climate Agreement. President Trump, prodded by oil and coal interests, refuses to endorse the agreement, citing damage to the u.s. economy and the inaction of other polluters, such as China and India. But virtually every nation in the world has failed to meet its carbon emission reduction commitments.[22]

Skeptics, who do not want to face the economic impact of climate change, argue that there has been extreme variability of climate in the planet's past. The difference is that previous change happened at a snail's pace. Today, it is like a locomotive barrelling towards us. There are still captains of industry who think human ingenuity can prevail in this disaster. They claim that experimental ideas such as spraying aerosols into the atmosphere to lessen sun exposure and cool temperatures would help. But this will not be enough to counteract the heating generated by methane released from millions of square kilometres of thawing tundra, or vehicle emissions from the vehicles that congest our urban centres, or carbon monoxide released into the air as forests increasingly burn out of control. Others, recognizing that we are in danger but unwilling to change their behaviour, go so far as to propose terraforming Mars or travelling into interstellar space in order to find "another Earth" after our natural home becomes uninhabitable.

Water Degradation

Only a miniscule one-hundredth of 1 percent of the world's fresh water is generally accessible for human consumption. It is a precious resource, indeed! As proof of the world's interconnectedness, chemicals such as PCBs and mercury produced in industrialized nations are found in higher concentrations in the Arctic—a sparsely inhabited region. The alarming melting of glaciers creates significant challenges in some of the world's most densely populated areas. In the Himalayan mountains, where the greatest concentration of ice exists apart from the poles, melting glaciers reduce the water supply that runs into the Indus and Ganges rivers. In nearby Bangladesh, melting of the Arctic and Antarctic icefields will flood the mega-deltas that currently support millions. Entire island nations such as Kiribati, Maldives, Tokelu, Tuvali, and the Marshall Islands will disappear.[23] This type of human-made catastrophe would have been unthinkable in Indigenous ecolizations that took seriously the effects of their actions on future generations.

Up to 40 percent of human-produced carbon dioxide is dissolved in oceans and other water bodies. This carbon absorption creates carbonic acid, causing acidification that bleaches and kills coral reefs, primary shelters of about a quarter of marine life such as crustaceans and mollusks. Most of the world's coral reefs are already damaged, and by 2050, 90 percent of the reefs may be destroyed. Acidification combined with warmer water further threatens marine life due to lower oxygen levels.

There are about 380 million tons of plastics produced annually. Of this only about 20 percent is recycled or incinerated. Ten million tons of plastics enters the ocean each year in multiple forms, including plastic bottles, cups, packaging, cigarette butts, disposable napkins, shampoos, and fishing gear. Most of these are single-use items. It is estimated that there are as many as five trillion pieces of plastics of various sizes floating in the oceans. Plastics can take centuries to decompose. In the process of decomposition, particles become increasingly smaller. Microplastics easily enter marine organisms and end up in the human food chain. Plastics release toxins such as bisphenol, which is understood to be carcinogenic and affects reproduction and immunity. Marine animals such as turtles and whales are becoming entangled in netting. Millions of fish, sea turtles, and birds rot on shores because they have mistaken plastics for food. It is projected that by 2050 there could be more plastics by weight in the oceans than fish.[24]

Indigenous Responses

The 1,172-mile-long Dakota Access Pipeline transports oil from the Bakken oil fields of North Dakota to refineries on the Gulf Coast. After protests from Montana municipal officials, the Army Corps of Engineers changed the route to run under the Missouri River near the Standing Rock Indian Reservation. The Lakota protested that an oil spill would permanently damage their water supplies. Hundreds of water protectors from across the world rallied, setting up their own encampment. Police from six states used armoured vehicles, rubber bullets, tasers, concussion grenades, and mace to force demonstrators away from the construction site. During the demonstrations, over five hundred water protectors were strip-searched and arrested. In December 2016, the protests led President Barack Obama to deny the necessary construction easement. However, in 2017, newly elected President Donald Trump, an investor in the pipeline project, quickly reversed the decision and waived any remaining requirements for environmental review. Increasingly aggressive police tactics led to the camp site being dismantled by February 2017. Water protectors left to prevent fatalities. The Indigenous Environmental Network warned that if the government granted an easement without any environmental review or tribal consultation, they would only fight harder.[25]

Indigenous Peoples cannot remained idle in the face of threats to Mother Earth. In September 2017, twenty prominent Elders and non-Indigenous scientists, along with 150 observers, gathered at the Turtle Lodge on the Sagkeeng First Nation in Manitoba. The Lodge was created by Elder Dave Courchene Jr. in 2002 following a vision of the Turtle, which represents truth. He saw the necessity to promote traditional learning to bring about healing and peace for all peoples. Elder Courchene has carried his message to the United Nations and around the world.[26]

The impetus for bringing Elders and scientists together was Prime Minister Justin Trudeau's remark that "Indigenous peoples have known for thousands of years how to care for our planet. The rest of us have a lot to learn and no time to waste."[27] Elders focus on the importance of spirituality and ceremony as the foundation of their approach. The natural laws followed by Indigenous Peoples call for respect for the environment. Scientists acknowledged that scientific knowledge, privileged as providing the solutions to world technological problems, is not enough.

Speaking on behalf of scientists, David Suzuki acknowledged that Indigenous knowledge provides vital perspectives on the environment. The gathering concluded with the Turtle Lodge Declaration, which states:

> Around the globe, traditional knowledge and wisdom embedded in place has enabled people and culture to flourish for millennia. . . . Suffused throughout the rituals and teachings is acknowledgement that there are spirits and forces beyond human understanding and control. . . . our Mother [Earth] cries out in pain and warns that human greed, ignorance and thoughtlessness are tearing at her ability to support life. . . . We forget to give thanks and acknowledge our responsibilities as self-indulgence blinds us to Nature's gifts upon which we depend. . . . Knowledge without spirit is soulless, lacking in love, humility and responsibility that must guide and constrain its application.[28]

The gathering concluded with an adoption ceremony in which the scientists, now allies, were accepted into the Aboriginal community. With that comes the duties and responsibilities to follow natural and supernatural laws.

Stopping the War against Nature

Dismal treatment of the environment is a major symptom of Wetiko civilization. Spiritual connection to land has been lost in favour of commercial use. Humans are living increasingly unnatural and unspiritual lifestyles. In Indigenous philosophy, all created beings have their place whether it is simply to learn to grow, to move, to breed, to hunt and be hunted, and so on. It is their spiritual mission, just as humans as a whole and as individuals have a purpose for existing. Under Indigenous worldview, animals, plants, and people must recognize and play their roles in the web of life.

People depend on all other species, but none of them need us. In fact, scientists note that in the absence of humanity, nature would once again blossom and proliferate. Indigenous Peoples did not believe they had the authority to employ technologies without the consent and affirmation of the Grandfather Spirits of nature and Ancestors.

The contemporary world is in deep denial about the implications of climate change and global warming. A 2017 article in *New York Magazine*, "The Uninhabitable Earth," which has become their most read press article, makes the shocking prediction that humanity could become extinct within just over a century.[29] While this seems alarmist, it should give pause for thought. Imagine that global average temperature rise does not stop at four degrees. It could conceivably rise to eight degrees or higher beyond pre-industrial levels, at which point humans will be battered by unimaginably destructive extreme heat and storms. By this time the natural environment will be largely devastated with only the hardiest of plants and insects hanging on. So what do humans do? Do we retreat into human-made caves with little gardens and barns holding whatever domesticated animals can be managed? By that time, the face of civilization and population as we know it will be unrecognizable. Unless fundamental change in attitude and practices occurs over the next few decades, Earth will be on a course of such degradation that humans may not feel survival is worthwhile.

Human Extinction?

Optimists believe there is still time to stop and reverse global warming before it reaches the four-degree mark. This, however, will take an immediate and extraordinary change in attitudes and practices. Witness all the places people have adapted to around the globe. We have been able to survive in the most inhospitable environments. But cleverness will not be the issue when it comes to survival. Rather, it will be the ability of all other species to survive, be they plant or animal, which do not have the privilege of picking up stakes and moving.

The ultimate irony is that the destruction of the natural environment, home of our spiritual kin, will spell doom for humanity as well. Population expansion has been abetted by the Industrial Revolution and advanced transportation technology that began in the late 1700s and was further exacerbated by globalization in the twentieth century. The estimated human population around 1800 CE was 900 million. In 1930, the number reached two billion. Now, in 2019, it is approaching eight billion. An additional billion people are being added to the world every decade.[30]

The world is overpopulated because of man's aggressive stance against and domination of nature. Optimum human population for Earth is between 1.5 to 2 billion people.[31] Burgeoning megacities are severely out of balance with their environment. Governments continue to blithely promote rapid economic growth as the panacea for public happiness. We now have hyper-consumption, with products reaching ever-expanding markets around the world. Put in another context, if the last 10,000 years of civilization could be put on a twenty-four-hour clock, this explosive expansion is occurring within the last ten seconds.

The average mammal species is expected to survive at least one million years.[32] So far humans have completed 200,000 years, only 20 percent of that journey. Even with our cleverness, will we be capable of lasting another 800,000 years given our current rate of planetary destruction? One wonders whether our descendants will ever reach their full potential given the current trajectory. People are unlikely to dramatically disappear unless there is a nuclear conflagration. It is more likely that as conditions worsen we will no longer see Earth as a desirable place to propagate and will simply vanish with barely a whimper.

Aboriginal Peoples are strongly committed to nurturing relationships with the natural environment. The individual covered in leather and feathers is honouring his ties to the natural world. Yet this image is tied to primitivism and backwardness. Contrast that with the stereotypical modern man sitting in his Cadillac and smoking a cigar. The latter's apparent prosperity is based upon an ideology of exploitation of nature. Which has the best prospects for long-term survival extending into millions of years?

In 1992 Hopi Elder Thomas Banyaca spoke to the United Nations about the Hopi's ancient obligation to act as stewards and the consequences of ignoring it.

We made a sacred covenant to follow his [Creator's] life plan at all times, which includes the responsibility of taking care of this land and life for his divine purpose. We have never made treaties with any foreign nation, including the United States, but for many centuries we have honoured this sacred agreement. Our goals are not to gain political control, monetary wealth nor military power, but rather to pray and to promote the welfare of all living beings and to preserve the world in a natural way. . . . This line [pointing to his ceremonial rattle] is a time line and indicates that we are in the final days of the prophecy. What have you, as individuals, as nations and as the whole world body been doing to care for this Earth? . . . If we as humans do not wake up to the learnings, the great purification will come to destroy this world just as previous worlds were destroyed.[33]

Former Isleta Pueblo governor and environmental activist Verna Williamson-Teller notes the connection between spirituality and environmental work.

The environmental issue is a very spiritual one. It takes an understanding and a recognition that water, and all natural resources, are really spirits. Indian people recognize that and so when those spirits are wounded or soiled, then it is very much a degradation of that spirit. Moreover, we are all going to pay and we are all paying for it now. Therefore, it is very important that we recognize the power of these spirits. We have no control over them. They are very powerful and if we're not really careful how we treat them, we may be seeing some very serious end to us, because the spirits can only put up with so much, and we have to be very careful to work with them. They are very real.[34]

Onondaga Chief Oren Lyons points out warnings in Haudenosaunee prophecy.

The prophecies said that there was going to be a degradation of the Earth. We were told that you could tell the extent of the degradation of the Earth because there would be two very important systems to warn you. One would be the acceleration of the winds. We were told that the winds would accelerate and continue to accelerate. When you see that the acceleration of the winds are growing, then you know you are in dangerous times. They said the other way to tell that the Earth was in degradation was how people treated their children. They said that will be very important to note how people treat their children, and that will tell you how the earth is degrading. So when you open up the newspapers today and they talk about exploitative sex and children, they talk about homeless children, and you can count the homeless children by the millions. To us, it's a severe indication of the degradation. Society doesn't care.[35]

Environmentalist David Suzuki recognizes that traditional peoples have that "something" which is missing in modern discourse. After all, they have proven to be capable of coexisting successfully with complex ecosystems for millennia: "In this new millennium, after a century of explosive growth in science and technology, it is fitting that leading members of the scientific community are starting to understand that science alone cannot fulfill humankind's needs: indeed, it has become a destructive force. We need a new kind of science that approaches the traditional knowledge of Indigenous communities; the search for it has already begun."[36]

The World Commission on Environment and Development observed: "[Indigenous] communities are the repositories of vast accumulations of traditional knowledge and experience that links humanity with its ancient origins. Their disappearance is a loss for the larger society, which could learn a great deal from their traditional skills in sustainably managing very complex ecological systems. It is a terrible irony that as formal development reaches deeply into rainforests, deserts, and other isolated environments, it tends to destroy the cultures that are thriving in these environments."[37]

The numinous is something that hard-boiled materialists need to learn to accept. In *The Machinery of Nature*, Paul Erlich contends that "a quasi-religious movement, one concerned with the need to change the values that now govern much of human activity, is essential to the persistence of our civilization. But agreeing that science, even the science of ecology, cannot answer all questions—that there are 'other ways of knowing'—does not diminish the absolutely critical role that good science must play if our over-extended civilization is to save itself."[38]

This acknowledges what Elders say—that learning and knowledge are desirable; however, in the absence of a sacred framework, severe mistakes are inevitable. While our peoples tenaciously cling to their values and culture, pessimism can settle in. Elder Phil Lane made an interesting observation when he asked why it is that First Peoples always seem to experience a disproportionally large amount of suffering. They endure this suffering to preserve the memory of humanity's original spiritual mission, he pointed out.[39] But there are those in mainstream societies who are coming to appreciate our resolve and are becoming allies. It is here that hope exists that humanity's outlook will change and a large-scale transformation of consciousness will occur.

Artificial Intelligence

Artificial intelligence (AI) is still in the stage of early development. Devices with intelligence, be they computers, digital home devices, or industrial robots, can only do basic tasks as programmed. Advocates of artificial intelligence such as Max Tegmark, president of the Future of Life Institute, state that all will be well, as long as the creators and managers of these innovations implement safe and ethical frameworks in which the goals of this technology align with human needs.[40] The truth is that there will never be consensus about what proper and ethical use of AI entails. Mavericks, criminals, and enemies will do what they want. Others say that artificial technology will free up people to enjoy leisure time and create opportunities to pursue personal interests. However, this technology has enslaved us, distancing and divorcing us from nature and the broader social environment.

The ability to learn lessons from the consequences of personal decisions will be diminished. In the broader sense, technology erodes human purpose and mission. Artificial intelligence takes us further away from what the Elders call the Good Path. It can enable the worst aspects of civilization while continuing to sever meaningful relationships. Along with fake news, it seems that the political and economic elite, who benefit from the status quo, are disconnecting people's brains with the message that there is nothing to worry about. Rather, the message is to continue to play with gadgets, enjoy consuming products, and watch entertainment on the media. This is abandonment of our natural purpose to learn from life's experiences. And what happens when the artificially maintained bubble bursts?

There are reasons why influential people such as Stephen Hawking, Bill Gates, and Elon Musk are concerned.[41] The ability of computers to process enormous amounts of data and execute increasingly sophisticated actions is increasing exponentially. In science fiction, one shudders at the idea of killing machines programmed to indiscriminately kill people. However, robots and digital devices may be the least one has to worry about. Programs that are sophisticated even beyond the comprehension of their makers will begin to make critical decisions. This already occurs to an extent in financial markets, government programs, and military strategies that become too complex to manage. In this scenario, humans will have little choice but to live with the consequences.

AI takes us further from the normalcy of natural living step by step. It appears to create relationships but actually erodes them. Artificial intelligence exacerbates global profiteering that is rapidly depleting the world's resources. Yet, we do not know what the limits of our inventiveness versus the dangers posed to our existence are. The complexities of artificial intelligence are laying bare the limits of human intellectual capability. Only under supernal wisdom can these technologies become safe tools.

Master of the Universe Fantasy

Man in his hubris is beginning to behave like the creator and master of the universe. Governments are working on initiatives for exploratory missions to Mars by the 2030s. Private companies such as Mars One and Space X believe that permanent colonies are possible in the next decade or two. Visions of colonizing Mars are based upon the suspicion that humanity will not survive in the long term because of environmental degradation or destruction by some other means. The solution touted to ensure continuity is travel to other planets where new human habitation can be established. Mars is the closest planet with an environment even remotely resembling Earth's.[42]

Mars has some characteristics, such as a twenty-four-and-a-half-hour day and an axial tilt similar to Earth's, that would create seasons. However, the seasons would be twice as long given Mar's orbit around the sun. Sunlight itself is only about half as strong as Earth's, so temperatures are much colder, consistently hovering below the freezing point. There are other equally challenging differences. Gravity is less than 40 percent of our planet, meaning that it would be impossible to maintain bone density and muscle mass. Damaging cosmic rays and ultraviolet light due to lack of significant atmosphere constantly bombard Mars. What little of the atmosphere exists is primarily carbon dioxide. Oxygen is virtually non-existent. Health complications would include cardiovascular problems, osteoporosis, cancer, and cognitive problems to mention only a few. Any child born in that environment would carry genetic defects. One can hardly imagine a more hostile environment. Mars will never be a second Earth.[43]

Mastery of the environment is different from, and does not have to imply, domination over it. Humans lived successfully and meaningfully for 194,000 years prior to the development of modern civilization. It is in the last 6,000 years, or 3 percent of our sojourn, that civilization has come to be considered the crown jewel of human achievement. Because of abandoning genuine spirituality, humanity has truly deceived itself. It turns out that the enemy is within, not in the environment that surrounds us. The real challenge will be to overcome the pride that is leading to self-destruction. It would be especially useful to start over with humility and honesty. It is the ultimate folly to imagine that people will successfully colonize a planet that is hostile in every imaginable manner after being unable to live in harmony with the Earth.

Secular scientists and scholars still prefer to think that spirituality is purely imagination and fabrication. A great deal of time and energy is spent dismissing pre-modern peoples as uninformed and hapless victims of their environments. The fact is, mainstream intellectuals do not understand the ideology of prehistoric peoples any more than they understand the philosophy of Indigenous Peoples today. The time has come to accept that so-called primitive peoples did indeed have a viable philosophy and worldview.

In the midst of angst over deteriorating world conditions, there are people in both Indigenous and mainstream cultures who continue to search for the meaning of life. Scientists and other researchers are elevating the public's awareness that more exists than "just meets the eye." Combining non-Indigenous discoveries with Indigenous spiritual knowledge can reveal answers to those who seek healing of the self and society.

CHAPTER 9
SEARCHING FOR HEALING

Indigenous Wisdom

I n the midst of materialism and secularism, people instinctively search for ways to better understand their purpose in life. While Indigenous thought provides a solid foundation, there are mainstream knowledge systems that complement Indigenous belief in the transcendent. These include studies of reincarnation and of near-death experiences. Marrying ancient healing practices with insights gained by modern science can produce new avenues for recovery in today's troubled times.

Gregory Cajete notes the tendency of Western science to eliminate uncertainty by controlling nature. "Western science is committed to increasing human mastery over nature, to go on conquering until everything natural is under absolute human control. In this vision, when we have fusion power, when we farm the oceans, when we can turn the weather on and off, when all things natural can be controlled, everything will be just fine. Western science and technology are seen as the great panacea and as the ultimate means for human survival."[1]

He maintains that Native science is not just about observing objective reality but involves active participation with the natural world. Native science needs to include respect for the ancient covenant that humans had with plants, animals, and other aspects of the universe.[2] Such science is a way of understanding the world that includes and validates Indigenous spirituality.[3]

Indigenous people have learned to flow with the stream of chaos and creativity that is an inherent part of nature. That involves a higher order of responsibility.

> Native science reflects a celebration of renewal. The ultimate aim is not explaining an objectified universe, but rather learning about and understanding responsibilities and relationships and celebrating those that humans establish with the world, native science is also about mutual reciprocity, which simply means a give and take relationship with the natural world and which presupposes a responsibility to care for, sustain and respect the rights of other living things, plants, animals and places in which one lives.[4]

Understanding Cycles

One of the fundamental differences between Indigenous Eden and Wetiko civilization are their philosophies of practising spiritual relationships, which is how Indigenous people fostered an environment of positive cyclical growth. Today, the art of spiritual healing is largely lost, which results in continual weakening of relationships and downward spirals of deterioration.

Almost everyone has a story of some paranormal occurrence in their lives. Yet most are reluctant to talk about it seriously because of a lack of a rational theory of how this could occur. But there are avenues available for considering such phenomena. A number of initiatives being conducted by scientists, doctors, and other researchers challenge the notion that nothing exists beyond what can be perceived through physical senses and scientific instruments. These researchers also challenge the materialist viewpoint of life. However, they remain at the fringes of university research because it is extremely difficult to posit a scientifically verifiable theory. As well, it is uncertain how such knowledge would produce concrete economic benefits in daily lives.

Rebirth: The Human Cycle

Reincarnation is one of those areas of research. Belief in rebirth, or reincarnation, exists across Native American cultures and is a virtually universal human concept. It existed within Christianity before the doctrine was expunged at the Council of Constantinople. The Division of Perceptual Studies at the University of Virginia is a leader in reincarnation and near-death studies research and houses the world's largest repository of reincarnation cases. Dr. Ian Stevenson, a psychiatrist who graduated with the top grades in his class at McGill University Medical School, pioneered the inquiry. Stevenson was intrigued as to why some very young children experienced phobias or possessed unusual talents not readily explainable through heredity. He wondered if memory transference from a previous life could be the cause and whether claims of reincarnation could be investigated in a systematic and empirical manner.[5]

Reincarnation research methodology is based upon spontaneous recollection of past-life memories of young children. The child who recalls a previous life is adamant and expresses strong convictions about having had such experience. Many of the children who are part of the research were precocious, both in richness of vocabulary and ability to articulate ideas. Some startle their parents by spontaneously uttering unusual words and phrases. The child begins to describe the previous life as soon as he or she is able to communicate.[6]

Data is collected and analyzed systematically. Statements of youngsters reporting past-life memories are recorded as soon as possible before their recollections are corrupted by others who might influence them. Stevenson devised a rigorous set of interviews with the child's family and acquaintances, for both the present and previous claimed life. Researchers locate documents and records pertinent to claimed events such as medical records and police and media reports. In numerous cases, accounts of the claims agree highly with verifiable facts.[7]

In 1960, Stevenson wrote an article describing forty-four cases. He detected unusual patterns in the accounts. The youngsters spoke insistently about a previous life, but those memories invariably faded by the age of seven or eight. Two-thirds of the children reported experiencing a violent ending in the previous life. They often exhibited unusual skills and attributes characteristic of the previous personality. Some bore birthmarks resembling wounds inflicted in the former life.[8]

Stevenson travelled the world, eventually collecting almost 3,000 cases.[9] One of the most fascinating aspects of the research links congenital markings such as birthmarks and physical defects to previous life occurrences. Stevenson describes examples in two of his books: *Reincarnation and Biology: A Contribution to the Etiology of Birth Marks and Birth Defects*,[10] an impressive collection of 225 cases, and *Where Reincarnation and Biology Intersect*, a summary of 112 significant accounts of reincarnation stories.[11] In cases involving violent death, children almost always recall their manner of perishing, including detailed descriptions of wounds. Some marks resemble scars from knife lacerations; others looked like entry and exit bullet marks of the wounds the children reported. Stevenson reported forty-nine cases in which medical reports were available; in forty-three of those, birthmarks matched so well that he deemed them to be more than coincidental.

Theorists propose that one process of reincarnation involves deprogramming or cleansing after death of the previous life memory. Stevenson believes that in cases of children reporting a violent demise, the individual was drawn back to life because their previous life ended prematurely, resulting in a sense of unfinished business. Within that context, the individual re-enters physical life before the full cycle of rejuvenation is complete. Past-life memories imply that some form of memory persists after death and resurfaces in the newborn strong enough to manifest itself physically.[12]

Stevenson's work challenges orthodox beliefs about the nature of existence and consciousness. Critics ridicule the idea that memory can survive death, let alone that a person might be born again. Others suggest Stevenson was duped by the imaginative stories of children and wishful thinking of adults. To counter arguments that cases he examined were from cultures with a pre-existing belief in reincarnation, Stevenson produced examples of cases of past-life memory in Europe and America, where society rejects the notion of reincarnation.

Indigenous Insights on Rebirth

Affirmation of rebirth is prevalent in areas such as the North West Coast. However, Plains Cree and Saulteaux Elders do not to talk openly about the subject. It is considered a sacred and highly personal topic discussed only within ceremonial context. In some cases, a mother can have a precognitive dream that heralds the arrival of a child.[13] At birth, infants are seen as innocent and pure because they are freshly arrived from the spirit realm and must be treated with respect. Mosôm Danny Musqua said the first step of life is choosing our parents. People are part of the Creator's web of life and can be born into different circumstances.[14]

> We are born seven times. We go through all of the difficulties, including being born of the opposite gender. You are born to face all of the trials of life. You will be born into a life of violence, into a life of peace, with wise people where you can become a healer or a prophet, you learn to become a leader. During these seven lives we learn the various lessons necessary until the Creator deems us perfected.[15]

The Elders' version of rebirth varies somewhat from the popular conception of reincarnation. The common perception is that one's identity is reborn in a new body to carry on life in a new opportunity. Under this view, John Doe would essentially be a reincarnation of himself, but in a new body. Elder Noel Starblanket told me that Ahcahk (soul, spirit) undergoes a type of metamorphosis in which it can draw upon a pool of attributes of its Ancestors for the purpose of pursing a new mission.[16] This implies that John Doe never exists again as the same personality it was in a particular body at a particular time, as it is part of a group soul. Mosôm maintained that the child who recollects a previous life is, in fact, communicating with his or her Ancestor. What emerges as a birth is the manifestation of supernal wisdom and individual incarnations serve a higher collective purpose.

Theories

Psychiatrist Dr. Jim Tucker, who carries on Ian Stevenson's work,[17] has an interesting theory about reincarnation based upon quantum science. He rejects the materialist view of the world, stating that everything is in a state of ever-changing flux. It is the simple act of observation that creates what appears to be reality. Tucker's theory draws on another mental phenomenon—the dream. As we visualize our dreams, they become created worlds. He maintains that as one observes the physical world, one's life unfolds similarly, according to the choices and judgments one makes. All of humanity is participating in a vast, shared dream based on our common observation of the physical world.[18] When one dies, one moves into pure consciousness, which is the essence of our being. When one reincarnates, a new dream begins. However, for children who recall previous lives, the memory of the previous life dream has not been totally erased. That past life cannot be resumed, which explains why the child's obsession with the previous experience fades by the age of seven.

There is value to learning about rebirth. Awareness of a higher plane of existence can foster physical, emotional, and psychic healing. Although we appear to be islands of consciousness in the physical world, people are in fact connected to a larger entity that supersedes time and space. Realizing that current generations will also be those of the future provides a fuller perspective to history.

Near-death experiences [NDES] are another area of empirical research that is too readily ignored because there is no discernable rational explanation. Raymond Moody, a pioneer of near-death experience study, published the seminal *Life After Life* in 1975. His research found a high degree of similarity in experiences of individuals who had close contact with death. Moody identified fifteen recurring features. Although NDES never include all of them, he describes typical elements.

A man is dying and, as he reaches the point of greatest physical distress, he hears himself pronounced dead by his doctor. He begins to hear an uncomfortable noise, a loud ringing or buzzing, and at the same time feels himself moving very rapidly through a long dark tunnel. After this, he suddenly finds himself outside of his own physical body, but still in the immediate physical environment, and he sees his own body from a distance, as though he is a spectator. He watches the resuscitation attempt from his unusual vantage point and is in a state of emotional upheaval. After a while, he collects himself and becomes more accustomed to his odd condition. He notices that he still has a 'body,' but one of a very different nature and with very different powers from the physical body he has left behind. Soon other things begin to happen. Others come to meet and to help him. He glimpses the spirits of relatives and friends who have already died, and a loving warm spirit of a kind he has never encountered before—a being of light—appears before him. This being asks him a question, non-verbally, to make him evaluate his life and helps him by showing him a panoramic, instantaneous playback of the major events of his life.[19]

Studies show that up to one-fifth of people going through cardiac arrest and clinical death report lucid thought, reasoning, and detailed recall of what transpired.[20] Experiences are similar regardless of religion, education, or upbringing. This suggests that the phenomenon is universal and transcends cultural and religious limitations.

The Human Consciousness Project, launched in September 2008 at a symposium at the United Nations, consists of a multidisciplinary consortium of scientists and physicians joining forces to research the nature of consciousness and its relationship to the brain.[21] The project is conducting the world's first large-scale scientific study of the relationship between mind and brain during clinical death. Studies in resuscitation examine cognitive functioning and the state of the human mind during and subsequent to cardiac arrest.

What makes NDEs and the Human Consciousness Project remarkable are findings that individuals retain detailed perceptions.

This indicates a high level of consciousness despite the absence of measurable brain activity. Awareness does, in fact, function in the absence of brain activity and body. This bears profound implications for the understanding of death and consciousness.

Science as Ally?

Science has made tremendous leaps over past decades in challenging conventional ideas about "reality." Albert Einstein made great strides in understanding the relationship between the speed of light and the passage of time.[22] He was a powerful dreamer whose insights came in the form of visionary or meditative thinking. He maintained that imagination was more potent than reason. Indigenous Medicine Persons would agree, as they realize that the greatest knowledge comes through inner insight.

By imagining accelerating to the speed of light, Einstein realized that time would slow down for the observer. He discovered that energy and matter are connected. It was known that the sun loses four million tons of mass per second. This energy can be described as sheets of light leaving the sun's surface. Matter never simply disappears but, rather, becomes transmuted. In this case, the transformation is into pure light energy. Hence, Einstein's equation $E=mc^2$, energy equals mass times the square of the speed at which light left the sun's surface.[23] This theory was proven when other scientists built the nuclear bomb, converting a tiny particle of matter into pure energy.

In realizing that time is not absolute, Einstein concluded that objects affected by gravity can be understood as being supported by a net of fabric-like space–time. This brilliant insight showed that space was not empty, but actually consists of something because it had the ability to bend. Other observations show that dark matter and dark energy constitutes as much as 95 percent of what exists. Yet this essence cannot be perceived by scientific instruments. How can one claim to know about reality if one ignores the non-physical realm that constitutes 95 percent of all that exists? Is this perhaps the medium in which consciousness and spirit thrives? Einstein once said that those who are intellectual but have no sense of the transcendent are lost: "religion without science is blind, science without religion is lame."[24]

Quantum Mysteries

An interesting question is whether subatomic physics, in particular dark matter, is related to the nature of consciousness. Scientist Niels Bohr, founder of quantum physics, noted how subatomic particles, or quanta, sometimes chose to act as waves.[25] Bohr concluded that what we perceive as reality occurs only when observation takes place and physical sight and senses working with consciousness collapses the waves to make the world seem real. This implies that what we perceive as material is essentially a form of illusion. Our senses are merely capturing fleeting glimpses of what is an underlying quantum world, an ethereal universe inhabited by dark matter and dark energy that constitutes 95 percent of all that exists.

For a long time, ideas from Newtonian physics dominated scientific thinking. It conformed well with the world of the senses, and time and space were steady and fixed. The physical world was, therefore, perfectly predictable. Now, a new science that recognizes that there is another level of consciousness that lurks behind physical reality is direly needed.

Consciousness Everywhere

There are great difficulties in arriving at a definitive understanding of the inherent nature of consciousness. Dictionary definitions include "inward awareness of an external object, state or fact"; "mind in the broadest sense: something in nature that is distinguished from the physical"; "awareness or perception of an inward or spiritual fact"; "the totality in psychology of sensations, perceptions, ideas"; and, the most succinct, "concerned awareness."[26]

Scientists wedded to the Newtonian view of the universe approach the question from a materialist perspective. They are skeptical that non-physical consciousness exists and that it is simply an offshoot of our biology. Nagging questions include whether animals have consciousness or if insects, plants, and even rocks have it. Experiments indicate that animals can demonstrate awareness by recognizing themselves in a mirror. Stephen Hawking and several other scientists felt compelled to sign the "Cambridge Declaration on Consciousness" in which they state: "We decided to reach a consensus and make a statement directed to the public that is not scientific. It is obvious to everyone in this room that animals have consciousness, but it is not obvious to the rest of the world. . . . Convergent evidence indicates that non-human animals . . . including all mammals and birds, and other creatures . . . have the necessary neural substrates of consciousness and the capacity to exhibit intentional behaviors."[27] Max Plank, the founder of quantum theory, described it this way: "I regard consciousness as fundamental. I regard matter as derivative from consciousness."[28] In other words, our physical perception creates what we perceived as the world, but it is inadequate.[29]

Who knew that even plants could have feelings? They not only respond to natural surroundings like light and temperature, but also to injury, music, and even to positive or negative human feelings. One of the pioneers in this field, Chandra Bose of India, was interested in investigating behavioural similarities between all things, including plants, animals, humans, and non-living metals. He began by comparing fatigue and recovery in metals and in muscle, and concluded that not only were there similarities, but that the boundary between living and non-living might not be as dramatic as usually thought. He tried other experiments such as applying chloroform anesthetic to both animals and plants. Again, he concluded that there were similar reactions to anesthesia; for example, plants would experience much less shock from transplantation after being anesthetized.

Biologists and animal scientists treated Bose's research with quiet contempt, especially after he suggested that, despite not having nerves and organs, plants nevertheless displayed awareness that approached that of animals. Bose protested: "The physicist, the chemist and the biologist come in by different doors, each one his department of knowledge, and each comes to think that his is a special domain unconnected with that of the other. Hence has arisen our present division of phenomena into the worlds of inorganic, vegetal and sentient. This philosophical attitude of mind may be denied.

We must remember that all inquiries have as their goal the attainment of knowledge in its entirety."[30]

German poet Johann Wolfgang von Goethe was interested in the philosophical understanding of plant life. He arrived at a conclusion that is markedly similar to what Elders say about Grandfather Spirits: "All plants are thus seen as specific manifestations of the archetypal plant that controls the entire plant kingdom and gives value to nature's artistry in creating forms. It is in ceaseless play within the world of plant form, capable of moving backward and forward, up and down, through the scale of forms."[31] This element or force, Goethe concluded, must exist beyond the material world.

What does this imply about differing levels of consciousness? In humans, it is widely accepted that dreaming is another level of consciousness and such experiences can include elements that seem as real as in physical life. Mystics understand that there are levels of consciousness that humans can attain which are not being utilized. People can perceive the world in different ways—some see it as a hostile place, others as a means to get what they want for themselves without regard for others. Those who believe that consciousness is an illusion would say morals don't matter because awareness of others is also illusory. Yet others feel that they are connected and fulfilled by a sense of a higher purpose to life.

Searching for Spirit

Parapsychology, a term coined by professor J.B. Rhine of Duke University, raises the question of whether supernatural knowledge could be subjected to scientific experimentation. It is the difficulty in reproducing consistently verifiable results, combined with continual objections by critics that one or another possible flaws exists, that makes this research so challenging. Investigators like Rhine have worked to see whether there are telepathic aspects to dreams.[32] Others have explored lucid or precognitive dreams, as well as "announcing dreams" that herald the birth of a reincarnating individual. Claims that there is psychic potential in dreams are invariably denied by experiments that fail to replicate results. Parapsychology becomes consigned to the realms of fantasy, illusion, magic, and myth. It is a conundrum that no experimental model appears capable of capturing psychic phenomena. Even if a legitimate event were to occur, skeptics would come up with a way to explain it away.

Collective Consciousness

Psychologist Carl Jung's interest in parapsychology began in 1895 when, as part of his doctoral dissertation, "On the Psychology and Pathology of So-Called Occult Phenomena," he studied the case of his fifteen-year-old cousin Helene Prieswerk. Helene had demonstrated mediumistic ability and claimed contact with a grandfather she had never known. She conveyed the voice and mannerisms of the grandfather and other deceased relatives with uncanny accuracy.[33]

Jung understood collective human unconscious as an array of archetypes that complement waking consciousness and serve as collective signposts for behaviours: "There exists a second psychic system of a collective, universal and impersonal nature which is identical in all individuals. It consists of pre-existent forms, the archetypes, which can only become conscious secondarily and which give definite form to certain psychic contents."[34] Jung believed this was an inheritance from ancient peoples. He concluded that the archetypes form the basis of spirituality but that organized religion is more concerned with ordinary daily life than with symbols. This battle between the exigencies and temptations of daily life versus the subconscious pull of archetypes can be portrayed as the struggle between good and evil.

Looking at the animus and anima, the male and female aspect within each person, Jung also suggested the common roots of collective experience: "They bring into our ephemeral consciousness an unknown psychic life belonging to a remote past. It is the mind of our unknown Ancestors, their way of thinking and feeling, their way of experiencing life and the world, gods and men. The existence of these archaic strata is presumably the source of man's belief in reincarnations and in memories of previous experiences."[35] Jung maintained that such archetypes cannot be studied within laboratory settings but are knowable through empirical observation. He believed that phenomena such as synchronicity and extrasensory perception demonstrate that there is psychic ability that transcends the ordinary mind and that parapsychology can contribute to the understanding of the collective unconscious. Jung believed that humans will always seek to connect to this transcendent sense of identity.

Jung came to appreciate that there is an external source of collective consciousness that is part of the human psyche, although he attributed it to heredity only.

> My thesis then is as follows: In addition to our immediate consciousness, which is of a thoroughly personal nature and which we believe to be the only empirical psyche (even if we tack on the personal unconscious as an appendix), there exists a second psychic system of a collective, universal and impersonal nature which is identical in all individuals. This collective unconscious does not develop individually but is inherited. It consists of pre-existent forms, the archetypes, which can only become conscious secondarily and which give definite form to certain psychic contents.[36]

Initially, Jung subscribed to the theory that such experiences were due to connecting with the unconscious. However other events, such as a trip to study the Bugishu people of British East Africa, where much of life involves interaction with ancestral spirits, caused Jung's thinking to evolve further. He began to experience dream visitations by an elderly figure he called Philemon and found that this personage provided him with insights he would not have otherwise received.[37]

This led Jung to hypothesize the existence of the collective unconscious and its relationship to a more fundamental reality.

> The collective unconscious is part of the psyche which can be negatively distinguished from a personal unconscious by the fact that it does not, like the latter, owe its existence to personal experience and consequently is not a personal acquisition. . . . Whereas the personal unconscious consists for the

most part of complexes, the content of the collective unconscious is made up essentially of archetypes. The concept of
the archetype, which is an indispensable correlate of the idea
of the collective unconscious, indicates the existence of definite forms in the psyche which seem to be present always and
everywhere. . . . It consists of pre-existent forms, the archetypes, which can only become conscious secondarily and
which give definite form to certain psychic contents.[38]

Carl Jung had been using the *I Ching* oracular system for personal guidance and as part of his analytical practice for close to
thirty years.[39] He liked to evoke the *I Ching*'s synchronicity as an
explanation of the oracle's effectiveness, but privately admitted that
the answers were prompted by "spiritual agencies" that formed the
"living soul of the book." Although in his earlier years Jung insisted
apparitions, and even physical manifestations, must be projections
of the unconscious, he later became convinced that a purely psychological explanation was inadequate. In a private letter to the psycho-
therapist Fritz Kunkel, he admitted that "metaphysical phenomena
could be explained better by the hypothesis of spirits than by the
qualities and peculiarities of the unconscious."[40]

Indigenous mystics understand that everything has spirit and is,
therefore, consciousness. As kindred spirits, one can connect with
the consciousness of these spiritual relatives with the appropriate
attitude, training, and Protocols. That consciousness existed was
never questioned—it was simply taken for granted. Multitudinous
innovations by Indigenous Peoples, whether in astronomy, architecture, animal relations, or horticulture, were accomplished not
with rationalist theories and technologies but through spiritual Protocols—going "inside" oneself to connect with the numinous. An
important function of this process is to seek wisdom. As stewards,
people are given the opportunity to use human intelligence in a
manner that could uplift other entities' existences. All living beings,
not only humans, could benefit from the human gift of intelligence,
self-awareness, and choice.

Need for "Spiritual Science"

David Bohm, a physicist who worked with Albert Einstein, suggests that what we see with our senses is the product of an "implicate order" or a hidden "field of energy."[41] This field cannot be perceived by physical senses, but plays a vital role in how life events unfold, something Bohm described as quantum potential. Subatomic particles cross the line between matter and energy, behaving like matter in one instant and waves the next. Under quantum mechanics, seemingly inexplicable phenomena occur. These include the ability to be in more than one place at the same time and being able to communicate instantaneously while at great distance. Bohm suspected that thought is an important structure of decision making within the field of energy. Bohm believed that Indigenous sages understood this "field." He took the opportunity to consult with Mosôm Danny and other Elders at Banff in 1992.[42]

Well-known scientists such as Einstein, Bohm, and Bohr were open to the possibility that the supernal exists and contended that it is important to keep an open mind. But that is not true of all scientists: One would think that if scientists can understand only 5 percent of Creation, they would have some humility. From the Indigenous perspective, it is possible to explore the numinous using consciousness alone because one's experience is the only means of "verification," and it can be accomplished only after the individual has employed spiritual methodology.

Spirituality and Healing

Regardless of the many advances by science and medicine, Indigenous healers understand that forces operate outside of the physical world. Elders realize all humans share consciousness at the individual and group levels and that there are different levels of awareness. Higher consciousness is strengthened through development of inner senses as in dreams, visions, and meditation. Belief in the reality of spirit is not blind—it is verifiable by the inner senses, a proof that is accessible to all. Different societies are at different stages of evolution in terms of understanding and balancing the four quadrants of being. Intellectual development is the area heavily promoted by contemporary civilization, but it is insufficient if not aided by the sacred.

Mosôm Danny commented on the application of spirituality in psychology.

> Yes we knew and know about the unconscious, and it's in part like you [Dick Katz] say, Freud described it—a place where the junk of our everyday lives can build up and without our knowing, it can hold us down. . . . Yet there is also another part, another dimension to that unconscious . . . a deeper more spiritual part . . . the unconscious is also the pathway through which the spirits and spiritual understandings can sometimes enter our world. . . . Sometimes we're so troubled we can't feel that spiritual presence—sometimes our unconscious spills into our daily lives with these bad memories and anxieties. . . . Sometimes our dreams give us messages from the spirit world. Sometimes our dreams can help us see into the future.[43]

An inmate who has had problems with alcoholism describes how traditional beliefs brought about personal transformation.

> There was still a vacuum in my life, and I could never pinpoint what it was. But there were benefits in terms of life for falling off the wagon. Materially, I lost everything. It was after about five years of drinking, that I reached out again. In my drunken state, I reached out and sought help, and that help was freely given to me by my other Elders. I didn't go back to A.A. I went back to the traditional way, understanding the way our forefathers lived and learning about the value system of life. Learning the life of creation, how it supports mankind. And then I began my journey towards spiritual healing, mental healing, physical healing. It was through the patience of other Elders that I began to understand who I was, my identity as a Native person.[44]

The emphasis within the Indigenous world has been on reconciliation, healing and fitting back in rather than on punishment and isolation.[45] One Elder points out the importance of accepting the supernatural ability to heal: "There is nothing I can do to heal anybody. The only thing that I can do is give him direction and guidance. Now whether he accepts that direction and that guidance is entirely up to him. If he refuses that, then there is nothing I can do, nothing. I can take him to the Sweat Lodge. If he still refuses to open up, he's wasting his time and he's wasting my time. He's got to open up himself in order for that self-healing to come. I believe that we all possess a healing process that is in the mind."[46]

Mental Illness as Spiritual Disease

In mental illness, anxiety and mood disorders top the list, together comprising nearly one-third of cases in developed countries. Others include depression, substance abuse, post-traumatic stress disorder, violence, and suicide. About one in three persons are expected to experience a major mental problem during their lifetime. Environmentalist Melissa Nelson concludes that there is a global health crisis, and "Eurocentric ideology where hierarchy, competition, individualism, materialism, sexism and a punitive system of education and justice" are creating what she calls "a worldwide psycho-spiritual meltdown."[47] Questions can be asked to what extent mental or emotional problems are linked to relationship issues, and whether they can be seen as psychic in origin. Was mental illness less of a problem in Indigenous ecolizations because individuals had a more positive sense of self and purpose, lived in more supportive communities, and had generally healthier environments?

Modern psychology and psychiatry uses materialist models to explain mental illness. These range from chemical imbalance to genetic defects to brain trauma. Treatments tend to take the form of psychotropic drugs—uppers and downers—intended to alter brain chemistry. Unfortunately such medications run the danger of causing more harm than good. But one thing seems certain—almost all mental illness is rooted in problematic and deteriorating relationships. Individuals that do not have support mechanisms, whether they are parents, communities, friends, or health services, tend to be most at risk. Traditional communities with their emphasis on strong and positive relationships were able to support individuals during times of crisis. In cases like depression and anxiety, mental illness can be viewed as diseases of the soul, and spirituality can provide a powerful tool to heal the mind.

In order to make sense of the dilemmas facing today's world, it is crucial to recognize the divide that has occurred between Indigenous and non-Indigenous people. Looking back at history, one will realize that the ways of ancient peoples include answers that can stabilize and rejuvenate today's societies. However, the task, which requires global reconciliation with Indigenous ways, is monumental.

CHAPTER 10

NEED FOR RECONCILIATION

Revisiting History

There are two variations of the definition of reconciliation. The first, "a situation in which two people or groups of people become friendly again after they have argued" is the definition most often used and easier to achieve. It is the sort of reconciliation that takes place after the subjugated group is offered opportunities to participate in the lifestyle of the victor. Generally, the onus is on the subjugated to compromise or sacrifice their beliefs and values in order to reconcile.

The second definition, "the process of making two opposite beliefs, ideas or situations agree,"[1] is far more difficult to achieve, particularly when the two sides had never seen eye to eye. The only way in which the second, more fundamental reconciliation can be achieved is if dominant society realizes that it has not been right about what it has done and decides wholeheartedly to change. The elites of dominant society have a particularly critical role to play in leading such a change.

The notion that an Indigenous Eden could have existed is not taken seriously. It is a blatant oversight to dismiss 97 percent of humanity's earliest existence as if it were of no consequence for modernity. This is a major disservice—to Indigenous Peoples whose knowledge and traditions are systematically being erased, as well as to non-Indigenous people who could benefit from ancient knowledge gathered over millennia. Mythologies hint at ancient stories of origin and life experience; however, since they were never written down, they are negated as meaningless. The rise of modern civilization can be interpreted as the overthrow of ancient knowledge and rejection of the original understanding of humanity's purpose. Ancestors have been dismissed as being under the thrall and control of nature. Given the harm that all life on this planet is facing, it is more important than ever to rediscover interpretations of our origins and purpose by revisiting ancient wisdom.

Non-Indigenous peoples have carefully documented and studied the rise of their civilization and the knowledge systems that accompanied it. They meticulously analyze the development of "ancient" Mesopotamian and Egyptian art and architecture, Greek thought, Roman bureaucracy, and the emergence of Christianity. Yet, there remains little understanding of the Indigenous cultures that are the precursors of those societies. The emergence of civilization in the Middle East and, later, Europe came at the cost of critical ties to the natural world. In contrast, despite their superior numbers, civilization centres such as China and India did not embark on such aggressive domination of nature and aggression towards others' lands. Those cultures retained ancient wisdom and did not fully embrace the notion that humans are the central focus of Creation. This does not mean that such societies did not make mistakes such as overcrowding and pollution. Even such powerful cultures are not immune from having to embrace destructive economic and technological practices in order to adapt to modernity.

Ecolizations were overwhelmed and unable to counteract Wetiko ideology and its program of conquest and colonization. Diseases spread from Europe and devastated original populations. Resisting the invaders by matching their deceit, cruelty, and barbarity would have meant Indigenous abandonment of their own values.

The situation in which humanity now finds itself is the result of historical choices. Changes have accelerated since the industrial revolution of the early 1800s. Overpopulation; stress on the natural environment, including animals, plants, and marine life; and catastrophic effects of climate change are harbingers of worse to come. Yet, humanity continues to live in a bubble perpetuated by the illusion of material prosperity and technological comfort. Efforts by world governments to solve problems are ineffective and will never work. Only a higher spiritual authority can bring universal order. In order to understand what is happening, one needs to look not at yearly or even decade-long results, but at centuries and millennia. The conclusions for those who are paying attention should be alarming.

Re-evaluating Civilization

Indigenous Peoples regard their sacred duty as one of respect for and living in harmony as stewards with the rest of Creation. The action of placing humanity and its interests above all else was a critical mistake. It resulted in unresolved ideological conflict that has critical implications for the destiny of humankind.

"Prehistoric" peoples did have a distinct ideology and belief that led them to behave in certain ways. Fundamental to this is the concept that humans are spirit beings experiencing a temporary physical existence. Aboriginal people understood that upon arriving on Earth, their challenge, in return for being in the presence of the Creator's gifts, was to learn to treat all other beings with respect and to coexist harmoniously. It is inaccurate to censure Indigenous people for polytheism, because they perceive only one Creator. They did recognize spirit helpers who aided in relating to the rest of Creation. This is little different than seeking help through the veneration of angels in Christianity and Islam.

Indigenous beliefs are the progenitor of all religions and remain the closest to authentic connection with the transcendent. In contrast, organized religions that are products of civilization, in particular Christianity and Islam, became instruments of the state and its agendas of exploitation and colonization. At the least, they had little effect in mitigating exploitation of the land and oppression of its original inhabitants. Unfortunately, spirituality is not recognized as having the same status as mainstream religions. If it were, Indigenous belief systems would have to be categorized as one of the great traditions of the world. They would attract many more adherents, particularly as individuals come to a fuller understanding of what happened to their original heritage.

Renewing Spirituality

In Indigenous Eden, ceremonies, prayer, and healing rituals produced societies that were healthy and happy. However, fear of the unknown, one of the first failings of "civilized" people who no longer trusted the benevolence of Creation, took over. By abandoning ties to Indigenous healing and spiritual accountability, modern civilizations produced systems in which humanity's original mission on Earth has been forgotten. People are becoming increasingly divorced from the environment and hostile towards one another. Crime is rampant and there appears to be no bottom to the depth of depravity that occurs. Cynicism and despair breed mental illness and self-destruction.

Rationalists are quick to dismiss Indigenous spirituality, visions, or healing as being the result of imagination or hallucination and, therefore, not worthy of serious consideration. Some think Indigenous knowledge systems are irrational because they include consultation with the numinous—something considered unknowable and unreliable. Elder Jim Ryder, one of the first to serve at First Nations University, pondered why, if Christians were so certain they have the correct religion, they are so threatened by Indigenous beliefs. In traditional culture, the supernatural forms an overarching reality. Spirit is tangible and it is possible to interact and have a meaningful relationship with the transcendent. In fact, the way in which ancient peoples interrelated with the world was highly organized. It was a holistic system with predictable patterns and it was the source from which ultimate wisdom and guidance was received. Balancing mind and spirit produced stable and enhancing results. Elders view the failure to take the incorporeal aspect of life seriously and to cultivate a relationship with the sacred as a serious error. Poverty of the soul inevitably leads to deterioration in all other aspects of our existence.

Unfortunately, European colonizers engaged in an ideological war in which the culture and worldview of Indigenous Peoples was suppressed and sidelined. It took only the slightest inkling of resistance, "dishonesty," or "theft" by Indigenous people—no matter how spurious the accusation—for colonizers to authorize punitive actions. This was despite hospitality shown by Indigenous Peoples, who were following the imperative to create harmonious relations. While European explorers used the pretext of saving souls, their true objective was to colonize and exploit Indigenous lands.

The challenge of Indigenous intellectuals is to correctly interpret the message of the Elders based on the premise that humans are, in essence, spiritual beings. The English language does not have a rich vocabulary dealing with the experiences of visions, dreams, ceremonies, healing, and other phenomena. Terminology used by Elders in ceremonies is specialized and learning this lexicon involves spending many years in tutelage. Many Native scholars have experienced severe language loss, yet Elders confirm that it is necessary to be able to talk about our beliefs in English. It just takes more work to clearly explain the main spiritual laws and concepts, such as wâhkôhtowin and miyo-wîchetowin.[2]

It is said that humans themselves are the best predictors of what will happen on Earth because of their ability to manipulate their environment. However, there is a need to take an honest look and make an admission of the damage caused by those activities and resolve to rectify the harm. There are glimpses of optimism to be had—traditional peoples who maintain their integrity and refuse to be co-opted into the Wetiko system, mainstream scholars who are prepared to admit that errors have been made, intellectuals who are willing to explore knowledge systems that can corroborate or complement ancient knowledge, and activists who are prepared to act in responsible ways.

Understanding the Cycle

The Medicine Circle is a tool for diagnosing evolutionary issues and problems.[3] Indigenous Elders maintain a strong belief in the cyclical nature of all created things and recognize that the material world is in constant change and flux. All cycles have an ending that leads to the beginning of further cycles of growth. The circle makes a clockwise rotation beginning in the east, the direction of the rising sun, which signifies birth, beginnings, or vision. As Mosôm Danny pointed out, at birth, individuals come to Earth with a purpose deeply embedded in their consciousness, hence the association with the east. Likewise, humanity arrived with a collective vision and mission that it was coming to Earth on a learning journey.

South, where the sun nourishes life, is the direction of youthful development. Thus, relationships and community become vital as one seeks to find appropriate and healthy development. In this respect, humanity first needed to devote a great deal of effort to fostering respectful relationships with the natural world. This path could have allowed humanity to thrive for at least one million years if not longer. However, after 200,000 years, some people decided they were the central purpose of Creation and could abuse nature at will. Worse, they forced the rest to go badly off course.

West is the direction of the setting sun, the direction of maturity. The focus is on carrying out responsibilities, developing emotional maturity, and acquiring wisdom. This is the product of vision and healthy growth. Had humanity's growth taken place according to spiritual wisdom and had knowledge and technological development occurred carefully over thousands of years rather than a few feverish centuries, humanity would have created a brilliant and durable civilization in which peace, harmony, and happiness thrive.

North is the direction of the coming cold. It marks the end of the cycle. It is the time to harvest the cycle's activity, with the emphasis on reflecting about our experience through giving back and sharing wisdom. The end of a cycle ideally brings about fulfillment from having diligently and mindfully completed one's mission. Wisdom has been gleaned from physical experience and the spirit is ready to move on to other challenges. Given humanity's current path, will it culminate in such success?

Medicine Circle learning involves analyzing issues and developments that incorporate the four cardinal directions. The fifth direction, the nadir or Earth teachings, use the physical earth, including lessons to be learned from flora and fauna. The sixth direction, the zenith or Sky Teachings, include learning from spirit by connecting with spirit protectors or consulting Ancestors through ceremony.

Elder Oren Lyons observed: "The spiritual side of the natural world is absolute. The laws are absolute. Our instructions, and I'm talking about for all human beings, our instructions are to get along. Understand what these laws are. Get along with the laws and support them and work with them. We are told a long time ago that if you do that, life is endless. It just continues on in great cycles of regeneration, great powerful cycles of life regenerating and regenerating and regenerating." The success, power, and health of each cycle builds upon previous cycles, strengthening the potency of the life.[4]

Mainstream academics rarely appreciate how potent Indigenous philosophy is despite its simplicity. The cyclical view of history is not anti-evolutionary. If one looks carefully, one will realize that events in nature are actually cyclical rather than linear. This applies to days in which one builds on the events of the previous day, season, or year. It applies to human lives and to their collectivities manifested as societies. Even species and planets have their cycles.[5]

Viewing civilizations or economies as linear progressions leads one to false conclusions, such as the belief that there are never-ending resources that we can continue to exploit, that military power should be constantly increased, and that human longevity can be extended indefinitely. Some scholars suggest that the march from hunter-gatherer societies to contemporary "advanced" globalized economies is an immutable law of progress.[6] In reality, it is a choice. Aboriginal Peoples have suffered the most from the choices made by non-Indigenous societies and continue to sacrifice to keep humanity's original spiritual vision alive. Analyzing the human trajectory, the Old Ones are greatly concerned that a reckoning is imminent because of the severe imbalance that is occurring. Due to general loss of supernal connection and wisdom, it may well be the case that humanity, not having learned basic lessons, will end its cycle short of its goal.

It is a maxim that if instructions are not followed, one is doomed to repeat the challenge. In Indigenous Eden, an environment in which humans were far more in touch with the transcendent, healers performed miracles because everything was in harmony with nature, among communities, and with the transcendent. There is an understanding among Indigenous healers that individuals who have not previously developed a relationship with the supernal cannot expect miraculous healing. The expression used is that the patient is "too far gone" to be helped. The sad fact is that may now apply to humanity.

The reality is that death ultimately overtakes every living thing. New life miraculously and mysteriously reappears. Where that hidden ground between life and death exists is a mystery to scientists. But the cycle of life on Earth will not last forever, as the existence of the planet itself has a fixed time span. Humanity has chosen to abandon the Indigenous culture of life, adopting instead downward spirals of unhealed relationships and an increasingly toxic environment. In the expanse of earthly time, it appears that human life will be exceedingly short, like a mere blink of the eye.

If things turn out for the worst, my spiritual advisor, Danny Musqua, reassured me that "the Creator does not lose his children." Mosôm suggested that humans will transmigrate to another planet, just as they came to Earth. His assertion reminds one of recent news reports that there could potentially be eight billion Earth-like planets in the Milky Way galaxy alone, enough for one planet per every human on Earth.[7]

Another Elder similarly said: "When the Mother is starting to leave us again one more time and this circle we are working on today, all the people will go in there and that's going to be a Spirit World, and everybody is going to be in there, and when Mother is starting to leave we wouldn't know anything about it, but we will be all in here. We will be safe in the Spirit World and the Mother will leave. And a new one will come, a new Mother will come."[8]

If one grows up in a culture in which one's teachers say we came from the stars, what would a "rational" person in that society think? Is our interest in space and the universe another sign of unique human ability for interplanetary travel? Mosôm said that we are preparing to travel again in spirit form. But having betrayed the sacred covenant to respect and be stewards entered into with the other creatures of Earth, the question is whether the next planet humanity wakes up on will be as welcoming as the Garden of Eden.

Global Reconciliation

One hopes that humanity's sojourn on Earth will end up being dignified and meaningful. There needs to be recognition that all created entities have spirit and, therefore, deserve respect. This means major review and reform of all ideologies that promote exploitation of resources without proper consideration of the impacts. Simple environmental and ethical reviews will be inadequate unless they incorporate a genuine sense of spirituality and ceremony. Entire sciences and technologies would have to be assessed in terms of determining their wisdom—what the impacts are on human and natural welfare and whether they are beneficial for future generations. As long as damages to human and natural welfare continue to generate downward spirals, there will be little hope of a positive outcome.

Indigenous communities need to be allowed to thrive on their own with equitable resources for health maintenance and education consistent with their traditions. This will preserve what little remains of Indigenous Eden. There is an obligation for members of mainstream society to learn about and respect traditional culture and practices. It is in this manner that healthier attitudes can develop and change over the long term. First Peoples understand that everyone is accountable for their actions. Humanity needs to face the consequences now.

Virtually all nations that include Indigenous populations within their borders have adopted Wetiko behaviours of resource exploitation and environmental destruction purely for economic gain. The scourge of greed needs to be contained. It is imperative to recognize that the vast majority of individual citizens do not fully subscribe to Wetiko values. Many individuals value healthy relationships with each other and with plants and animals, even viewing them as conscious beings. They are sensitive to the needs of the environment. They still detect their ancient heritage in their genes. However, all have grown up within and have unwittingly become part of a Wetiko system. Elders at the First Nations University of Canada counsel students to "take the best of both worlds" while maintaining a personal foundation of Indigenous values. In other words, a Native person can live in Wetiko society, yet preserve his or her identity and values by remaining mindful of one's spiritual purpose on Earth.

The *United Nations Declaration on the Rights of Indigenous Peoples* (UNDRIP), hard-won over decades of lobbying, recognizes that wrongs have been committed against Original Peoples. The declaration was approved on September 13, 2007, with the support of 144 countries of the United Nations General Assembly. Australia, Canada, New Zealand, and the United States initially voted against the resolution over uncertainty as to how it would affect existing laws and control of resources. All four have since changed their position.[9]

Article 12.1 of UNDRIP states: "Indigenous peoples have the right to manifest, practise, develop and teach their spiritual and religious traditions, customs and ceremonies." Unfortunately, the Declaration is largely a hollow gesture. It is lofty but has no force in law and no ability for recourse to international court as tribal peoples are not recognized as nations. It serves as guidance only and, even if implemented, will never go far enough to repair all the damage to the Indigenous world. It gives no increased power to Indigenous people to influence or coerce national governments. How each nation deals with Indigenous issues is left up to that jurisdiction. The vast majority are simply not motivated to make changes they perceive as diminishing their national sovereignty or economy.

In 2010, Bolivia's first Indigenous president, Evo Morales, a Quechua, was the first world leader to fully embrace UNDRIP. His government has sought to respect nature by granting rivers similar rights as humans. The move is driven by Native Peoples who contend that "we belong to a big family of plants and animals" and that Mother Earth is "sacred, fertile and the source of life that feeds and cares for all human beings."[10]

Scholar John Mohawk remains optimistic about the future for Indigenous teachings, humanity, and the Earth.

There's space for re-indigenization, which I say means to rebuild that which was there before that [colonization] happened, both in the form of human cultures and in the form of bringing back the biodiversity that existed prior to the colonization. At the same time, there's the possibility now of gathering consciousness among hundreds of millions of people about how this is not only necessary but is a very good thing, a positive thing. This new consciousness will help us rethink terms like modernism and progress, and re-examine where things are going, even to rethink what capitalism can mean. . . . We do not have a system that seeks to promote life. We have a system that seeks to promote profit, and the cost of the profit is hunger and death on a day-to-day basis.[11]

Is Reconciliation Possible?

The most flagrant part of humanity's self-destruction has occurred in the last two hundred years. However, this is a mere blink of the eye in terms of human existence. Over the course of written history, human-centred civilizations appear to be the victors as they hold virtually all of the power and wealth. Tribal peoples who continue to cling to the values of harmonious relationships with the environment are relegated to the sidelines. The world appears to be on the fast track to catastrophe.

Reconciliation with Indigenous Peoples, the modern remnants of Indigenous Eden, is an essential part of the solution. The Wetiko cultures that have set the course of world affairs pretend to solve the problems through a combination of rationalism and economic development. Unfortunately, they lack the moral authority and will never possess it until they reconcile with Indigenous Peoples and their ancient wisdom. Only a spiritual revolution can bring humanity back to its original path.

The only manner in which genuine change and reconciliation can be achieved with Indigenous Peoples is by recognizing that the oppression of their culture was wrong. There needs to be recognition by religions that Indigenous spirituality is more holistic and that direct individual connection with spirit is desirable. Individuals should not be dictated to by doctrines that eliminate any flexibility in beliefs. Religious leaders should be guides, not infallible authorities.

In traditional communities, when differences in beliefs arose, the first recourse was to join together in prayer and ceremony. That way, individual egos and pride were left at the door, and respectful dialogue under authority of the supernal could occur. Those involved in the debate would discuss the meanings of their dreams, visions, and meditations until consensus about the issue was reached. The genius of spirituality as a higher form of intelligence was able to assert itself, as the answers often came from a source that was over and above and the workings of the mind alone.

Indigenous philosophy and worldview challenges the heart and soul of modern society. Not until people recognize that every insect and blade of grass has equal validity will they be capable of living in harmony with nature. Humanity needs to confront one of its most intractable issues—admitting that our numbers have become too great—now at least four times more than is feasible if the balance with nature is to be maintained. Unfortunately, such change goes against every political and economic tenet of governments, which are based upon population and power. Clearly, the predicament the world now faces has been a result of choices. Are nations sophisticated or committed enough to devise effective strategies of planetary survival that can be implemented globally? The inability of people to deal effectively with critical issues will lay bare the immaturity of humanity in its current phase of evolution. Rediscovering our relationship to the Creator is the only way by which our integrity can be restored.

APPENDIX 1

COMPARING ECOLIZATIONS AND CIVILIZATIONS

	ECOLIZATION (INDIGENOUS)	CIVILIZATION (NON-INDIGENOUS)
WORLDVIEW	Humans are not central to Creation. All created entities have their own spirit and are interconnected.	Supremacy of people. Only humans have a spirit or soul. Nature is to be controlled, subdued, and exploited.
THEISM	Belief in one Creator but acknowledges spirits in plants, animals, and other entities.	God who has a special covenant with humans and has granted dominion over all of Creation.
WORSHIP	Direct connection to spirit through personal spiritual disciplines such as fasting, meditation, dreams, and visions.	Through institutions whose beliefs are interpreted in text and whose adherents must follow prescribed rituals.
MORALITY	Accountability to spirit and emphasis on repairing relationships.	Human laws dictating moral behaviours and punishment for transgressors.
CULTURE	Emphasis on harmony with Creation and other humans.	Human-centred arts, sciences, and philosophy that glorify humanity.

	ECOLIZATION (INDIGENOUS)	*CIVILIZATION (NON-INDIGENOUS)*
HISTORY	Knowledge is recorded orally. Everything occurs in cycles of life and learning so an objective past is not as important as a harmonious present.	Events that have occurred cannot be revisited; progress is linear—only moving forward. Recording the past is necessary or its context will be forgotten.
POLITICS	Social and economic equality is valued and wealth and power are distributed.	The wealthy and powerful control the cultural, political, and military apparatus.
ECONOMICS	Barter system promotes interdependence and reflects actual value of goods.	Monetary and banking systems are designed to rapidly expand jobs and artificially inflate wealth.
ACHIEVEMENTS	Advances in agriculture, social organization, and healthy relationships with environment under guidance of spirituality.	Global expansion of territory through colonization and resource exploitation and degradation of the environment and widespread conflict.

APPENDIX 2

UNITED NATIONS DECLARATION ON THE RIGHTS OF INDIGENOUS PEOPLES[1]

ARTICLE 1

Indigenous peoples have the right to the full enjoyment, as a collective or as individuals, of all human rights and fundamental freedoms as recognized in the Charter of the United Nations, the Universal Declaration of Human Rights and international human rights law.

ARTICLE 2

Indigenous peoples and individuals are free and equal to all other peoples and individuals and have the right to be free from any kind of discrimination, in the exercise of their rights, in particular that based on their indigenous origin or identity.

ARTICLE 3

Indigenous peoples have the right to self-determination. By virtue of that right they freely determine their political status and freely pursue their economic, social and cultural development.

ARTICLE 4

Indigenous peoples, in exercising their right to self-determination, have the right to autonomy or self-government in matters relating to their internal and local affairs, as well as ways and means for financing their autonomous functions.

ARTICLE 5

Indigenous peoples have the right to maintain and strengthen their distinct political, legal, economic, social and cultural institutions, while retaining their right to participate fully, if they so choose, in the political, economic, social and cultural life of the State.

ARTICLE 6

Every indigenous individual has the right to a nationality.

ARTICLE 7

1. Indigenous individuals have the rights to life, physical and mental integrity, liberty and security of person.

2. Indigenous peoples have the collective right to live in freedom, peace and security as distinct peoples and shall not be subjected to any act of genocide or any other act of violence, including forcibly removing children of the group to another group.

ARTICLE 8

1. Indigenous peoples and individuals have the right not to be subjected to forced assimilation or destruction of their culture.

2. States shall provide effective mechanisms for prevention of, and redress for:

(a) Any action which has the aim or effect of depriving them of their integrity as distinct peoples, or of their cultural values or ethnic identities;

(b) Any action which has the aim or effect of dispossessing them of their lands, territories or resources;

(c) Any form of forced population transfer which has the aim or effect of violating or undermining any of their rights;

(d) Any form of forced assimilation or integration;

(e) Any form of propaganda designed to promote or incite racial or ethnic discrimination directed against them.

ARTICLE 9

Indigenous peoples and individuals have the right to belong to an indigenous community or nation, in accordance with the traditions and customs of the community or nation concerned. No discrimination of any kind may arise from the exercise of such a right.

ARTICLE 10

Indigenous peoples shall not be forcibly removed from their lands or territories. No relocation shall take place without the free, prior and informed consent of the indigenous peoples concerned and after agreement on just and fair compensation and, where possible, with the option of return.

ARTICLE 11

1. Indigenous peoples have the right to practise and revitalize their cultural traditions and customs. This includes the right to maintain, protect and develop the past, present and future manifestations of their cultures, such as archaeological and historical sites, artefacts, designs, ceremonies, technologies and visual and performing arts and literature.

2. States shall provide redress through effective mechanisms, which may include restitution, developed in conjunction with indigenous peoples, with respect to their cultural, intellectual, religious and spiritual property taken without their free, prior and informed consent or in violation of their laws, traditions and customs.

ARTICLE 12

1. Indigenous peoples have the right to manifest, practise, develop and teach their spiritual and religious traditions, customs and ceremonies; the right to maintain, protect, and have access in privacy to their religious and cultural sites; the right to the use and control of their ceremonial objects; and the right to the repatriation of their human remains.

2. States shall seek to enable the access and/or repatriation of ceremonial objects and human remains in their possession through fair, transparent and effective mechanisms developed in conjunction with Indigenous peoples concerned.

ARTICLE 13

1. Indigenous peoples have the right to revitalize, use, develop and transmit to future generations their histories, languages, oral traditions, philosophies, writing systems and literatures, and to designate and retain their own names for communities, places and persons.

2. States shall take effective measures to ensure that this right is protected and also to ensure that indigenous peoples can understand and be understood in political, legal and administrative proceedings, where necessary through the provision of interpretation or by other appropriate means.

ARTICLE 14

1. Indigenous peoples have the right to establish and control their educational systems and institutions providing education in their own languages, in a manner appropriate to their cultural methods of teaching and learning.

2. Indigenous individuals, particularly children, have the right to all levels and forms of education of the State without discrimination.

3. States shall, in conjunction with indigenous peoples, take effective measures, in order for indigenous individuals, particularly children, including those living outside their communities, to have access, when possible, to an education in their own culture and provided in their own language.

ARTICLE 15

1. Indigenous peoples have the right to the dignity and diversity of their cultures, traditions, histories and aspirations which shall be appropriately reflected in education and public information.

2.   States shall take effective measures, in consultation and cooperation with the indigenous peoples concerned, to combat prejudice and eliminate discrimination and to promote tolerance, understanding and good relations among indigenous peoples and all other segments of society.

ARTICLE 16

1.   Indigenous peoples have the right to establish their own media in their own languages and to have access to all forms of non-indigenous media without discrimination.

2.   States shall take effective measures to ensure that State-owned media duly reflect Indigenous cultural diversity. States, without prejudice to ensuring full freedom of expression, should encourage privately owned media to adequately reflect indigenous cultural diversity.

ARTICLE 17

1.   Indigenous individuals and peoples have the right to enjoy fully all rights established under applicable international and domestic labour law.

2.   States shall in consultation and cooperation with indigenous peoples take specific measures to protect indigenous children from economic exploitation and from performing any work that is likely to be hazardous or to interfere with the child's education, or to be harmful to the child's health or physical, mental, spiritual, moral or social development, taking into account their special vulnerability and the importance of education for their empowerment.

3.   Indigenous individuals have the right not to be subjected to any discriminatory conditions of labour and, inter alia, employment or salary.

ARTICLE 18

Indigenous peoples have the right to participate in decision-making in matters which would affect their rights, through representatives chosen by themselves in accordance with their own procedures, as well as to maintain and develop their own indigenous decision-making institutions.

ARTICLE 19

States shall consult and cooperate in good faith with the indigenous peoples concerned through their own representative institutions in order to obtain their free, prior and informed consent before adopting and implementing legislative or administrative measures that may affect them.

ARTICLE 20

1. Indigenous peoples have the right to maintain and develop their political, economic and social systems or institutions, to be secure in the enjoyment of their own means of subsistence and development, and to engage freely in all their traditional and other economic activities.

2. Indigenous peoples deprived of their means of subsistence and development are entitled to just and fair redress.

ARTICLE 21

1. Indigenous peoples have the right, without discrimination, to the improvement of their economic and social conditions, including, inter alia, in the areas of education, employment, vocational training and retraining, housing, sanitation, health and social security.

2. States shall take effective measures and, where appropriate, special measures to ensure continuing improvement of their economic and social conditions. Particular attention shall be paid to the rights and special needs of indigenous Elders, women, youth, children and persons with disabilities.

ARTICLE 22

1. Particular attention shall be paid to the rights and special needs of Indigenous Elders, women, youth, children and persons with disabilities in the implementation of this Declaration.

2. States shall take measures, in conjunction with Indigenous peoples, to ensure that indigenous women and children enjoy the full protection and guarantees against all forms of violence and discrimination.

ARTICLE 23

Indigenous peoples have the right to determine and develop priorities and strategies for exercising their right to development. In particular, indigenous peoples have the right to be actively involved in developing and determining health, housing and other economic and social programmes affecting them and, as far as possible, to administer such programmes through their own institutions.

ARTICLE 24

1. Indigenous peoples have the right to their traditional medicines and to maintain their health practices, including the conservation of their vital medicinal plants, animals and minerals. Indigenous individuals also have the right to access, without any discrimination, to all social and health services.

2. Indigenous individuals have an equal right to the enjoyment of the highest attainable standard of physical and mental health. States shall take the necessary steps with a view to achieving progressively the full realization of this right.

ARTICLE 25

Indigenous peoples have the right to maintain and strengthen their distinctive spiritual relationship with their traditionally owned or otherwise occupied and used lands, territories, waters and coastal seas and other resources and to uphold their responsibilities to future generations in this regard.

ARTICLE 26

1. Indigenous peoples have the right to the lands, territories and resources which they have traditionally owned, occupied or otherwise used or acquired.

2. Indigenous peoples have the right to own, use, develop and control the lands, territories and resources that they possess by reason of traditional ownership or other traditional occupation or use, as well as those which they have otherwise acquired.

3. States shall give legal recognition and protection to these lands, territories and resources. Such recognition shall be conducted with due respect to the customs, traditions and land tenure systems of the Indigenous peoples concerned.

ARTICLE 27

States shall establish and implement, in conjunction with Indigenous peoples concerned, a fair, independent, impartial, open and transparent process, giving due recognition to Indigenous peoples' laws, traditions, customs and land tenure systems, to recognize and adjudicate the rights of indigenous peoples pertaining to their lands, territories and resources, including those which were traditionally owned or otherwise occupied or used. Indigenous peoples shall have the right to participate in this process.

ARTICLE 28

1. Indigenous peoples have the right to redress, by means that can include restitution or, when this is not possible, just, fair and equitable compensation, for the lands, territories and resources which they have traditionally owned or otherwise occupied or used, and which have been confiscated, taken, occupied, used or damaged without their free, prior and informed consent.

2. Unless otherwise freely agreed upon by the peoples concerned, compensation shall take the form of lands, territories and resources equal in quality, size and legal status or of monetary compensation or other appropriate redress.

ARTICLE 29

1. Indigenous peoples have the right to the conservation and protection of the environment and the productive capacity of their lands or territories and resources. States shall establish and implement assistance

programmes for indigenous peoples for such conservation and protection, without discrimination.

2. States shall take effective measures to ensure that no storage or disposal of hazardous materials shall take place in the lands or territories of indigenous peoples without their free, prior and informed consent.

3. States shall also take effective measures to ensure, as needed, that programmes for monitoring, maintaining and restoring the health of indigenous peoples, as developed and implemented by the peoples affected by such materials, are duly implemented.

ARTICLE 30

1. Military activities shall not take place in the lands or territories of Indigenous peoples, unless justified by a relevant public interest or otherwise freely agreed with or requested by the Indigenous peoples concerned.

2. States shall undertake effective consultations with the Indigenous peoples concerned, through appropriate procedures and in particular through their representative institutions, prior to using their lands or territories for military activities.

ARTICLE 31

1. Indigenous peoples have the right to maintain, control, protect and develop their cultural heritage, traditional knowledge and traditional cultural expressions, as well as the manifestations of their sciences, technologies and cultures, including human and genetic resources, seeds, medicines, knowledge of the properties of fauna and flora, oral traditions, literatures, designs, sports and traditional games and visual and performing arts. They also have the right to maintain, control, protect and develop their intellectual property over such cultural heritage, traditional knowledge, and traditional cultural expressions.

2. In conjunction with indigenous peoples, States shall take effective measures to recognize and protect the exercise of these rights.

ARTICLE 32

1. Indigenous peoples have the right to determine and develop priorities and strategies for the development or use of their lands or territories and other resources.

2. States shall consult and cooperate in good faith with the Indigenous peoples concerned through their own representative institutions in order to obtain their free and informed consent prior to the approval of any project affecting their lands or territories and other resources, particularly in connection with the development, utilization or exploitation of mineral, water or other resources.

3. States shall provide effective mechanisms for just and fair redress for any such activities, and appropriate measures shall be taken to mitigate adverse environmental, economic, social, cultural or spiritual impact.

ARTICLE 33

1. Indigenous peoples have the right to determine their own identity or membership in accordance with their customs and traditions. This does not impair the right of Indigenous individuals to obtain citizenship of the States in which they live.

2. Indigenous peoples have the right to determine the structures and to select the membership of their institutions in accordance with their own procedures.

ARTICLE 34

Indigenous peoples have the right to promote, develop and maintain their institutional structures and their distinctive customs, spirituality, traditions, procedures, practices and, in the cases where they exist, juridical systems or customs, in accordance with international human rights standards.

ARTICLE 35

Indigenous peoples have the right to determine the responsibilities of individuals to their communities.

ARTICLE 36

1. Indigenous peoples, in particular those divided by international borders, have the right to maintain and develop contacts, relations and cooperation, including activities for spiritual, cultural, political, economic and social purposes, with their own members as well as other peoples across borders.

2. States, in consultation and cooperation with indigenous peoples, shall take effective measures to facilitate the exercise and ensure the implementation of this right.

ARTICLE 37

1. Indigenous peoples have the right to the recognition, observance and enforcement of treaties, agreements and other constructive arrangements concluded with States or their successors and to have States honour and respect such treaties, agreements and other constructive arrangements.

2. Nothing in this Declaration may be interpreted as diminishing or eliminating the rights of indigenous peoples contained in treaties, agreements and other constructive arrangements.

ARTICLE 38

States, in consultation and cooperation with indigenous peoples, shall take the appropriate measures, including legislative measures, to achieve the ends of this Declaration.

ARTICLE 39

Indigenous peoples have the right to have access to financial and technical assistance from States and through international cooperation, for the enjoyment of the rights contained in this Declaration.

ARTICLE 40

Indigenous peoples have the right to access to and prompt decision through just and fair procedures for the resolution of conflicts and disputes with States or other parties, as well as to effective remedies for all infringements of their individual and collective rights. Such a decision shall give due consideration to the customs, traditions, rules and legal systems of the indigenous peoples concerned and international human rights.

ARTICLE 41

The organs and specialized agencies of the United Nations system and other intergovernmental organizations shall contribute to the full realization of the provisions of this Declaration through the mobilization, inter alia, of financial cooperation and technical assistance. Ways and means of ensuring participation of Indigenous peoples on issues affecting them shall be established.

ARTICLE 42

The United Nations, its bodies, including the Permanent Forum on Indigenous Issues, and specialized agencies, including at the country level, and States shall promote respect for and full application of the provisions of this Declaration and follow up the effectiveness of this Declaration.

ARTICLE 43

The rights recognized herein constitute the minimum standards for the survival, dignity and well-being of the Indigenous peoples of the world.

ARTICLE 44

All the rights and freedoms recognized herein are equally guaranteed to male and female indigenous individuals.

ARTICLE 45

Nothing in this Declaration may be construed as diminishing or extinguishing the rights Indigenous peoples have now or may acquire in the future.

ARTICLE 46

1. Nothing in this Declaration may be interpreted as implying for any State, people, group or person any right to engage in any activity or to perform any act contrary to the Charter of the United Nations or

construed as authorizing or encouraging any action which would dismember or impair, totally or in part, the territorial integrity or political unity of sovereign and independent States. In the exercise of the rights enunciated in the present Declaration, human rights and fundamental freedoms of all shall be respected. The exercise of the rights set forth in this Declaration shall be subject only to such limitations as are determined by law and in accordance with international human rights obligations. Any such limitations shall be non-discriminatory and strictly necessary solely for the purpose of securing due recognition and respect for the rights and freedoms of others and for meeting the just and most compelling requirements of a democratic society.

2. The provisions set forth in this Declaration shall be interpreted in accordance with the principles of justice, democracy, respect for human rights, equality, non-discrimination, good governance and good faith.

GLOSSARY

ABORIGINAL—existing in a land from earliest times, synonymous with Indigenous

AHCAHK—the Cree word for soul or spirit, also the word for star

ALL OUR RELATIONS—an expression that acknowledges kinship with all of Creation

ANISHINAABE—First Nation prevalent around the Great Lakes, also known as Ojibway

ATAHUALPA—leader of the Inca at the time of Spanish contact

ÂTAYÔHKANAK— spirit helpers, Cree

CAHOKIA—the largest urban centre in Indigenous North America

CALMECAC—the Aztec institution of higher education

CHOLULA—site in Mexico of the world's most massive pyramid

CIVILIZATION—a society based upon human-centredness and domination of nature

CODE OF HAMMURABI—one of the earliest codes of human law that espoused an "eye for an eye"

CULTURE OF DEATH—a culture where, through loss of spirituality, ills are no longer meaningfully mended, resulting in cycles of deterioration

CULTURE OF LIFE—a culture rooted in spirituality and practising constant healing that results in life-enhancing cycles

DALIT—Indigenous Peoples of India

ECOLIZATION—a society founded on the concept that humans are not the focus but one cog in a holistic Creation

EL CARACOL—the Mayan "observatory" at Chichen Itza, Mexico

ENKAI—Creator in Maasi

ETHISODA—a pretender who challenged Shonkwaia'tison, the Creator, in Haudenosaunee

FIRST NATION—a political term denoting an Indigenous community recognized under Canada's *Indian Act.*

GOOD PATH—the trajectory followed by individuals and groups when obeying spiritual laws

HAUDENOSAUNEE—the true name of the Iroquois

HUITZILOPOCHTLI—the Aztec god of discord

I CHING—the Chinese oracular system

INDIGENOUS EDEN—the world in which Indigenous Peoples respect and live in harmony with all created beings

ITEYIMIKOWISIYECIKEWINA—Cree name for treaty, agreement inspired by kise-manitow

KACHINA—spirits that interact with the Pueblo and are represented by carved figures

KAHUNAS—Hawaiian medicine practitioner

KICIWÂMINAWAK—Cree term for cousin, used in treaty discussion

KISE-MANITOW—Benevolent Creator, Cree

KOSÂPAHCIKAN—Spirit Lodge, Cree

MAASAW—Creator in Hopi

MANITOW—Creator, Cree

MAPUCHE—Indigenous people located in Chile and Argentina

MEDICINE CIRCLE (OR WHEEL)—an Indigenous analytical tool

MITEWIWIN—an Anishinaabe society for advancement in spiritual knowledge

MIYO-WÎCEHTOWIN—Laws of Relationships to promote harmony, Cree

MOSÔM—Grandfather, also a term of respect for Elders, Cree

NÊHIYAWÊWIN—Cree language

NIKÂWÎNÂN ASKIY—Mother Earth, Cree

NGENECHEN—Creator in Mapuche

NÔSISIM—grandchild, Cree

OMETEOTL—Aztec supreme being

ORIGINAL PEOPLES—another term for Indigenous Peoples

PAWÂKAN—spirit (dream) power, Cree

PAX ROMANA—peace that reigned after Roman conquest based on "protections" of prosperity and control by law enforcement.

PIMÂCIHOWIN—spiritual connection to the land, Cree

PIPE CEREMONY—a ceremony of welcoming and adoption into a sacred circle

POTLATCH—a ceremony of giving away property to establish social relationships

QUECHUA—the descendants of the Inca empire

QUETZALCOATYL—the exiled Aztec god of knowledge

QUR'AN—the Islamic holy book

SAULTEAUX—the Plains offshoot of the Anishinaabe

SEVEN DISCIPLINE—fasting, sharing, parenting, learning, teaching, praying, and meditating are tools that assist with spiritual development

SEVEN VIRTUES—humility, respect, courage, love, generosity, honesty, and wisdom are the gold standard of behaviour

SHAKING TENT—see Spirit Lodge

SHONKWAIA'TISON—
Creator in Haudenosaunee

SPIRIT LODGE—the Shaking
Tent Ceremony in which
spirit helpers are consulted

SPIRITUALITY—recognition
and acceptance that unseen
forces influence and guide life

SUMERIA—an ancient
part of Mesopotamia

SUN DANCE—the major
ceremony for renewal of life
held at summer solstice

TABLA RASA—an "empty
mind" waiting to be filled in

TANAK—Jewish scriptures
that form the basis of
the Old Testament

TAWANTNSUYU—the
Inca homeland

TENOCHTITLAN—the
capital city of the Aztecs

TEOTIHUACAN—sacred
site of ancient pyramids
located near Mexico City

TERRA NULLIUS—a legal term
that held that Indigenous lands
were not effectively occupied
and, therefore, could be wrested
away by Christian nations

TIWANACO—Gate of the
Sun sacred site in Bolivia

THIRST DANCE—see Sun Dance

TURTLE ISLAND—Indigenous
name for North America

UR—the first urban
centre in Sumeria and
epicentre of civilization

VISION QUEST—a ceremony for
establishing connection with and
guidance from the spirit world

WÂHKÔHTOWIN—the
spiritual integrity that humans,
as physical beings, must
struggle to maintain, Cree

WAKAN TANKA—Great
Mystery or Creator in Lakota

WETIKO—a cannibalistic
spirit representing the force
of greed and selfishness that
destroys all it touches

WETIKO WORLD—those regions
in which Wetiko ideology
dominates or is on the ascendant

WICCE—the term for pagan
healers that became the
basis of the word *witch*

WINDIGO—Anishinaabe
word for Wetiko

WÎSAHKECÂHK (ALSO CALLED
WESAHKECHAK)—Cree Elder
Brother Transformer Spirit

YOWA—Creator in Cherokee

NOTES

Chapter 1: Enchanted World

1 Thomas E. Mails, *Fools Crow: Wisdom and Power* (Graham, NC: Millichap Books, 2012), 52.

2 Danny Musqua, quoted in Harold Cardinal and Walter Hildebrandt, *Treaty Elders of Saskatchewan: Our Dream Is That Our Peoples Will One Day Be Clearly Recognized as Nations* (Calgary: University of Calgary Press, 2000), 40. "Our people" refers to the Saulteaux, the Plains offshoot of Anishinaabe. The name Anishinaabe means "People who came from the Heavens."

3 Danny Musqua, interview with the author, April 9, 2012.

4 Gregory Cajete, *Native Science: Natural Laws of Interdependence* (Santa Fe: Clear Light Publishers, 2000), 226.

5 Allen C. Ross, *Mitakuye Oyasin: We Are All Related* (Fort Yates: Bear Publishing, 1989), 76–77.

6 "Star Knowledge," www.michaelwassegijik.com, accessed January 18, 2019.

7 Cajete, *Native Science*, 37.

8 As the author understands Mosôm Danny, human consciousness travelled to Earth "from the stars" in spirit form, and not on physical spaceships. Human awareness entered and became the master consciousness of pre-existing hominid bodies, which were deemed suitable vehicles for humanity's earthly experience. While hominid bodies are well suited for survival on earth, human consciousness is far different and needs to learn how to live harmoniously with the rest of Creation. Humans struggle to control their movement of these physical bodies and the emotions that have been inherited from its hominid predecessor. The ability to travel in spirit, at which Indigenous spiritualists were adept, makes human consciousness a "denizen of the cosmos."

9   Niigaanwewidam James Sinclair and Warren Cariou, eds., *Manitowapow: Aboriginal Writings from the Land of Water* (Winnipeg: High Water Press, 2011), 61–68.

10   Robert Brightman, *Grateful Prey: Rock Cree Human-Animal Relationships* (Regina: Canadian Plains Research Centre, 2002), 37–75.

11   The four good Grandfather Spirits are those of the four directions. Wîsahkecâhk played the role of transformer and could employ various tools such as a sacred whistle to accomplish his goals. The assertion that women were created to join the men is opposite to other stories and may be the result of influence by Christianity.

12   Cardinal and Hildebrandt, *Treaty Elders of Saskatchewan*, 23–24.

13   Musqua, interview, April 9, 2012.

14   Danny Musqua, interview with the author, October 24, 2012.

15   Many Cree and Saulteaux words have similar spellings. The Saulteaux equivalent of the Cree word *ahcahk* is *ahtahsohkan*. The Cree word is used for convenience.

16   Musqua, interview, April 9, 2012.

17   Although soul and spirit are used interchangeably, soul is identified with the individual or egotistic aspects of spirit such as personality and intellect. Spirit relates to the eternal aspect of one's being.

18   Musqua, interview, October 24, 2012.

19   Ibid.

20   Ibid.

21   Ibid., The superior beings at a supernal level called Grandfather Spirits are comparable to angels. Mosôm said that some spirits have not experienced physical life. Superior beings appear to guide human direction from a higher level of understanding, with the intent that humans will benefit by learning from the physical experience.

22   William S. Lyon, *Spirit Talkers: North American Indian Medicine Powers* (Kansas City: Prayer Efficacy Publishing, 2012), 84–93.

23   Blair Stonechild, *The Knowledge Seeker: Embracing Indigenous Spirituality* (Regina: University of Regina Press, 2016), 79–80; Brightman, *Grateful Prey*, 187; Jean-Guy Goulet, *Ways of Knowing* (Vancouver: UBC Press, 1998), 62 and 73.

24   Stonechild, *The Knowledge Seeker*, 69–85.

25   Musqua, interview, October 24, 2012.

26   Vina Deloria Jr., *The World We Used to Live In: Remembering the Powers of the Medicine Man* (Golden, CO: Fulcrum Publishing, 2006), 108.

27   Lyon, *Spirit Talkers*, 154–7.

28   Ibid.

29   Danny Musqua, interview with the author, January 28, 2013.

30   Melissa Nelson, *Original Instructions: Indigenous Teachings for a Sustainable Future* (Rochester: Bear & Company, 2008), 49.

31   Fool's Crow quoted in Mails, *Fools Crow*, 124–25.

32　Danny Musqua quoted in Richard Katz, *Indigenous Healing Psychology: Honouring the Wisdom of the First Peoples* (Rochester: Healing Arts Press, 2017), 375.

33　Tony Sand quoted in Katz, *Indigenous Healing Psychology*, 178.

34　Velma Goodfeather, interview with the author, March 7, 2012.

35　Diane Knight, *The Seven Fires: Teachings of the Bear Clan as Recounted by Dan Musqua.* (Muskoday First Nation, SK: Many Worlds Publishing, 2001), 86.

36　William S. Lyon, *Encyclopedia of Native American Healing* (New York: Norton, 1996), 80–82.

37　Shawn Smallman, *Dangerous Spirits: The Windigo in Myth and History* (Victoria: Heritage House, 2014), 13.

38　Robert Roskind, *The Beauty Path* (Blowing Rock: One Love Press, 2006), 11.

39　*New World Encyclopedia Online*, s.v. "Hopi," accessed October 13, 2017, www.newworldencyclopedia.org.

40　Cajete, *Native Science*, 283.

41　An anonymous Elder made this statement during the Lodge of Nation gathering at World Parliament of Religions in Toronto, November 5, 2018.

42　Encyclopedia.com, s.v. "Mapuches," accessed October 13, 2017, www.encyclopedia.com.

Chapter 2: Indigenous Garden of Eden

1　The biblical Garden of Eden was an earthly paradise inhabited by Adam and Eve prior to their expulsion for disobeying God's commandment.

2　Personal communication, late Elder Ernest Tootoosis from Poundmaker First Nation, Saskatchewan, 1977.

3　United Nations Permanent Forum on Indigenous Issues, "Who Are Indigenous Peoples," www.un.org, accessed March 19, 2008.

4　United Nations, "State of the World's Indigenous Peoples," www.un.org, accessed March 19, 2018.

5　According to Iroquois (Haudenosaunee) tradition, the Great Law of Peace was the result of a vision that came to Huron prophet Degandawida and inspired the creation of the Iroquois Confederacy.

6　Cardinal and Hildebrandt, *Treaty Elders of Saskatchewan*, 14.

7　Ibid.

8　James B. Waldram, *The Way of the Pipe: Aboriginal Spirituality and Symbolic Healing in Canadian Prisons* (Peterborough, ON: Broadview Press, 1997), 84.

9　Knight, *The Seven Fires*, 30.

10　Cardinal and Hildebrandt, *Treaty Elders of Saskatchewan*, 18.

11　The spellings of Plains Cree and Saulteaux words quoted from sources such as *Grateful Prey* or the *Treaty Elders of Saskatchewan* generally do not follow the Standard Roman Orthography.

12　Our family's German shepherd Gracie displays great intelligence and sensitivity to feelings and words. How can one deny that such creatures have considerable consciousness?

13 Peter Kulchyski, Don McCaskill, and David Newhouse, eds. *In the Words of Elders: Aboriginal Cultures in Transition* (Toronto: University of Toronto Press, 1999), 129.

14 Waldram, *The Way of the Pipe*, 96.

15 Mandelbaum, *The Plains Cree*, 236; and Asikinack, "Sweat Lodge Ceremony," in *The Encyclopedia of Saskatchewan* (Regina, SK: Canadian Plains Research Centre, 2005), 918.

16 Brightman, *Grateful Prey*, 81.

17 See Thomas E. Mails, *The Mystic Warriors of the Plains* (New York: Doubleday, 1972) for an in-depth description of the spiritual path of the brave.

18 Basil Johnson, *Ojibway Ceremonies* (Toronto: McClelland and Stewart, 1982), 95–99.

19 In Saulteaux teachings, phases of life are referred to as "fires."

20 Knight, *The Seven Fires*, 58.

21 Walter Linklater, interview with the author, Saskatoon, April 12, 2012.

22 Knight, *The Seven Fires*, 76.

23 Nelson, *Original Instructions*, 156.

24 Noel Starblanket, interview with the author, October 14, 2013.

25 Kulchyski et al., *In the Words of Elders*, 297.

26 Sylvia McAdam, *Nationhood Interrupted: Revitalizing Nehiyaw Legal Systems* (Saskatoon, SK: Purich Publishing, 2015), 28–30.

27 Elder Dave Courchene told the author that the term "two spirit" is inaccurate. Gay individuals have one spirit that exhibits two aspects of gender.

28 Cardinal and Hildebrandt, *Treaty Elders of Saskatchewan*, 5.

29 Ibid., 7.

30 Ibid., 31.

31 Ibid., 14.

32 Ibid., 53.

33 "Haudenosaunee Confederacy's creation," www.haudenosauneeconfederacy.com, accessed March 31, 2019.

34 "How the Iroquois Great Law of Peace shaped US democracy," www.pbs.org, accessed November 8, 2017.

35 For more on the life of this warrior, statesman, and spiritual leader, see Hugh A. Dempsey, *Big Bear: The End of Freedom* (Vancouver, BC: Douglas & McIntyre, 1984).

36 Mails, *The Mystic Warriors of the Plains*, 550–78.

37 Harold Johnson, *Two Families: Treaties and Government* (Vancouver, BC: UBC Press, 2007), 40.

38 Arthur J. Ray, *Indians in the Fur Trade: Their Role as Trappers, Hunters and Middlemen in the Lands Southwest of Hudson Bay, 1660–1870* (Toronto: University of Toronto Press, 1998) 19–21.

39 Deloria, *The World We Used to Live In*, 98.

40 Ibid., 94.

41 Brown and Brightman, *The Orders of the Dreamed*, 8.

42 Ibid., 157.

43   Deloria, *The World We Used to Live In*, 101.

44   Both books take the notion of reality of spirit seriously.

45   Lyon, *Spirit Talkers*, 115.

46   Ibid.

47   Nancy Conner and Bradford Keeney, *Shamans of the World: Extraordinary First Person Accounts of Healings, Mysteries, and Miracles* (Boulder, CO: Sounds True, 2008), 47.

48   Deloria, *The World We Used to Live In*, 134–35.

49   Ibid., 67.

50   Ibid., 45–48.

51   Lyon, *Spirit Talkers*, 272–81.

52   Cardinal and Hildebrandt, *Treaty Elders of Saskatchewan*, 8.

53   William M. Denevan, *The Native Population of the Americas in 1492* (Madison, WI: University of Wisconsin Press, 1992).

54   Cajete, *Native Science*, 283.

55   "Teotihuacan," *Encyclopedia Britannica*, www.britannica.com, accessed October 17, 2017.

56   The author was invited by the Embassy of Canada to participate in an Indigenous dialogue on the occasion of Mexican bicentennial in 2010 and had the opportunity to visit Teotihuacan.

57   Cajete, *Native Science*, 228.

58   Ibid., 247.

59   "Tenochtitlan," www.encyclopedia.com, accessed October 8, 2017.

60   Cajete, *Native Science*, 248.

61   Jack Weatherford, *Indian Givers: How Indians of the Americas Transformed the World* (New York: Ballantine Books, 1989), 241–46.

62   Charles Mann, *1491: New Revelations of the Americas before Columbus*, 2nd edition (New York: Vintage Books, 2011), 243.

63   Cajete, *Native Science*, 75–79.

64   Weatherford, *Indian Givers*, 63–64.

65   Nelson, *Original Instructions*, 264.

66   Cajete, *Native Science*, 132.

67   Weatherford, *Indian Givers*, 187.

68   Ibid., 177.

69   Ibid., 121 and 135–49.

70   Kulchyski et al., *In the Words of Elders*, 246.

71   "Potlatch," www.encyclopedia.com, accessed March 31, 2019.

72   Smallman, *Dangerous Spirits*, 23–25; and Brightman, *Grateful Prey*, 136–58.

73   Brightman, *Grateful Prey*, 136–42.

74   Smallman, *Dangerous Spirits*, 61.

75   Ibid., 63.

76   Paul Thistle, *Indian-European Trade Relations in the Lower Saskatchewan River Region to 1840* (Winnipeg, MB: University of Manitoba Press, 1986), 18.

77   Brightman, *Grateful Prey*, 145.

Chapter 3: Betraying Indigenous Eden

1   *Sapiens* is the Latin word for "wise."

2   Quoted in David Suzuki, *The Sacred Balance: Rediscovering Our Place in Nature* (Vancouver, BC: Greystone Books, 2007), 21.

3   Ashley Montagu, *The Direction of Human Development* (New York: Harper, 1955).

4   Carpe Diem cartoon appeared in the *Regina Leader-Post* in 2017.

5   "Clovis/Llano," *The Canadian Encyclopedia*, www.thecanadianencyclopedia.ca, accessed March 3, 2018.

6   Mann, *1491*, 192.

7   "Origins: The Journey of Mankind—Spark of Civilization," *National Geographic Channel*, Asylum Entertainment, 2017.

8   New International Version, Genesis 1:28.

9   According to Reich, D.E., and D.B. Goldstein, "Evolution Genetic Evidence for a Paleolithic Human Population Expansion in Africa" (www.ncbi.nlm.nih.gov, 1998), at the dawn of human emergence, there was a functioning population of between 10,000 to 30,000 individuals in Africa. Due to drought those numbers dropped to less than 10,000 around 70,000 BCE. The population of Ur in Sumeria, the world's urban centre where civilization is believed to have emerged, was about 80,000. Estimates of world population from Colin McEvedy and Richard Jones, *Atlas of World Population History* (New York: Facts on File, 1978); John Durand, "Historical Estimates of World Population: An Estimate" (University of Pennsylvania, 1974); and Angus Maddison, *The World Economy: Historical Statistics*, vol. 2 (Paris: OECD, 2003), estimate human population around 1492 BCE to be from 430 to 540 million. Included in these estimates are China with 120 million, India with 100 million, Africa with 100 million, Europe with 60 million, the Americas with 50 million, and southeast Asia with 50 million. Estimates can vary considerably; for example, the population of pre-contact Americas has been estimated as being as high as 112 million. By the 1820s, global transportation, trade and colonization of Indigenous lands was well advanced. For example, in the Americas, most of the Indigenous population had perished due to disease or conquest. According to the United Nations, the current world population of Indigenous Peoples is 370 million.

10 International Commission for a History of the Scientific and Cultural Development of Mankind, *History of Mankind: Cultural and Scientific Development: Prehistory and the Beginnings of Civilization*, vol. 1 (London: George Allen & Unwin, 1965), xviii; and Richard Ovey, *The Times History of the World* (New York: New York Times Books, 2008), 2.

11 International Commission, *History of Mankind*, 3.

12 Ibid., 4.

13 Ibid., 8.

14 As an example, Ovey, *The Times History of the World*.

15 "Zoroastrianism," *Encyclopedia Britannica*, www.britannica.com, accessed December 19, 2017.

16 "Hammurabi's Code: An Eye for an Eye," http://www.ushistory.org/civ/4c.asp, accessed October 21, 2018.

17 In Plains culture, counting coup consisted of touching the opponent with one's weapon or lance, but not killing that person. The point of the combat was to demonstrate skill and ability to subdue the other, and not to kill them.

18 Mails, *The Mystic Warriors of the Plains*, 152–57.

19 Ray, *Indians in the Fur Trade*, 19–21.

20 Joshua J. Mark, "War," in *Ancient History Encyclopedia*, http://www.ancient.eu.war/, accessed August 30, 2017. Conflict between the Sumer and Elam in Mesopotamia in 2700 BCE is cited as the first recorded war.

21 W.D. Rubinstein, *Genocide: A History*. London (UK: Pearson Longman, 2004), 22.

22 Junius Rodriguez, *The Historical Encyclopedia of World Slavery*, vol. 1 (Oxford: ABC-CLIO, 1997), 49.

23 Dave Grossman, *On Killing: The Psychological Cost of Learning to Kill in War and Society* (New York: Back Bay Books, 1996).

24 Ashley Montagu, *The Nature of Human Aggression* (Oxford: Oxford University Press, 1976).

25 Julian Marais, *History of Philosophy* (New York: Dover Publications, 1967), 37.

26 Ibid., 39.

27 Ibid., 61.

28 Nicholas Smith, "Aristotle's Theory of Natural Slavery," www.researchgate.net, accessed April 2, 2019.

29 Nigel Cawthorne, *100 Tyrants* (London: Arcturus, 2010), 12–16.

30 J.P. Balsdon, *Romans and Aliens* (Chapel Hill, NC: University of North Carolina Press, 1979), 2.

31 Kevin McGeough, *The Romans: New Perspectives* (Santa Barbara: ABC-CLIO Inc., 2004), 167–74.

32 The Romans believed in strong bloodlines, which resulted in leaders being chosen because of heredity rather than competence.

33 Balsdon, *Romans and Aliens*, 65–66.

34 Ibid., 4.

35 J.H. Brennan, *Whisperers: The Secret History of the Spirit World* (London: Overlook Duckworth, 2013), 105.

36 The Gauls migrated from the Caucasus into western Europe but retained their Indigenous cultural practices.

37 "150,000 fled for their lives, but were slaughtered by Julius Caesar army, bones reveal," www.ancient-origins.net, December 14, 2015.

38 *Eight Days That Made Rome*, The Smithsonian Channel (2017) documentary series hosted by historian Bettany Hughes puts a human face to the Roman experience.

39 "The Extent of the Roman Empire," *Ancient History Encyclopedia*, www. ancient.eu, accessed April 4, 2019.

40 English Standard Version, Matthew 5:3–10.

41 "Constantine 1," *New World Encyclopedia*, www.newworldencyclopedia.org, accessed April 2, 2019.

42 Ibid.

43 Franz Volker Greifenhagen, "Islam(s)," *Introduction to Religious Studies*, 3rd ed., ed. Leona Anderson (Regina, SK: University of Regina, 2008), 202; and "Polytheism," www.oxfordislamicstudies.com, accessed April 10, 2018.

44 Malcolm Lambert, *God's Armies: Crusade and Jihad: Origins, History, Aftermath* (New York: Pegasus Books, 2016), 52–60.

45 Ibid., 61–64.

46 Ibid., 66–79.

47 Ibid., 82–95.

48 "What is Paganism? Frequently Asked Questions about Paganism," Papal Apology Project, 1999, 3.

49 Ibid.

50 Ibid., The modern pagan movement attempts to reconstruct the beliefs and practices of cultures long lost except for small pockets that remain in more isolated parts of Europe, such as Latvia.

51 "Charlemagne: Holy Roman Emperor," *Encyclopedia Britannica*, www. britannica.com, accessed April 2, 2019.

52 Mark Cartwright, "Northern Crusades," *Ancient History Encyclopedia*, www. ancient.eu, accessed November 8, 2018.

53 "Crusades," *Ancient History Encyclopedia*, www.ancient.eu, accessed November 8, 2018.

54 Skyforger/History, "The Baltic Crusades and European paganism's last stand against Christianity," http://history.skyforger.lv/2011/crusades-against-pagan-northern-europe/, accessed November 8, 2018.

55 Dr. Katharine Olsen, "10 Dangers of the Medival Period," BBC History Magazine, https://www.historyextra.com/period/medieval/10-dangers-of-the-medieval-period/, accessed May 2, 2018.

56 Eric R. Wolf, *Europe and the People Without History* (Berkeley: University of California Press, 1982).

57 Weatherford, *Indian Givers*, 63 and 71.

58 "Wars of the Roses," www.history.com, accessed December 10, 2018.

59 For world population estimates, see International Commission, *History of Mankind*.

60 The author was invited to attend the opening ceremony for the Sami University's new facility at Kautokieno, Norway, in 2009.

61 Today Indigenous populations are defined not only as being very non-technological and "tied to the land" but are also defined as marginalized. This disqualifies populations such as the Chinese, who are Indigenous to their lands but are also technologically and organizationally advanced.

62   The Celts migrated from the Caucasus region to Europe; however, they prac-
     tised Indigenous culture and spirituality that tied them closely to the land.

63   The episode "Boudica's Revenge" in the *Eight Days That Made Rome* series
     describes Roman derogatory relationships with the Indigenous Peoples of
     Britain.

64   The expression comes from the book by Wolf, *Europe and the People Without
     History*.

65   John Mohawk, "The Art of Thriving in Place," in Nelson, *Original Instruc-
     tions*, 127.

Chapter 4: Final Conquest of Eden

1   "Civilization," www.dictionary.com, accessed September 19, 2018.

2   "Eco" comes from the Greek word for "home." Its use in ecolizations is
     intended to evoke the idea of holism.

3   Weatherford, *Indian Givers*, 14–16.

4   Ibid., 37.

5   See Wolf, *Europe and the People Without History*.

6   *Terra nullius* or "empty land" is a legal concept that because Indigenous Peo-
     ples are not civilized, they do not effectively occupy or own the land they
     inhabit, making it legitimate to be legally owned by Christian nations.

7   Certainly concerns were raised at the spectacle of human sacrifices; how-
     ever, the basic nature and spiritual motives of these Indigenous practices
     were not understood.

8   Hans Koning, *Columbus: His Enterprise* (New York: Monthly Review Press,
     1991), 14.

9   Ibid., 37.

10   Nelson, *Original Instructions*, 164.

11   Koning, *Columbus*, 52–53.

12   Ibid., 95–96.

13   Brennan, *Whisperers*, 25.

14   Koning, *Columbus*, 63.

15   Ibid., 83–84.

16   Cajete, *Native Science*, 285.

17   Ibid., 284.

18   An even larger pyramid at Cholula, Mexico, is the most massive pyramid by
     volume ever created on Earth.

19   Bernat Hernandez, "The Cortés Conquest," *National Geographic*, December
     18, 2018.

20   Lawrence Clayton, *Bartolomé de las Casas: A Biography* (Cambridge: Cam-
     bridge University Press, 2012), 448.

21   "Native Americans and Europeans," www.encyclopedia.com, accessed
     October 13, 2018.

22 "Francisco Pizarro," *Encyclopedia Brittanica*, www.britannica.com, accessed April 4, 2019.

23 Michael Cartwright, "Pizarro and the Fall of the Inca Empire," *Ancient History Encyclopedia*, www.ancient.eu, accessed April 4, 2019.

24 Koning, *Columbus*, 51–53; and Olive Patricia Dickason, *A Concise History of Canada's First Nations* (Don Mills, ON: Oxford University Press Canada, 2006), 83.

25 Dickason, *A Concise History of Canada's First Nations*, 87.

26 John Webster Grant, *Moon of Wintertime: Missionaries and the Indians of Canada in Encounter Since 1534* (Toronto: University of Toronto Press, 1984), 34.

27 Dickason, *A Concise History of Canada's First Nations*, 135.

28 Arthur J. Ray, Jim Miller, and Frank J. Tough, *Bounty and Benevolence: A History of Saskatchewan Treaties* (Montreal: McGill-Queen's University Press, 2000), 32–35.

29 Ibid.

30 Sheldon Krasowski, *No Surrender: The Land Remains Indigenous* (Regina, SK: University of Regina Press, 2019), 277.

31 Olive Patricia Dickason, *Canada's First Nations: A History of Founding Peoples from Earliest Times* (Toronto: Oxford University Press, 2002), 198–99.

32 Alexander Morris, *The Treaties of Canada with the Indians of Manitoba and the North-West Territories* (Toronto: Coles Publishing Company, 1979), 296.

33 Cardinal and Hildebrandt, *Treaty Elders of Saskatchewan*, 14.

34 Treaty Commissioner for Saskatchewan, *Statement of Treaty Issues: Treaties as a Bridge to the Future* (Saskatoon, SK: Treaty Commissioner for Saskatchewan, 1998), 13–14.

35 Morris, *The Treaties of Canada*, 296–97.

36 See Richard Hofdstater, *Social Darwinism in American Thought* (Boston: Beacon Press, 1992).

37 Blair Stonechild, "Recovering the Heritage of Treaty Number Four," in *Plain Speaking: Essays on Aboriginal Peoples and the Prairie*, eds. P. Douaud and B. Dawson (Regina, SK: Canadian Plains Research Center, 2002), 1–10; and James Daschuk, *Clearing the Plains: Disease, Politics of Starvation, and the Loss of Aboriginal Life* (Regina, SK: University of Regina Press, 2013), 162–64.

38 Deanna Christensen, *Ahtahkakoop: The Epic Account of a Plains Cree Head Chief, His People, and their Struggle for Survival, 1816–1896* (Shell Lake, SK: Ahtahkakoop Publishing, 2000), 159–62.

39 Thomas Moore Keesig came from Muscowpetung Indian Reserve.

40 Kent McNeil, "Social Darwinism and Judicial Conceptions of Indian Title in Canada in the 1880s," *Journal of the West* 38, no.1 (January 1999): 71–72.

41 Frederick Hoxie, ed., *Encyclopedia of North American Indians* (New York: Houghton Mifflin, 1996), 101.

42 J.R. Miller, *Shingwauk's Vision: A History of Native Residential Schools* (Toronto: University of Toronto Press, 1996), 191–192.

43 John Milloy, *A National Crime: The Canadian Government and the Residential School System, 1879–1986* (Winnipeg, MB: University of Manitoba Press, 1999), 40.

44 Kulchyski et al., *In the Words of Elders*, 291.

45 Waldram, *The Way of the Pipe*, 53.

46 Milloy, *A National Crime*, 95.

47 Raven Sinclair, *Wicihitowin* (Winnipeg, MB: Fernwood Publishing, 2009), 90–93.

48 Truth and Reconciliation Commission of Canada, *Summary of the Final Report*, issued in June 2015, declared that residential schools amounted to "cultural genocide."

49 Call to Action #48, from *Truth and Reconciliation Commission of Canada: Calls to Action*, 2012, 5.

50 Johnson, *Two Families*, 50 and 81.

51 Ibid., 47.

52 Jacob Olupona, "The Spirituality of Africa," *Harvard Gazette*, October 6, 2015.

53 Ibid.

54 Ibid.

55 The author participated in the "Celebrating the Ancient/Contemporary Wisdom of the Fourth World" conference at Acharya Nagarjuna University in Vijiawada, India, in December 2015, at which Dalit literature was highlighted.

56 "Ancestor Worship in Ancient China," *Ancient History Encyclopedia*, www.ancient.eu.

57 Tim Hannigan, *A Brief History of Indonesia* (North Clarendon, VT: Tuttle Publishing, 2015), 11–17.

58 Tang Alisa, "Indonesia's Land Transfer a Breakthrough for Indigenous Rights," *Reuters*, January 11, 2017.

59 Ibid., 62

60 Ibid., 83–84.

61 Asian Indigenous Peoples Pact, "Joint Stakeholder's Submission on the Situation of Human Rights of Indigenous Peoples in Indonesia," https://iphrdefenders.net, May 2017.

62 "Indonesia's Orang Rimba: Forced to Renounce Their Faith," http://www.bbc.com/news/world-asia-41981430, November 17, 2017.

63 Ibid.

64 Ibid.

65 Ibid.

66 Ibid.

67 Michael Bachelard, "Papuan Children Taken to Jakarta to Be Converted to Islam," http://www.smh.com.au/world/papuan-children-taken-to-jakarta-to-be-converted-to-islam-20140301-33s0q.html, March 2, 2014.

68 Carl Ernst, *Rethinking Islam in the Contemporary World* (Edinburgh: Edinburgh University Press, 2004), 35–43. Two major foundations of Western

civilization are the revelations of Judaism, including monotheism, and the philosophy of reasoning of the Greeks. Islam claims the same two foundations, as well as Muhammad of course. When the Ottomans conquered Constantinople in 1453 they inherited and adopted much of the apparatus of the Roman Empire. There is a concept of "Pax Islamica": "The Prophet made efforts to establish friendly relations with outside tribes whenever the opportunity offered itself, the purpose being to organize resistance to aggression and to secure freedom of conscience and belief for everyone. This was the beginning of Pax Islamica." (Muhammad Zafrullah Khan, *Islam: Its Meaning for Modern Man*, 59–60.) . . . "Delegations now poured in from all parts of Arabia offering their submission and announcing their acceptance of Islam. In a short time the whole of Arabia adhered to the Pax Islamica." (Ibid., 97.)

69 "Australian Aborigine," *New World Encyclopedia,* www.newworldencyclo-pedia.org, accessed March 31, 2019.

70 "Maori," *Encyclopedia Britannica,* www.britannica.com.

Chapter 5: Religion Overtakes the World

1 Musqua, interview, January 28, 2013.

2 "Spirituality," *Merriam-Webster,* www.merriam-webster.com and www.dic-tionary.com.

3 Richard J. Neuhaus, ed., *Unsecular America* (Grand Rapids, MI: William B. Eerdmans Publishing Company, 1986), 115–42.

4 John (Fire) Lame Deer and Richard Erdoes, *Lame Deer, Seeker of Visions* (New York: Simon & Schuster, 1994), 61.

5 "Relativism," *Merriam-Webster,* www.merriam-webster.com, accessed January 29, 2019.

6 Darlene Juschka, "Religious Studies and the Study of Religion," *Introduction to Religious Studies*, 3rd ed., ed. Leona Anderson (Regina, SK: University of Regina, 2008), 4–17.

7 John Paul II in Vertitas Spendor encyclical on moral teaching, 1993.

8 Shakespeare, *As You Like It,* Act 2 Scene 7.

9 Stonechild, *The Knowledge Seeker,* 166.

10 Brown and Brightman, *The Orders of the Dreamed,* 146–148.

11 Jack Forbes, *Columbus and Other Cannibals* (New York: Seven Stories Press, 2008), 74. The concept of Machi Manitow (bad Creator) is a recently introduced idea that is inconsistent with Indigenous theology since Manitow was always benevolent.

12 "FBI Investigation into Las Vegas Shooting Finds No Motive," *The Guardian,* January 29, 2019, https://www.theguardian.com/us-news/2019/jan/29/las-vegas-shooting-motive-fbi-investigation.

13 Brennan, *Whisperers,* 34.

14 Ibid., 16.

15 Ibid., 40–42.

16 Ibid., 45.

17 Ibid., 55–56.

18 Ibid., 34–35.

19 Ibid., 82.

20 Karen Armstrong, *The Bible: A Biography* (New York: Grove Press, 2007), 11.

21 Ibid., 63–65.

22 The Torah are the five books of Moses from Genesis to Deuteronomy.

23 New International Version, Genesis 1:26–28.

24 Ibid., Genesis 2:16–17.

25 Ibid., Genesis 3:6–7.

26 Ibid., Genesis 3:1–12.

27 Ibid., Exodus 20:3 and 5–9.

28 English Standard Version, Matthew 24:10–12.

29 Ibid., Second Timothy 3:1–5.

30 New International Version, Luke 21:11.

31 In other words humans become responsible for their own sin and determining the punishment.

32 Brennan, *Whisperers*, 106–7.

33 Ibid., 108–110.

34 Tom Harpur, *The Pagan Christ* (Toronto: Thomas Allen Publishers, 2004), 3.

35 Ibid., 12.

36 Ibid., 23.

37 Ibid., 38.

38 Ibid., 151.

39 Brennan, *Whisperers*, 107.

40 Harpur, *The Pagan Christ*, 178.

41 Quoted in Gretta Vosper, *With or Without God: Why the Way We Live Is More Important Than What We Believe* (Toronto: HarperCollins Canada, 2008), 79.

42 Brennan, *Whisperers*, 108.

43 Ibid., 110–11.

44 "Martin Luther," *Encyclopedia Britannica*, www.britannica.com, accessed November 23, 2018.

45 Vosper, *With or Without God*, 75.

46 Ernst, *Rethinking Islam in the Contemporary World*, 43.

47 Vosper, *With or Without God*, 28.

48 Ibid., 34.

49 William Arnal, "Christianity," in *Introduction to Religious Studies*, 3rd ed., ed. Leona Anderson (Regina, SK: University of Regina, 2008), 70–106.

50 "Second Vatican Council," *Encyclopedia Britannica*, www.britannica.com, accessed November 18, 2018.

51 Tolly Bradford and Chelsea Horton, *Mixed Blessings: Indigenous Encounters with Christianity in Canada* (Vancouver, BC: UBC Press, 2016), 30.

52 Kulchyski et al., *In the Words of Elders*, 127.

53 *First Peoples Theological Journal* (Indigenous Theological Training Institute, 2000), ii.

54　"Humanism," www.encyclopedia.com, accessed January 27, 2019.

55　Brennan, *Whisperers*, 375.

56　Elder Eva McKay quoted in Kulchyski et al., *In the Words of Elders*, 303.

57　Elder Wilfred Tootoosis quoted in Kulchyski et al., *In the Words of Elders*, 341.

58　Nelson, *Original Instructions*, 140.

59　Ibid., 322.

60　Lambert, *God's Armies*, 13–19.

61　Tilman Nagel, *The History of Islamic Theology* (Princeton: Markus Wiener Publishers, 2006), 20.

62　History Classics. *Mysteries of the Bible, The Bible's Greatest Heroes*. (DVD) Disc 1. Indigenous people were not polytheists in the sense that they worshipped nature "gods." Indigenous people saw flora and fauna as gifts from the Creator and allies from whom they could learn about physical living. They utilized ceremonies to communicate with these beings, but did not hold them in the reverence that they had for the Creator.

63　"Islam—Foundations of Islam," *Encyclopedia Britannica*, www.britannica.com, accessed April 18, 2019.

64　"Qur'an," *Encyclopedia Britannica*, www.britannica.com, accessed April 13, 2019.

65　"Pillars of Islam," *Encyclopedia Britannica*, www.britannica.com, accessed April 15, 2019.

66　Lambert, *God's Armies*, 15–42 and 128–30.

67　The word "Sufi" refers to coarse garments worn by the poor.

68　This response was to a question raised by the author at the Lodge of Nations, World Parliament of Religions conference, Toronto, Canada, November 6, 2018.

69　Anderson, ed., *Introduction to Religious Studies*, 43 and 63.

70　Brennan, *Whisperers*, 92.

71　Stonechild, *The Knowledge Seeker*, 100–101.

72　Brennan, *Whisperers*, 92–94.

73　The author was a member of a delegation from the First Nations University that was invited to China in 1984 to visit National Minorities in Inner Mongolia and Xingiang Autonomous Region.

74　For example, joss paper or spirit money is burned during traditional Chinese ancestor worship ceremonies.

75　Brennan, *Whisperers*, 100.

76　"The Brutal Brilliance of Genghis Khan," www.historyextra.com, accessed February 13, 2019.

77　Cawthorne, *100 Tyrants*, 36.

78　Marc Fonda, "Canadian Census Figures on Aboriginal Spirituality Preferences: A Revitalization Movement?" *Religious Studies and Theology* 30, no. 2 (May 2012).

79　Reginald Bibby and James Penner, *The Emerging Millennials: How Canada's Next Generation Is Responding to Change and Choice* (Lethbridge, AB: Project Canada Books, 2009).

80 Lawrence Kirmayer and Gail Guthrie Valaskakis, *Healing Traditions: The Mental Health of Aboriginal Peoples in Canada* (Vancouver, BC: UBC Press, 2009), 98.

Chapter 6: Knowledge, Sacred and Profane

1 Marais, *History of Philosophy*, 10–14.
2 International Commission, *History of Mankind*, 10.
3 "Nicolaus Copernicus," *Encyclopedia Britannica*, www.britannica.com, accessed February 9, 2019.
4 Immanuel Kant, *Religion and Rational Thought* (Cambridge: Cambridge University Press, 1996), 13 and 57.
5 Ibid., 61.
6 "John Locke," *New World Encyclopedia*, www.newworldencyclopedia.org, accessed December 2, 2018.
7 "Thomas Hobbes," *Internet Encyclopedia of Philosophy*, www.iep.utm.edu, accessed December 4, 2018.
8 "John Locke," *New World Encyclopedia*, www.newworldencyclopedia.org, accessed December 2, 2018.
9 John Dunn, *Rethinking Modern Political Theory* (Cambridge: Cambridge University Press, 1985), 61.
10 Richard Gale, *On the Nature and Existence of God* (Cambridge: Cambridge University Press, 1991).
11 Peter Van Inwagen, *Existence: Essays in Ontology* (Cambridge: Cambridge University Press, 2014).
12 "Cogito, ergo sum," *Encyclopedia Britannica*, www.britannica.com, accessed December 5, 2018.
13 "Indus Valley Civilization," *New World Encyclopedia*, www.newworldencyclopedia.com, accessed March 10, 2019.
14 "Iroquois Confederacy," *Encyclopedia Britannica*, www.britannica.com, accessed March 31, 2019.
15 "Knowledge," www.dictionary.com, accessed November 23, 2018.
16 Leanne Simpson, *Dancing on Our Turtle's Back* (Winnipeg, MB: Arbeiter Ring Publishing, 2011), 32.
17 Frances Widdowson, "Academic Freedom and Indigenization: Should the Dissemination of Pseudoscientific 'Ways of Knowing' be Protected?" (paper presented at the Pseudo-Science and Academic Freedom Colloquium, Saint Mary's University, Halifax, November 4, 2016), 4 and 11.
18 Ibid., 21.
19 Ibid., 28.
20 Albert Howard, "Indigenizing the University: When Reason is Afraid to Speak," *Society for Academic Freedom and Scholarship* newsletter, September 2016.

21　"Herodotus," *Ancient History Encyclopedia*, https://www.ancient.eu, accessed March 1, 2019.

22　"Science," *Oxford Dictionaries*, www.oxforddictionaries.com, accessed February 22, 2019.

23　Indigenous Peoples explored science; however, such development was subservient to spirituality.

24　Kulchyski et al., *In the Words of Elders*, 56.

25　Nelson, *Original Instructions*, 178–79 and 262.

26　Ibid., 305.

27　Cajete, *Native Science*, 212.

28　Nelson, *Original Instructions*, 108.

29　Anonymous.

30　Cajete, *Native Science*, 79.

31　Ibid., 271.

32　Albert Einstein, *Albert Einstein, The Human Side: New Glimpses from His Archives* (Princeton: Princeton University Press, 1981), 32–33; and Alan Hugenot, *The New Science of Consciousness Survival* (Indianapolis: Dog Ear Publishing, 2016), 43.

Chapter 7: The Big Rush

1　Here Indigenous would include populations such as the Chinese, which although industrialized to a degree, have not subscribed to an ideology of disrespect of ancestors, rampant abuse of the environment, or global encroachment on the lands of others.

2　Paul R. Ehrlich, *The Population Bomb* (New York: Ballantine Books, 1968).

3　McAdam, *Nationhood Interrupted*, 28.

4　Suzuki, *The Sacred Balance*, 38

5　Ibid., 43

6　Mass psychosis is a form of mental disconnection that can occur on a mass scale.

7　Forbes, *Columbus and the Cannibals*, 22.

8　Ibid., 81.

9　Ibid., 146.

10　Ibid., xviii.

11　Paul Levy, *Dispelling Witeko: Breaking the Curse of Evil* (Berkeley,: North Atlantic Books, 2013), 228.

12　Ibid., 12.

13　Forbes, *Columbus and the Cannibals*, 160.

14　Ibid., 51.

15　Levy, *Dispelling Wetiko*, 105.

16　Forbes, *Columbus and the Cannibals*, 171.

17　Kulchyski et al., *In the Words of Elders*, 77.

18　Forbes, *Columbus and the Cannibals*, 61.

19　Ibid., 97.

20 Kulchyski et al., *In the Words of Elders*, 112.

21 Forbes, *Columbus and the Cannibals*, 108.

22 Ibid., 172.

23 Ibid., 15–16.

24 Levy, *Dispelling Wetiko*, 37.

25 Ibid., 54.

26 Stonechild, *The Knowledge Seeker*, 189.

27 Forbes, *Columbus and the Cannibals*, 52.

28 Levy, *Dispelling Wetiko*, 150.

29 Weatherford, *Indian Givers*, 46.

30 Ibid., 46, 49, and 55.

31 John H. Bodley, *Victims of Progress* (Mountain View, CA: Mayfield Publishing, 1982), 2.

32 James Otteson, ed., *Adam Smith: Selected Philosophical Writings* (Exeter, UK: Imprint Academic, 2012), 32.

33 "5 Shocking Facts about Extreme Global Inequality and How to Even It Up," Oxfam International, https://www.oxfam.org/en/5-shocking-facts-about-extreme-global-inequality-and-how-even-it, accessed December 2017.

34 Alexander C. Kaufman, "Pope Francis: 'Inequality Is the Root of Social Evil,'" *Huffington Post*, https://www.huffingtonpost.ca/2014/04/28/pope-francis-tweet-inequality_n_5227563.html, accessed December 2017.

35 "War," *Ancient History Encyclopedia*, www.ancient.eu, accessed August 30, 2017.

36 Joshua Mark, "War in Ancient Times," *Ancient History Encyclopedia*, www.ancient.eu, accessed September 14, 2019.

37 Mails, *The Mystic Warriors of the Plains*, 552–54.

38 President Dwight Eisenhower, Farewell Address to the Nation, January 17, 1961.

39 Nelson, *Original Instructions*, 9.

40 Kulchyski et al., *In the Words of Elders*, 53.

41 "Malaysian Airlines 370 Flight Disappearance," *Encyclopedia Britannica*, https://www.britannica.com/event/Malaysia-Airlines-flight-370-disappearance, accessed March 10, 2019.

42 "No 'Clear Motivating Factor' Inspired Las Vegas Gunman, FBI Says," *New York Times*, January 29, 2019.

43 "Trump Visits Shooting Victims, First Responders in Las Vegas," National Public Radio, www.npr.org, October 4, 2017.

44 Kulchyski et al., *In the Words of Elders*, 165.

45 Ibid., 61.

Chapter 8: Harming Our Relatives

1 "Great Chain of Being," *New World Encyclopedia*, www.newworldencyclopedia.org, accessed January 24, 2019.

2   "Anthropocene Epoch," www.encyclopedia.com, accessed April 4, 2019.

3   A significant amount of the current precipitous decline in various whale species can be attributed to ingestion of plastics or becoming entangled in nylon nets.

4   Elena Becatoros, "More Than 90 Percent of the World's Coral Reef Will Die by 2050," www.independent.co.uk, accessed March 13, 2017.

5   "What's New at the Honolulu Zoo," Honolulu Zoo Society, http://honoluluzoo.org/endangered-species-day/, accessed December 2017.

6   "Endangered Species," *National Geographic*, www.nationalgeographic.org, accessed April 10, 2017.

7   "Extinction," *Oxford Research Encyclopedia of Environmental Science*, https://oxfordre.com/environmentalscience, accessed April 19, 2017.

8   Martine Conservation Institute, "Destructive Fishing," www.marineconservation.org, accessed March 17, 2019.

9   "Passenger Pigeon," *New World Encyclopedia*, www.newworldencyclopedia.org, accessed May 30, 2017.

10   Suzuki, *The Sacred Balance*, 218.

11   "The Extinction Crisis," *Center for Biological Diversity*, http://www.biologicaldiversity.org/programs/biodiversity/elements_of_biodiversity/extinction_crisis/ accessed June 27, 2017.

12   Elizabeth Brown, "Widely Misinterpreted Report Still Shows Catastrophic Animal Decline," www.thenationalgeographic.com, November 1, 2018.

13   Mark Niemeyer, *Water: The Essence of Life* (London: Duncan Baird Publishers, 2008), 71–73.

14   Max Wilbert, "46% of Forests Have Been Destroyed by Civilization . . . and Counting," https://dgrnewsservice.org/civilization/ecocide/habitat-loss/46-of-forests-have-been-destroyed-by-civilizationand-counting/, July 24, 2018.

15   Ibid.

16   "Haze from Indonesian Fires May Have Killed More Than 100,000 People—Study," *The Guardian*, September 19, 2016, https://www.theguardian.com/world/2016/sep/19/haze-indonesia-forest-fires-killed-100000-people-harvard-study.

17   Robinson Meyer, "The Amazon Rainforest Was Profoundly Changed by Ancient Humans: The Region's Ecology Is a Product of 8,000 Years of Indigenous Agriculture," www.theatlantic.com, March 2, 2017, accessed September 10, 2019.

18   Dom Philips, "Bolsonaro Declares 'the Amazon Is Ours and Calls Deforestation Data Lies," www.theguardian.com, July 19, 2019.

19   Douglas Main, "Why Insect Populations Are Declining—And Why It Matters," www.nationalgeographic.com, February 14, 2019.

20   Laurie Goering, "Cities Face Dramatic Rise in Heat, Flood Risks by 2050, Researchers Say," https://www.100resilientcities.org/cities-face-dramatic-rise-in-heat-flood-risks-by-2050-researchers-say/, accessed March 28, 2019.

21 Jonathan Watts, "We Have 12 Years to Limit Climate Change Catastrophe, Warns UN," *The Guardian*, October 8, 2018.

22 See Climate Action Tracker for performance of each nation: https://climateactiontracker.org/.

23 Lyn Mettler, "Thirteen Islands that Will Disappear in the Next 80 Years," *Readers Digest*, https://www.rd.com/advice/travel/islands-will-disappear-80-years/, accessed April 15, 2019.

24 Sarah Kaplan, "By 2050,There Will Be More Plastic than Fish in the World's Oceans, Study Says," *Washington Post*, January 20, 2016, https://www.washingtonpost.com/news/morning-mix/wp/2016/01/20/by-2050-there-will-be-more-plastic-than-fish-in-the-worlds-oceans-study-says/.

25 *Dakota Pipeline Protests*, NBC News, https://www.nbcnews.com/storyline/dakota-pipeline-protests, accessed March 3, 2018.

26 "Turtle Lodge," *Onjisay Aki*, http://onjisay-aki.org/turtle-lodge, accessed January 18, 2019.

27 "Justin Trudeau Tells World Climate Fight Begins at Home," www.macleans.ca, November 30, 2015.

28 The Turtle Lodge Declaration was signed at the Turtle Lodge on Sagkeeng First Nation in September 2017.

29 David Wallace-Wells, "The Unihabitable Earth," *New York Magazine*, July 10, 2017.

30 Eric McLamb, "Impact of the Industrial Revolution," www.ecology.com, September 18, 2011.

31 Gretchen Daily, Anne Ehrlich, and Paul Ehrlich, "Optimum Population Size," Stanford University, July 1994. 1994, www.dieoff.com, accessed September 28, 2018.

32 "The Current Mass Extinction," https://www.pbs.org/wgbh/evolution/library/03/2/l_032_04.html, accessed April 10, 2019.

33 Nelson, *Original Instructions*, 8.

34 Ibid., 125.

35 Ibid., 23.

36 Suzuki, *The Sacred Balance*, 47.

37 Ibid.

38 Ibid.

39 This response was made by Elder Phil Lane in response to a question by the author at the Lodge of Nations, World Parliament of Religions, November 6, 2018.

40 Max Tegmark, "Benefits and Risks of Artificial Intelligence," https://futureoflife.org/background/benefits-risks-of-artificial-intelligence/, accessed December 2017.

41 Quincy Larson, "A Warning from Bill Gates, Elon Musk and Stephen Hawking,"https://www.freecodecamp.org/news/a-warning-from-bill-gates-elon-musk-and-stephen-hawking-f339e4bbfa9d/, accessed January 26, 2019.

42 "Why Should We Go to Mars?" www.mars-one.com, accessed October 19, 2017.

43   Steve Dent, "Getting To and Living on Mars Will Be Hell on Your Body," https://www.engadget.com/2017/10/27/getting-to-and-living-on-mars-will-be-hell-on-your-body/.

Chapter 9: Searching for Healing

1   Cajete, *Native Science*, 16.

2   Ibid., 5.

3   Ibid., 2–3.

4   Ibid., 19–21.

5   Jim B. Tucker, *Life Before Life: A Scientific Investigation of Children's Memories of Previous Lives* (New York: St. Martin's Press, 2005), 17–18.

6   Antonia Mills and Richard Slobodin, eds., *Amerindian Rebirth: Reincarnation Belief among North American Indians and Inuit* (Toronto: University of Toronto Press, 1994), 13.

7   Tucker, *Life Before Life*, 22–26.

8   Ibid., 9–10.

9   Dr. Ian Stevenson's work on the North West coast in Canada has been carried on by Dr. Antonia Mills, with whom the author has had the privilege of corresponding.

10   Ian Stevenson, *Reincarnation and Biology: A Contribution to the Etiology of Birthmarks and Birth Defects* (Westport, CT: Praeger Publishers, 1997).

11   Stevenson, *Where Reincarnation and Biology Intersect* (Westport, CT: Praeger Publishers, 1997).

12   Tucker, *Life Before Life*, 82–85.

13   Velma Goodfeather, interview with the author, Standing Buffalo First Nation, March 7, 2012. Velma passed into the spirit world two weeks after the interview. She told me that she had no fear of death.

14   Barry Ahenakew, interview with the author, Saskatoon, October 23, 2012.

15   Danny Musqua, interview with the author, Regina, April 12, 2012.

16   Noel Starblanket, interview with the author, October 14, 2013.

17   Dr. Jim Tucker, child psychiatrist at the University of Virginia School of Medicine (Charlottesville), had no previous belief in reincarnation.

18   Ibid., 212.

19   Raymond Moody, *Life After Life* (San Francisco: Harper, 2001), 77.

20   Jeffrey Long and Paul Perry, *Evidence of the Afterlife: The Science of Near-Death Experiences* (New York: Harper One, 2010), 102.

21   http://www.nourfoundation.com/events/Beyond-the-Mind-Body-Problem/The-Human-Consciousness-Project/researchers-and-scientific-advisory-group.html.

22   Denis Brian, *Einstein: A Life* (New York: John Wiley & Sons, 1996), 65; and John D. Norton, "Chasing the Light: Einstein's Most Famous Thought Experiment," in *Thought Experiments in Philosophy, Science and the Arts*, eds. Frappier, Meynell, and Brown (New York: Routledge, 2013), 123–40.

23 Energy equals mass times the speed of light squared.

24 James Randerson, "Childish Superstition: Einstein's Letter Makes View of Religion Relatively Clear," *The Guardian*, May 13, 2008.

25 F. David Peat, *Einstein's Moon: Bell's Theorem and the Curious Quest for Quantum Reality* (Chicago: Contemporary Books, 1990), 19 and 54.

26 "Consciousness," www.dictionary.com, accessed February 8, 2018.

27 Phillip Low, "The Cambridge Declaration on Consciousness" (proclaimed atthe Francis Crick Memorial Conference on Consciousness in Human and Non-Human Animals, at Churchill College, University of Cambridge, July 7, 2012), http://fcmconference.org/img/CambridgeDeclarationOnConsciousness.pdf, accessed February 9, 2018.

28 Quoted in Tucker, *Life Before Life*, 168.

29 Ibid., 166.

30 Peter Tompkins and Christopher Bird, *The Secret Life of Plants* (New York: Harper Perennial, 1973), 96.

31 Ibid., 114.

32 "Telepathy," *New World Encyclopedia*, www.newworldencyclopedia.org, accessed January 14, 2018.

33 Brennan, *Whisperers*, 307.

34 C.G. Jung, "The Concept of the Collective Unconscious," *The Jung Page*, http://www.cgjungpage.org/learn/articles/analytical-psychology/527-the-concept-of-the-collective-unconscious, accessed December 2017.

35 Anthony Storr, *The Essential Jung* (Princeton: Princeton University Press, 1983), 233.

36 Brennan, *Whisperers*, 341.

37 Ibid., 338–39.

38 Ibid., 341.

39 Ibid., 97–98.

40 Ibid., 100.

41 Einstein and Bohm were close, with Einstein once referring to Bohm as his "spiritual son." www.thebohmdocumentary.org, accessed February 12, 2019.

42 Katz, *Indigenous Healing Psychology*, 392–94. Bohm proposed his theory in *Thought as a System* (New York: Routledge, 1994).

43 Ibid., 385–86.

44 Waldram, *The Way of the Pipe*, 102.

45 Nelson, *Original Instructions*, 46.

46 Waldram, *The Way of the Pipe*, 115.

47 Nelson, *Original Instructions*, 184.

Chapter 10: Need for Reconciliation

1 "Reconciliation," *Cambridge English Dictionary* (online).

2 Tyrone Tootoosis, interview with the author, Saskatoon, April 11, 2012.

3   Jennifer Dockstator, "Widening the Sweetrass Road" (PhD diss. Trent University, 2014) gives an excellent description of how the Medicine Circle is utilized.

4   Nelson, *Original Instructions*, 24.

5   Larry J. Zimmerman, *Sacred Wisdom of the American Indians* (London: Watkins Publishing, 2011), 254.

6   Widdowson, "Academic Freedom and Indigenization," 22.

7   "Billions of Earth-like Planets in Milky Way," http://www.cbc.ca/news/technology/billions-of-earth-like-planets-in-milky-way-study-1.2356237, accessed November 4, 2013.

8   Kulchyski et al., *In the Words of Elders*, 52.

9   United Nations Department of Economic and Social Affairs, "United Nations Declaration on the Rights of Indigenous Peoples—Historical Overview," www.un.org/development/desa, accessed March 22, 2019.

10 "Bolivia Enshrines Natural World's Rights with Equal Status for Mother Earth," *The Guardian*, April 10, 2011, https://www.theguardian.com/environment/2011/apr/10/bolivia-enshrines-natural-worlds-rights.

11 Nelson, *Original Instructions*, 258–59.

Appendix 2

1   United Nations, *Declaration on the Rights of Indigenous Peoples* (New York, 2007).

BIBLIOGRAPHY

Elders and Knowledge Keepers Cited:

Albert Ward, Mi'kmaq
Allan Ross, Lakota
Buffy Sainte-Marie, Cree
Campbell Papequash, Saulteaux
Danny Musqua, Saulteaux
Dave Courchene, Jr., Anishinaabe
Ernest Benedict, Haudenosaunee
Ernest Tootoosis, Cree
Eva Mckay, Dakota
Evehema, Hopi
Fool's Crow, Lakota
Gordon Oakes, Cree
Gregory Cajete, Tewa
Harold Cardinal, Cree
Harold Johnson, Cree
Jack Forbes, Powhatan-Renapé
Jim Ryder, Assiniboine

John Mohawk, Seneca
John Trudell, Lakota
Katsi Cook, Mohawk
Noel Pinay, Cree
Noel Starblanket, Cree
Oren Lyons, Onondaga
Paula Gunn Allen, Laguna-Sioux
Phil Lane, Dakota
Thomas Banyaca, Hopi
Tony Sand, Cree
Wilfred Tootoosis, Cree
Velma Goodfeather, Dakota
Vine Deloria, Jr., Lakota
Walter Linklater, Anishinaabe
Wilfred Buck, Cree
Willam Asikinack, Anishinaabe

Works Consulted:

Ahenakew, Freda. *âh-âyîtaw isi ê-kî-kiskêyihtahkik maskihkiy / They Knew Both Sides of Medicine: Cree Tales of Curing and Cursing Told by Alice Ahenakew.* Winnipeg, MA: University of Manitoba Press, 1998.

Akbar, Ahmed. *Islam Under Siege.* Cambridge: Polity Press, 2003.

Allen, Paula Gunn. *Grandmothers of the Light: A Medicine Woman's Sourcebook.* Boston, MA: Beacon Press, 1991.

———. *The Sacred Hoop, Recovering the Feminine in American Indian Traditions.* Boston, MA: Beacon Press, 1992.

Anderson, Leona, ed. *Introduction to Religious Studies,* 3rd edition. Regina, SK: University of Regina, 2008.

Armstrong, Karen. *The Bible: A Biography.* New York: Grove Press, 2007.

Arnal, William. "Christianity." In *Introduction to Religious Studies,* 3rd edition, edited by Leona Anderson. Regina, SK: University of Regina, 2008.

Asikinack, William. "Sweat-Lodge Ceremony." In *The Encyclopedia of Saskatchewan.* Regina, SK: Canadian Plains Research Center, 2005.

Atleo, E. Richard. *Principles of Tsawalk: An Indigenous Approach to Global Crisis.* Vancouver: UBC Press, 2012.

Balsdon, J.P. *Romans and Aliens.* Chapel Hill, NC: University of North Carolina Press, 1979.

Barnosky, Anthony. *Dodging Extinction: Power, Food, Money and the Future of Life on Earth.* Oakland, CA: University of California Press, 2014.

Battiste, Marie Ann, and James Youngblood Henderson. *Protecting Indigenous Knowledge and Heritage: A Global Challenge.* Saskatoon, SK: Purich Publishing, 2000.

Bennett, Hal Zina. *Spirit Circle: A Story of Adventure & Shamanic Revelation.* Arkansas City, KS: Tenacity Press, 1998.

Bibby, Reginald, and James Penner. *The Emerging Millennials: How Canada's Next Generation Is Responding to Change and Choice.* Lethbridge, AB: Project Canada Books, 2009.

Bird, Louis. *The Spirit Lives in the Mind.* Montreal: McGill-Queen's Press, 2007.

Bitterli, Urs. *Cultures in Conflict.* Cambridge: Polity Press, 1989.

Bjarnason, Paul. *Stargazers: Stories of the First Philosophers.* Winchester, UK: O. Books, 2007.

Black Elk, Wallace, and William S. Lyon. *Black Elk: The Sacred Ways of a Lakota.* New York: HarperOne, 1991.

Blackman, Sushila, ed. *Graceful Exits: How Great Beings Die.* New York: Weatherhill, 1997.

Blaisdell, Bob. *Great Speeches by Native Americans.* Mineola, NY: Dover Publications, Inc., 2000.

Bloomfield, Leonard. *Sacred Stories of the Sweet Grass Cree.* Ottawa, ON: National Museum of Canada, 1930.

Boatman, John. *My Elders Taught Me: Aspects of Western Great Lakes American Indian Philosophy.* Lanham, MD: University Press of America, 1992.

Bodley, John H. *Victims of Progress.* Mountain View, CA: Mayfield Publishing, 1982.

Bohm, David. *Thought as a System.* New York: Routledge, 1994.

———. *Wholeness and the Implicate Order.* New York: Routledge, 1980.

Boulter, Michael. *Extinction: Evolution and the End of Man.* New York: Columbia University Press, 2002.

Bradford, Tolly, and Chelsea Horton. *Mixed Blessings: Indigenous Encounters with Christianity in Canada.* Vancouver, BC: UBC Press, 2016.

Brennan, J.H. *Whisperers: The Secret History of the Spirit World.* London: Overlook Duckworth, 2013.

Brian, Denis. *Einstein: A Life.* New York: John Wiley & Sons, 1996.

Brightman, Robert. *Grateful Prey: Rock Cree Human-Animal Relationships.* Regina, SK: Canadian Plains Research Center, 2002.

Brown, Dee. *Bury My Heart at Wounded Knee.* New York: Bantam Books, 1973.

Brown, Harold O.J. *Heresies: The Image of Christ in the Mirror of Heresy and Orthodoxy from the Apostles to the Present.* Toronto: Doubleday & Company, 1984.

Brown, Jennifer S.H., and Robert Brightman. *The Orders of the Dreamed: George Nelson on Cree and Northern Ojibwa Religion and Myth, 1823.* Winnipeg, MB: University of Manitoba Press, 1988.

Brown, Joseph Epes. *Teaching Spirits: Understanding Native American Religious Traditions.* New York: Oxford University Press, 2001.

Bryce, P.H. *The Story of a National Crime: Being an Appeal for Justice to the Indians of Canada.* Ottawa, ON: James Hope and Sons Limited, 1922.

Cairns, Alan C. *Citizens Plus: Aboriginal Peoples and the Canadian State.* Vancouver, BC: UBC Press, 2000.

Cajete, Gregory. *Native Science: Natural Laws of Interdependence.* Santa Fe, NM: Clear Light Publishers, 2000.

Cardinal, Harold. *The Unjust Society: The Tragedy of Canada's Indians.* Edmonton, AB: M.G. Hurtig, 1969.

Cardinal, Harold, and Walter Hildebrandt. *Treaty Elders of Saskatchewan: Our Dream Is That Our Peoples Will One Day Be Clearly Recognized as Nations.* Calgary, AB: University of Calgary Press, 2000.

Carter, Sarah. *Aboriginal People and Colonizers of Western Canada to 1900.* Toronto: University of Toronto Press, 1999.

———. *Lost Harvests: Prairie Indian Reserve Farmers and Government Policy.* Montreal: McGill-Queen's University Press, 1990.

Cawthorne, Nigel. *100 Tyrants.* London: Arcturus, 2010.

Choquette, Robert. *The Oblate Assault on Canada's Northwest.* Ottawa: University of Ottawa Press, 1995.

Christensen, Deanna. *Ahtahkakoop: The Epic Account of a Plains Cree Head Chief, His People, and Their Struggle for Survival, 1816–1896.* Shell Lake, SK: Ahtahkakoop Publishing, 2000.

Clayton, Lawrence. *Bartolomé de las Casas: A Biography.* Cambridge: Cambridge University Press, 2012.

Conner, Nancy, and Bradford Keeney. *Shamans of the World: Extraordinary First Person Accounts of Healings, Mysteries, and Miracles.* Boulder, CO: Sounds True, 2008.

Crow Dog, Leonard, and Richard Erdoes. *Crow Dog: Four Generations of Sioux Medicine Men.* New York: Harper Perennial, 1995.

Daschuk, James. *Clearing the Plains: Disease, Politics of Starvation, and the Loss of Aboriginal Life*. Regina, SK: University of Regina Press, 2013.

Davis, James. *The Human Story: Our History from the Stone Age to Today*. New York: Harper Collins, 2004.

Dawkins, Richard. *The God Delusion*. Boston, MA: Houghton Mifflin Company, 2006.

Deloria, Vine, Jr. *Custer Died for Your Sins: An Indian Manifesto*. Norman, OK: University of Oklahoma Press, 1969.

———. *God Is Red: A Native View of Religion*. New York: G.P. Putnam's Sons, 1973.

———. *The World We Used to Live In: Remembering the Powers of the Medicine Man*. Golden, CO: Fulcrum Publishing, 2006.

Dempsey, Hugh A. *Big Bear: The End of Freedom*. Vancouver, BC: Douglas & McIntyre, 1984.

Dempsey, James. "The Persistence of a Warrior Ethic among the Plains Indians." *Alberta History* 36, no. 1 (Winter 1988).

Denevan, William M. *The Native Population of the Americas in 1492*. Madison, WI: University of Wisconsin Press, 1992.

Diamond, Jared. *Guns, Germs & Steel: The Fates of Human Societies*. New York: W.W. Norton & Company, 1999.

Dickason, Olive Patricia. *A Concise History of Canada's First Nations*. Don Mills, ON: Oxford University Press Canada, 2006.

———. *Canada's First Nations: A History of Founding Peoples from Earliest Times*. Toronto: Oxford University Press, 2002.

———. *The Myth of the Savage: And the Beginnings of French Colonialism in the Americas*. Edmonton, AB: University of Alberta Press, 1997.

Dockstator, Jennifer. "Widening the Sweetgrass Road: Re/Balancing Ways of Knowing for Sustainable Living with a Cree-Nishnaabe Medicine Circle." (PhD dissertation), Trent University, 2014.

Dunn, John. *Rethinking Modern Political Theory*. Cambridge: Cambridge University Press, 1985.

Eagle, Chokecherry Gall. *Beyond the Lodge of the Sun: Inner Mysteries of the Native American Way*. Rockport, MA: Element Books, 1997.

Eagle Feather, Ken. *Traveling with Power: The Exploration and Development of Perception*. Charlottesville, NC: Hampton Roads Publishing, 1992.

Einstein, Albert. *Albert Einstein, The Human Side: New Glimpses from His Archives*. Princeton: Princeton University Press, 1981.

Eliade, Mircea. *Shamanism: Archaic Techniques of Ecstasy*. Princeton: Princeton University Press, 1964.

Endredy, James. *Shamanism for Beginners: Walking with the World's Healers of Earth and Sky*. Woodbury, MN: Llewellyn Worldwide, 2009.

Erdoes, Richard. *The Sun Dance People: The Plains Indian, Their Past and Present*. New York: Random House, 1972.

Ehrlich, Paul R. *The Population Bomb*. New York: Ballantine Books, 1968.

Ernst, Carl. *Rethinking Islam in the Contemporary World*. Edinburgh: Edinburgh University Press, 2004.

Federation of Saskatchewan Indians. *Elders' Interpretation of Treaty 4: A Report on the Treaty Interpretation Project*. Saskatoon, SK: Federation of Saskatchewan Indians, 1978.

Ferguson, Niall. *Civilization*. London: Penguin Press, 2011.

Fiola, Chantal. *Rekindling the Sacred Fire: Métis Ancestry and Anishinaabe Spirituality*. Winnipeg, MA: University of Manitoba Press, 2014.

Forbes, Jack. *Columbus and Other Cannibals*. New York: Seven Stories Press, 2008.

Fonda, Marc. "Canadian Census Figures on Aboriginal Spirituality Preferences: A Revitalization Movement?" In *Religious Studies and Theology* 30, no. 2 (May 2012): 169–185.

Friesen, Gerald. *The Canadian Prairies: A History*. Toronto: University of Toronto Press, 1987.

Friesen, John W. *Aboriginal Spirituality and Biblical Theology: Closer Than You Think*. Edmonton, AB: Brush Education, 2000.

Gale, Richard. *On the Nature and Existence of God*. Cambridge: Cambridge University Press, 1991.

Gill, Sam D. *Native American Religions: An Introduction*. Boston: Wadsworth Publishing, 1982.

Goulet, Jean-Guy. *Ways of Knowing*. Vancouver, BC: UBC Press, 1998.

Goulet, Jean-Guy, and Bruce G. Miller. *Extraordinary Anthropology*. Lincoln, NB: University of Nebraska Press, 2006.

Grant, John Webster. *Moon of Wintertime: Missionaries and the Indians of Canada in Encounter Since 1534*. Toronto: University of Toronto Press, 1984.

Greifenhagen, Franz Volker. "Islam(s)." In *Introduction to Religious Studies*, edited by Leona Anderson. Regina, SK: University of Regina, 2008.

Grossman, Dave. *On Killing: The Psychological Cost of Learning to Kill in War and Society*. New York: Back Bay Books, 1996.

Hamid, Shadi. *Islamic Exceptionalism: How the Struggle over Islam Is Reshaping the World*. New York: St. Martin's Press, 2016.

Hannigan, Tim. *A Brief History of Indonesia*. North Clarendon, VT: Tuttle Publishing, 2015.

Harner, Michael. *The Way of the Shaman*. New York: Harper One, 1980.

Harpur, Tom. *The Pagan Christ*. Toronto: Thomas Allen Publishers, 2004.

Helewa, Sami. *Models of Leadership in the Adab Narratives of Joseph, David and Solomon*. New York: Lexington Books, 2018.

Hofdstater, Richard. *Social Darwinism in American Thought*. Boston: Beacon Press, 1992.

Hogan, Linda, ed. *The Inner Journey: Views from Native Traditions*. Sandpoint, ID: Morning Light Press, 2009.

Hotaling, Ed. *Islam Without Illusions: Its Past, Its Present, and Its Challenge for the Future*. Syracuse, NY: Syracuse University Press, 2003.

Howard, Albert. "Indigenizing the University: When Reason is Afraid to Speak." In *Society for Academic Freedom and Scholarship* newsletter, September 2016.

Hoxie, Frederick, ed. *Encyclopedia of North American Indians.* New York: Houghton Mifflin, 1996.

Hultkrantz, Åke. *Native Religions of North America: The Power of Visions and Fertility.* New York: Harper & Row, 1987.

Hultkrantz, Åke, and Walter Capps. *Seeing with a Native Eye: Essays on Native American Religion.* New York: Harper Forum Books, 1976.

Hugenot, Alan. *The New Science of Consciousness Survival.* Indianapolis: Dog Ear Publishing, 2016.

Human Consciousness Project. http://www.nourfoundation.com/events/Beyond-the-Mind-Body-Problem/The-Human-Consciousness-Project.html. Accessed February 11, 2018.

Huntington, Samuel. *The Clash of Civilizations and Remaking of World Order.* New York: Simon & Schuster, 1996.

"Indigenous Religions Today." In *Atlas of World Religions.* London: Laurence King Publishing, 2005.

First Peoples Theology Journal. Tucson: Indigenous Theological Training Institute, 2000.

Indian Act, 1880, SC 1880, c 28.

Innes, Robert Alexander. *Elder Brother and the Law of the People: Contemporary Kinship and Cowessess First Nation.* Winnipeg, MA: University of Manitoba Press, 2013.

International Commission for a History of the Scientific and Cultural Development of Mankind. *History of Mankind: Cultural and Scientific Development: Prehistory and the Beginnings of Civilization,* vol. 1. London: George Allen & Unwin, 1965.

Irwin, Lee. *Native American Spirituality: A Critical Reader.* Lincoln, NB: University of Nebraska Press, 2000.

Jefferson, Warren. *Reincarnation Beliefs of North American Indians: Soul Journeys, Metamorphosis, and Near-Death Experiences.* Summertown, TN: Native Voices Books, 2008.

Jenkins, Philip. *Dream Catchers: How Mainstream America Discovered Native Spirituality.* Oxford: Oxford University Press, 2004.

Johnston, Basil. *The Manitows: The Spiritual World of the Ojibway.* St. Paul, MN: Minnesota Historical Society, 2001.

———. *Ojibway Ceremonies.* Toronto: McClelland and Stewart, 1982.

———. *Ojibway Heritage.* Toronto: McClelland and Stewart, 1976.

Johnson, Harold. *Two Families: Treaties and Government.* Vancouver, BC: UBC Press, 2007.

Jorgensen, Joseph G. *The Sun Dance Religion: Power for the Powerless.* Chicago: University of Chicago Press, 1972.

Juschka, Darlene. "Religious Studies and the Study of Religion." In *Introduction to Religious Studies*, 3rd edition, edited by Leona Anderson. Regina, SK: University of Regina, 2008.

Kant, Immanuel. *Religion and Rational Thought*. Cambridge: Cambridge University Press, 1996.

Katz, Richard. *Boiling Energy: Community Healing Among the Kalahari Kung*. Cambridge: Harvard University Press, 1984.

———. *Indigenous Healing Psychology: Honoring the Wisdom of the First Peoples*. Rochester, NY: Healing Arts Press, 2017.

———. *The Straight Path*. Reading, MA: Addison-Wesley, 1993.

Katz, Richard, and Stephen Murphy-Shigematsu. *Synergy, Healing and Empowerment: Insights from Cultural Diversity*. Edmonton, AB: Brush Education, 2012.

Kawagley, Angayuqaq Oscar. *A Yupiaq Worldview: A Pathway to Ecology and Spirit*. Long Grove, IL: Waveland Press, 1995.

Kearney, Richard, and Jens Zimmerman. *Reimagining the Sacred*. New York: Columbia University Press, 2016.

Keeley, Lawrence. *War Before Civilization: The Myth of the Peaceful Savage*. New York, NY: Oxford University Press, 1996.

Kehoe, Alice Beck. *Saskatchewan Indian Religious Beliefs*. Regina: Saskatchewan Museum of Natural History, 1963.

Khan, Muhammad Zafrullah. *Islam: Its Meaning for Modern Man*. London: The London Mosque, 2004.

Kimmerer, Robin W. *Braiding Sweetgrass*. Minneapolis: Milkweed Editions, 2013.

King, Victor. *The Peoples of Borneo*. Oxford: Blackwell Publishers, 1993.

Kingsnorth, Paul. *Confessions of a Recovering Environmentalist and Other Essays*. London: Faber and Faber, 2017.

Kirkness, Verna J. *Creating Space: My Life and Work in Indigenous Education*. Winnipeg, MB: University of Manitoba Press, 2013.

Kirmayer, Lawrence, and Gail Guthrie Valaskakis. *Healing Traditions: The Mental Health of Aboriginal Peoples in Canada*. Vancouver, BC: UBC Press, 2009.

Knight, Diane. *The Seven Fires: Teachings of the Bear Clan as Recounted by Dan Musqua*. Muskoday First Nation, SK: Many Worlds Publishing, 2001.

Koning, Hans. *Columbus: His Enterprise*. New York: Monthly Review Press, 1991.

Krasowski, Sheldon. *No Surrender: The Land Remains Indigenous*. Regina, SK: University of Regina Press, 2019.

Krickenberg, Walter, et al. *Pre-Columbian American Religions*. London: Weidfeld and Nicolson, 1968.

Kulchyski, Peter, Don McCaskill, and David Newhouse, eds. *In the Words of Elders: Aboriginal Cultures in Transition*. Toronto: University of Toronto Press, 1999.

Lambert, Malcolm. *God's Armies: Crusade and Jihad: Origins, History, Aftermath*. New York: Pegasus Books, 2016.

Lame Deer, Archie Fire, and Richard Erdoes. *Gift of Power: The Life and Teachings of a Lakota Medicine Man*. Rochester, VT: Bear & Company, 1992.

Lame Deer, John (Fire), and Richard Erdoes. *Lame Deer, Seeker of Visions*. New York: Simon & Schuster, 1994.

Lane, Phil Jr., et al. *The Sacred Tree: Reflections on Native American Spirituality*. Surrey, BC: Four Worlds International Institute, 1984.

Levy, Paul. *Dispelling Witeko: Breaking the Curse of Evil*. Berkeley, CA: North Atlantic Books, 2013.

Levy-Bruhl, Lucien. *How Natives Think*. Princeton: Princeton University Press, 1985.

Lightning, Albert. "The Compassionate Mind: Implications of a Text Written by Elder Louis Sunchild." (MA thesis), University of Alberta, Edmonton, 1992.

Long, Jeffrey, and Paul Perry. *Evidence of the Afterlife: The Science of Near-Death Experiences*. New York: Harper One, 2010.

Lyon, William S. *Encyclopedia of Native American Healing*. New York: Norton, 1996.

———. *Spirit Talkers: North American Indian Medicine Powers*. Kansas City: Prayer Efficacy Publishing, 2012.

Maddison, Angus. *The World Economy: Historical Statistics*, vol. 2. Paris: OECD iLibrary, 2003. https://doi.org/10.1787/9789264104143-en.

Mails, Thomas E. *Fools Crow*. Lincoln: University of Nebraska Press, 1979.

———. *Fools Crow: Wisdom and Power*. Graham, NC: Millichap Books, 2012.

———. *The Mystic Warriors of the Plains*. New York: Doubleday, 1972.

———. *Secret Native American Pathways: A Guide to Inner Peace*. San Francisco: Council Oak Books, 1998.

Mandelbaum, David G. *The Plains Cree: An Ethnographic, Historical and Comparative Study*. Regina, SK: Canadian Plains Research Center, 1979.

Mann, Charles. *1491: New Revelations of the Americas before Columbus*, 2nd edition. New York: Vintage Books, 2011.

Manuel, Arthur, and Grand Chief Ronald M. Derrickson. *Unsettling Canada: A National Wake-up Call*. Toronto: Between the Lines, 2015.

Marais, Julian. *History of Philosophy*. New York: Dover Publications, 1967.

Mark, Joshua J. "War." In *Ancient History Encyclopedia*. http://www.ancient.eu.war/.

Marshall, Joseph. *The Lakota Way: Stories and Lessons for Living*. New York: Penguin, 2002.

McAdam, Sylvia. *Nationhood Interrupted: Revitalizing Nehiyaw Legal Systems*. Saskatoon, SK: Purich Publishing, 2015.

McGaa, Ed. *Mother Earth Spirituality*. New York: Harper One, 1990.

McGeough, Kevin. *The Romans: New Perspectives*. Santa Barbara, CA: ABC-CLIO Inc., 2004.

McNeil, Kent. "Social Darwinism and Judicial Conceptions of Indian Title in Canada in the 1880s." *Journal of the West* 38, no.1 (January 1999): 68–76.

Meadows, Kenneth. *Shamanic Spirit: A Practical Guide to Personal Fulfillment.* Rochester, VT: Bear & Company, 1995.

Mehl-Madrona, Lewis. *Narrative Medicine: The Use of History and Story in the Healing Process.* Rochester, VT: Bear & Company, 2007.

Miller, J.R. *Shingwauk's Vision: A History of Native Residential Schools.* Toronto: University of Toronto Press, 1996.

Milloy, John. *A National Crime: The Canadian Government and the Residential School System, 1879–1986.* Winnipeg, MB: University of Manitoba Press, 1999.

———. *The Plains Cree: Trade, Diplomacy and War, 1790–1870.* Winnipeg, MB: University of Manitoba Press, 1988.

Mills, Antonia, and Richard Slobodin, eds. *Amerindian Rebirth: Reincarnation Belief among North American Indians and Inuit.* Toronto: University of Toronto Press, 1994.

Mithen, Steven. *The Prehistory of the Mind.* London: Thames and Hudson, 1996.

Monroe, Robert A. *Far Journeys.* New York: Doubleday, 1985.

———. *Journeys Out of the Body.* New York: Doubleday, 1971.

Montagu, Ashley. *The Direction of Human Development.* New York: Harper, 1955.

———. *The Nature of Human Aggression.* Oxford: Oxford University Press, 1976.

Moody, Raymond. *Life After Life.* San Francisco: Harper, 2001.

Morris, Alexander. *The Treaties of Canada with the Indians of Manitoba and the North-West Territories.* Reprint. Toronto: Coles Publishing Company, 1979.

Nagel, Tilman. *The History of Islamic Theology.* Princeton: Markus Wiener Publishers, 2006.

Neihardt, John G. *Black Elk Speaks: Being the Life Story of a Holy Man of the Ogalala Sioux.* Lincoln, NB: University of Nebraska Press, 1932.

Nelson, Kevin, M.D. *The Spiritual Doorway to the Brain.* New York: Dutton, 2011.

Nelson, Melissa. *Original Instructions: Indigenous Teachings for a Sustainable Future.* Rochester, VT: Bear & Company, 2008.

Neuhaus, Richard J., ed. *Unsecular America.* Grand Rapids, MI: William B. Eerdmans Publishing Company, 1986.

Newton, Michael. *Journey of Souls: Case Studies of Life Between Lives.* Woodbury, MN: Llewellyn Worldwide Publications, 2008.

Niemeyer, Mark. *Water: The Essence of Life.* London: Duncan Baird Publishers, 2008.

Norton, John D. "Chasing the Light: Einstein's Most Famous Thought Experiment." In *Thought Experiments in Philosophy, Science and the Arts*, edited by Mélanie Frappier, Letitia Meynell, and James Robert Brown, 123–40. New York: Routledge, 2013.

Otteson, James, ed. *Adam Smith: Selected Philosophical Writings.* Exeter, UK: Imprint Academic, 2012.

Ovey, Richard. *The Times History of the World.* New York: New York Times Books, 2008.

Paper, Jordan. *Native North American Religious Traditions: Dancing for Life.* Westport, CT: Praeger, 2007.

Peat, F. David. *Blackfoot Physics: A Journey into the Native American Universe.* Newburyport, MA: Phanes Press, 2002.

———. *Einstein's Moon: Bell's Theorem and the Curious Quest for Quantum Reality.* Chicago: Contemporary Books, 1990.

———. *Infinite Potential: The Life and Times of David Bohm.* New York: Perseus Books, 1996.

Pettipas, Katherine. *Severing the Ties That Bind: Government Repression of Indigenous Religious Ceremonies on the Prairies.* Winnipeg, MB: University of Manitoba Press, 1994.

Plato. *The Republic.* Translated by Benjamin Jowett. The Internet Classics Archives. http://classics.mit.edu/Plato/republic.html.

Pratt, Doris, Harry Bone, and the Treaty and Dakota Elders of Manitoba. *Untuwe Pi Kin He: Who We Are.* Winnipeg, MB: Treaty Relations Commission of Manitoba, 2014.

Radin, Paul. *Primitive Man as Philosopher.* Hicksville, NY: Maudsley Press, 1927.

Ray, Arthur J. *Indians in the Fur Trade: Their Role as Trappers, Hunters and Middlemen in the Lands Southwest of Hudson Bay, 1660–1870.* Toronto: University of Toronto Press, 1998.

Ray, Arthur J., Jim Miller, and Frank J. Tough. *Bounty and Benevolence: A History of Saskatchewan Treaties.* Montreal: McGill-Queen's University Press, 2000.

Relland, Michael Roger. "The Teachings of the Bear Clan: As Told by Saulteaux Elder Danny Musqua." (MEd thesis), University of Saskatchewan, 1998.

Rice, Brian, Jill Elizabeth Oakes, and Roderick R. Riewe. *Seeing the World with Aboriginal Eyes: A Four Directional Perspective on Human and Non-Human Values, Cultures and Relationships on Turtle Island.* Winnipeg, MB: Aboriginal Issues Press, 2005.

Starblanket: A Spirit Journey. (DVD and soundtrack). Ocate, NM: Rites of Passage, 2006.

Rodriguez, Junius. *The Historical Encyclopedia of World Slavery,* vol. 1. Oxford: ABC-CLIO, 1997.

Roskind, Robert. *The Beauty Path.* Blowing Rock, NC: One Love Press, 2006.

Ross, Allen C. *Mitakuye Oyasin: We Are All Related.* Fort Yates, ND: Bear Publishing, 1989.

Royal Commission on Aboriginal Peoples. *The Report of the Royal Commission on Aboriginal Peoples.* Ottawa: Government of Canada, 2005.

Rubinstein, W.D. *Genocide: A History.* London, UK: Pearson Longman, 2004.

Saskatchewan Indian Cultural Centre. *Cultural Teachings.* Saskatoon, SK: Saskatchewan Indian Cultural Centre, 2009.

Schaef, Anne Wilson. *Native Wisdom for White Minds: Daily Reflections Inspired by the Native Peoples of the World.* New York: Random House, 1995.

Shroder, Tom. *Old Souls: Compelling Evidence from Children Who Remember Past Lives.* New York: Simon & Shuster, 2001.

Simon, Sarah, et al. *Bridges in Spirituality: First Nations Christian Women Tell Their Stories*. Toronto: United Church Publishing House, 1997.

Simpson, Leanne. *Dancing on Our Turtle's Back*. Winnipeg, MB: Arbeiter Ring Publishing, 2011.

Sinclair, Niigaanwewidam James, and Warren Carriou. *Manitowapow*. Winnipeg, MB: High Water Press, 2011.

Sinclair, Raven. *Wicihitowin*. Winnipeg, MB: Fernwood Publishing, 2009.

Sioui, Georges E. *For an Amerindian Autohistory: An Essay on the Foundations of a Social Ethic*. Montreal: McGill-Queen's University Press, 1992.

———. *Huron Wendat: The Heritage of the Circle*. Vancouver, BC: University of British Columbia Press, 1999.

Smallman, Shawn. *Dangerous Spirits: The Windigo in Myth and History*. Victoria, BC: Heritage House, 2014.

Smith, Linda Tuhiwai. *Decolonizing Methodologies: Research and Indigenous Peoples*. London: ZED Books, 2012.

Spencer, Herbert. "Progress: Its Law and Cause." *Westminster Review* 67 (April 1857).

Sprague, D.N. *Canada and the Métis, 1869–1885*. Waterloo, ON: Wilfrid Laurier University Press, 1988.

Stead, Christopher. *Philosophy in Christian Antiquity*. Cambridge: Cambridge University Press, 1994.

Stevenson, Ian. *Reincarnation and Biology: A Contribution to the Etiology of Birthmarks and Birth Defects*. Westport, CT: Praeger Publishers, 1997.

———. *Twenty Cases Suggestive of Reincarnation*. Charlottesville, NC: University Press of Virginia, 1966.

———. *Where Reincarnation and Biology Intersect*. Westport, CT: Praeger Publishers, 1997.

Stonechild, Blair. *Buffy Sainte-Marie: It's My Way*. Toronto: Fifth House, 2012.

———. *The Knowledge Seeker: Embracing Indigenous Spirituality*. Regina, SK: University of Regina Press, 2016.

———. *The New Buffalo: The Struggle for Aboriginal Post-Secondary Education in Canada*. Winnipeg, MB: University of Manitoba Press, 2006.

———. "Recovering the Heritage of Treaty Number Four." In *Plain Speaking: Essays on Aboriginal Peoples and the Prairie*, edited by P. Douaud and B. Dawson, 1–10. Regina, SK: Canadian Plains Research Center, 2002.

Stonechild, Blair, and Bill Waiser. *Loyal Till Death: Indians and the North-West Rebellion*. Toronto: Fifth House, 1997.

Storm, Hyemeyohsts. *Seven Arrows*. New York: Ballentine Books, 1972.

Storr, Anthony. *The Essential Jung*. Princeton: Princeton University Press, 1983.

Sulkin, Carlos David Londoño. *People of Substance: An Ethnography of Morality in the Colombian Amazon*. Toronto: University of Toronto Press, 2012.

Sun Bear and Wabun. *The Medicine Wheel: Earth Astrology*. Toronto: A Fireside Book, 1980.

Suzuki, David. *The Sacred Balance: Rediscovering Our Place in Nature.* Vancouver, BC: Greystone Books, 2007.

Tahko, Tuomas. *An Introduction to Metametaphysics.* Cambridge: Cambridge University Press, 2015.

Tarasoff, Koozma. *Persistent Ceremonialism: The Plains Cree and Saulteaux.* Ottawa, ON: National Museums of Canada, 1980.

Taylor, John William. "The Development of an Indian Policy in the Canadian North-West, 1869–79." (PhD dissertation), Queen's University, 1975.

Tegmark, Max. "Benefits and Risks of Artificial Intelligence." https://futureof-life.org/background/benefits-risks-of-artificial-intelligence/. Accessed March 5, 2018.

Thistle, Paul. *Indian-European Trade Relations in the Lower Saskatchewan River Region to 1840.* Winnipeg, MB: University of Manitoba Press, 1986.

Trafzer, Clifford. *American Indian Medicine Ways: Spiritual Power, Prophets and Healing.* Tucson, AZ: University of Arizona Press, 2017.

Tompkins, Peter, and Christopher Bird. *The Secret Life of Plants.* New York: Harper Perennial, 1973.

Treaty Commissioner for Saskatchewan. *Statement of Treaty Issues: Treaties as a Bridge to the Future.* Saskatoon, SK: Treaty Commissioner for Saskatchewan, 1998.

Truth and Reconciliation Commission of Canada. "Calls to Action." In *Honoring the Truth, Reconciling for the Future: Summary of the Final Report of the Truth and Reconciliation Commission of Canada,* 319–37. Winnipeg, MB: The Truth and Reconciliation Commission of Canada, 2015.

———. *Interim Report.* Winnipeg, MB: The Truth and Reconciliation Commission of Canada, 2012.

Tucker, Jim B. *Life Before Life: A Scientific Investigation of Children's Memories of Previous Lives.* New York: St. Martin's Press, 2005.

United Nations. *Declaration on the Rights of Indigenous Peoples.* New York, 2007.

Van Evera, Stephen. *Causes of War: Power and the Roots of Conflict.* Ithaca, NY: Cornell University Press, 1999.

Van Inwagen, Peter. *Existence: Essays in Ontology.* Cambridge: Cambridge University Press, 2014.

Virilio, Paul, and Sylvere Lotringer. *Pure War.* Los Angeles: Semiotext(e), 2008.

Vosper, Gretta. *With or Without God: Why the Way We Live Is More Important Than What We Believe.* Toronto: HarperCollins Canada, 2008.

Waldram, James B. *The Way of the Pipe: Aboriginal Spirituality and Symbolic Healing in Canadian Prisons.* Peterborough, ON: Broadview Press, 1997.

Wall, Steve, and Henry Arden. *Wisdom Keepers: Meetings with Native American Spiritual Elders.* Hillsboro, OR: Beyond Words Publishing, 2006.

Walsh, Roger. *The World of Shamanism: New Views of an Ancient Tradition.* Woodbury, MN: Llewellyn Worldwide, 2007.

Walzer, Michael. *Arguing About War.* New Haven, CT: Yale University Press, 2004.

Weatherford, Jack. *Indian Givers: How Indians of the Americas Transformed the World*. New York: Ballantine Books, 1989.

Wedgewood, C.V. *The Spoils of Time: A History of the World from Earliest Times to the Sixteenth Century*. New Haven, CT: Phoenix Press, 1984.

Wheeler, John Archibald. "Bohr, Einstein and the Strange Lesson of the Quantum." In *Mind in Nature*, edited by Richard Quentin Elvee and John Archibald Wheeler, 1–30. New York: Harper & Row, 1982.

Widdowson, Frances. "Academic Freedom and Indigenization: Should the Dissemination of Pseudoscientific 'Ways of Knowing' be Protected?" Paper presented at the Pseudo-Science and Academic Freedom Colloquium, Saint Mary's University, Halifax, November 4, 2016.

Wilkins, David. *Red Prophet: The Punishing Intellectualism of Vine Deloria Jr.* Golden, CO: Fulcrum, 2018.

Wilson, Shawn. *Research Is Ceremony: Indigenous Research Methods*. Black Point, NS: Fernwood Publishing, 2009.

Wolf, Eric R. *Europe and the People Without History*. Berkeley, CA: University of California Press, 1982.

Wolf, Fred Alan. *The Eagle's Quest: A Physicist's Search for Truth in the Heart of the Shamanic World*. New York: Touchstone, 1992.

Wolfe, Alexander. *Earth Elder Stories: The Pinayzitt Path*. Toronto: Fifth House, 1988.

Wooley, Leonard. *The Sumerians*. New York: W.W. Norton & Company, 1965.

Woolf, Alex. *The History of the World*. London: Arcturus Publishing Ltd., 2017.

Wright, Ronald. *Stolen Continents: The "New World" Through Indian Eyes*. New York: Penguin Books, 1993.

Yogananda, Paramahansa. *Autobiography of a Yogi*. Los Angeles: Self-Realization Fellowship, 1971.

Young, David, Grant Ingram, and Lise Swartz. *Cry of the Eagle: Encounters with a Cree Healer*. Toronto: University of Toronto Press, 1989.

Young, David, Robert Rogers, and Russell Willier. *A Cree Healer and His Medicine Bundle*. Berkeley, CA: North Atlantic Books, 2015.

Zimmerman, Larry J. *The Sacred Wisdom of the American Indians*. London: Watkins Publishing, 2011.

INDEX

A

Aboriginal Peoples. *See*
    Indigenous Peoples
Abrahamic religions: as created by
    humans, 149; differences with
    Indigenous spirituality, 146;
    as dominating the world, xvi,
    83, 157; foundations of, 72; with
    human-centric ideology, 137, 156;
    and Islam, 82; as leading to aggres-
    sion, 190; as monotheistic, 88, 145;
    values of, 79. *See also* religions
Adam and Eve, 135
Age of Enlightenment /Reason:
    as engine of human prog-
    ress, 164; ideology of, 162, 181;
    knowledge systems of, 175; and
    prominence of physical world,
    161, 166, 174; values of, 147
agriculture: as contributing to
    deforestation, 206; and hoard-
    ing of plants and animals, 179;
    Indigenous agriculture as col-
    laborating with nature, 56–57;
    loss of, 61; as modifying Earth's
    surface, 202; and private prop-
    erty, 70, 132; as subsistence, 86

Ahcahk (human soul), 8–9,
    11, 17, 20, 24, 38, 225
Alexander the Great of
    Macedonia, 76–77
Allah, 149
Allen, Paul Gunn, 148
Amazonian tribes, 206
Amazon rainforest. *See* rainforests
ancient peoples. *See* primitive peoples
Andean people, 57–58
Anglican Church, and res-
    idential schools, 113
animals and plants, 13, 16, 18–19, 92,
    159, 237; animal urge as root of
    warfare, 194; communication with,
    34; and consciousness, 230; domes-
    tication of, 70; as "dumb," 174; as
    endangered, 203–4, 207; exploita-
    tion of, 67; and habitat destruction,
    203; Indigenous approach to, 70;
    as overhunted, 66–68, 202, 204;
    philosophical understanding of,
    231. *See also* natural world; species
Anishinaabe people, 5, 25,
    38, 60, 105, 183, 199
Arawak peoples, 96, 98

archetypes, in spirituality, 232–34

Aristotle: and Theory of Natural Slavery, 76, 102, 159, 165–66; as tutor to Alexander the Great, 76

artificial intelligence (AI), 217–18

ashe (or nyama, as life force), 117

Asian Aboriginal Peoples, 120, 152, 166; as under control of colonizers, 119

Askeew Pim Atchi howin (making a living off of the land), 108

assimilation policy, 109, 113–14, 125, 182

Atahualpa (Inca leader), 103

âtayôhkanak (spirit helpers), 20, 35, 37–39, 44–45, 51, 129–30, 145, 150

Augustus, Romulus, 79, 141

Australian Aboriginals, 124

avarice, 183, 185–88, 191

Aztec people, 4, 103; civilization of, 26–27, 53, 194; and human sacrifice, 54–55, 166; mythology of, 99; prophecy of, 100; as slaughtered by Spanish, 101

B

balance: and gender roles, 40; living in, 27, 29, 52, 116, 179, 193–94, 213, 250; as spiritual, 33, 53

Banyaca, Thomas, 214

Benedict, Ernest, xiii, 35

Big Bear, 44

bison, North American: mass slaughter of, 204

Blackfoot people, 45

Bohm, David, 235

Bohr, Niels, 229, 235

Bolsonaro, President Jair, 206–7

Book of Revelation, 137

Bose, Chandra, 230

bravery, 44, 72–73, 166, 195. See also courage

Brennan, J.H., 131–32, 134, 147

Brigham, William, 50

Bryce, Peter, 113–14

Buck, William, 4

Buddhism, 150, 152

Bugishu people, 233

C

Caesar, Julius, 78–79

Cahokia, 55

Cajete, Gregory, 4, 57, 99, 174–75, 221

Cambridge Declaration on Consciousness, 230

capitalism, 151, 171, 180, 249; as causing deterioration of country, 193; and exploitation, 182, 191

Carpenter, James, 58

Catholic Church, 139, 143, 165; as condemning human sacrifice, 55; as discrediting science, 161; inquisitions of, 138, 141, 144, 161; as opening to Indigenous spirituality, 144; and residential schools, 113; spread of, 83, 87, 96, 148, 155; as state religion, 138, 184; and treatment of Indigenous Peoples, 81, 95, 101

Cayuga people, 43

Celts, 84–85

ceremonies, 129–30, 137, 151, 176, 242–43; as connection with the transcendent, 36, 117, 125, 128, 150, 177; as conquering evil, 23; considered as superstitious, 95; as creating social cohesion, 2; for finding game, 35; for living in balance, 33; as making contact with the deceased, 24, 34, 84; as outlawed through policy, 108–9, 115; as part of spirituality, xii, 7, 25, 27, 32, 40, 103, 108, 127, 145, 211, 247; and prayer, 10, 12, 14; to prepare for bravery, 73; resurgence of, 155; right to practice, xiv; role in healing, 60, 152; roles for different genders, 42; and sacred learning, 16, 19, 21; as traditional, 52, 58; of world renewal, 174. See also rituals

Hudson's Bay Company, 46, 94
Huitzilopochtli deity, 54
human consciousness, transformation of, 216
Human Consciousness Project, 227
humanism, 147, 162, 165, 188
humanity: as abandoning Indigenous culture, 219, 246; as accountable for its actions, 247; connection to natural world, 6, 57, 72, 84, 89, 159–60, 163–64, 172, 202; as dependent on Creator, 70; effects on from military and industrial development, 196; God's New Covenant with, 135; as having free will, 72, 161–62; and human relationships, 38, 115, 153, 181; image of in portrayals of deities, 80; immaturity of, 250; and intellect, 175; morality of, 136, 143, 163, 189; portrayed as violent, 75; purpose of, 5, 7, 156, 164, 240, 242, 245; and pursuit of wealth, 199; as sharing consciousness, 235; as spirit beings, 8; survival of, xvii, 3, 205, 207, 212–13, 218, 221, 244, 249; and warfare, 75
human sacrifice, Aztec, 26–27, 54–55, 99–100, 166
human unconscious, 232
humility, 13–15, 76, 81, 219, 235
Huron people, 43, 104–5

I

I Ching (or *Book of Changes*), 152, 234
ideology: of belief systems, xi; as human-centred, 137, 156; of Indigenous Peoples, xii, 3, 89, 125, 194; of prehistoric people, 2, 241; of Wetiko, 240. *See also* Indigenous beliefs/philosophy
Iliad, 133
Inca civilizations, 27, 56, 61, 102–3, 166, 194, 206
incarnations. *See* reincarnation
Indian Act, 59, 109

Indigenous Africa, 117–19
Indigenous beliefs/philosophy, 2, 73, 75, 82, 89, 108, 151, 212; as ancient wisdom, 140, 175, 240, 249; attack on, 114, 125; fundamental role of, 94; lack of understanding of, 194; place of Creation in, 212; as potent, 245; and supernal experience, 128, 241–42
Indigenous children/youth, 146, 155, 168; as converted to Christianity, 109; and forcing of religion on, 123–24; in residential schools, 109, 111, 114, 124
Indigenous communities, xiii, 22–23, 181, 247; and alien diseases, 58; as conquered, 77; economic ethos of, 35; as using health to measure progress, 57; vulnerabilities of, 91. *See also* traditional communities
Indigenous cosmology, 115, 128, 130, 152, 163; and harmony, 34, 58, 60, 150
Indigenous cultures, xi–xii, 66, 92, 137, 181, 240, 246; as egalitarian, 75; oppression of, 249; portrayed as inferior, 74; revitalizing of, xiii; as undervalued, xv; and violence, 74. *See also* traditional cultures
Indigenous Eden, xv, 93, 117, 240, 249; characteristics of, 63; demise of, 90, 135, 247; environment of, 26, 31, 60, 156, 180, 242, 246; and harmonious relations, 60, 89; and miraculous healing, 48, 197; and respect for life, 59, 192; spirituality of, 80, 155
Indigenous Elders, xii, 146, 244
Indigenous Environmental Network, 210
Indigenous ethics, 79–80, 134–35, 170, 179–80, 191
Indigenous hegemony, 29–30
Indigenous knowledge, xiv, 94, 168–69, 211, 242

Indigenous lands, 95, 125; clearance of, 206; conquest of, 102, 105–6, 115, 147; defense of, 107; as plundered, 90

Indigenous Peoples: accomplishments of, 61; codes of behaviours, 115; connection to Creation, 60, 67, 71, 93, 211, 214, 241; definition of, 29–30, 88, 121; destruction of, 98, 183; domination of, 79, 90, 190–91; exploitation of, 76, 96, 119, 183; and healing/reconciliation, 187, 235, 249; history and story of, 147, 170; independence of, 204; and male/female attributes, 42; as monotheists, 149; persecution of, 81, 87, 125; regarded as backward, 167, 174; regarded as inferior, 75, 102, 160, 187; regarded as savages, 95, 110, 145, 173–74, 194; strengths of, 57, 62, 74, 78, 102, 248; sufferings of, 83, 92, 101, 216, 245; as thinking people, 16, 52, 61, 167, 177; as viewed as backward, 89, 108, 164; as "White Man's burden," 111

Indigenous spirituality, 31, 91, 150; basis of, 130; and conjuring, 46–47; consequences of loss of, 118; as different from rationalist approach, 146, 167; discovering of, xiii; as holistic, 249; as inconsistent with secular education, 169; and religions, 117, 122, 124, 145; as in resurgence, 154; and return to Good Path, 3; traditional values of, xv, 81, 110, 135, 180, 182, 248; understanding of, 9, 127, 161, 219, 242; viewed as lacking worth, xiii, 105, 108, 114, 160, 168. *See also* spirituality

Indigenous worldview, xv, 104, 114, 155; in conflict with colonizer view, xi, xiii, 170, 243; and female spirit, 40; and regard for Creation, 31, 64, 212, 250

Indonesia Indigenous Peoples, 120–21

industrialization, 89, 192

Industrial Revolution, 184, 202, 204, 241; and global expansion, 190; impacts of, 191; negative effect on peace and harmony, 195; and population expansion, 213

inequality: as based on spiritual accomplishment, 180; as basis for war, 194; consequences of, 193; and hoarding, 179; as root of evil, 192

Inter Caetera bull, 96

Intergovernmental Panel on Climate Change, 208

International Monetary Fund, 192

Inuit communities, xiii

Iroquois people, 4, 30, 105

Isis (goddess), 133

Islam: as dominant/state religion, xvi, 79, 83, 120–23, 134, 156; growth of, 149–50, 184, 190; and subjugation of original populations, 82–83, 117; and trade, 121; and traditional beliefs, 118, 174, 241

iteyimikowisiyecikewina (treaty), 43

J

Javanese people, 121

Jefferson, Thomas, 43, 58

Jehovah (Yahweh), 132, 134

Johnson, Harold, 44, 115–16

Judaism, 80, 132, 134, 149, 156, 174

Jung, Carl, 152, 232–34

Jupiter (god of the sky), 133

K

Kachina spirits, 25–26

Kane, Paul, 46

Kant, Immanuel, 161

Khan, Genghis, 153

kiciwâminawak (White people), 43

Kise-Manitou (also Kitche Manitow, Benevolent Father), 3, 33

knowledge. *See* Indigenous knowledge; spiritual knowledge; traditional knowledge

money: as drug of modern development, 181; as false sense of fulfillment, 182, 192; and greed, 186; and inequality, 179; as not employed by Original Peoples, 59, 171; as undermining sharing, 180. *See also* currency

monotheism, 82, 88, 132, 134, 145, 149, 179

Montagu, Ashley, 65, 75

Moody, Raymond, 226

Moon Time Ceremony, 39

Morales, Evo, president of Bolivia, 248

morality, 150, 160–63, 196

Morris, Alexander, 108

Mother Earth, 211, 248

mound building, 55–56

Muhammad, 82, 149–50

Musk, Elon, 217

Musqua, Danny: and the challenge of physical life, 10, 32; and difference between traditional beliefs and mainstream religions, 127; and gender balance, 40; and humans as spirit beings, 4, 7–9, 16, 130, 225, 244, 246; as Indigenous Elder, xiii, 235; as Knowledge Keeper, xii; as mentor, 3; and reaching sacred knowledge, 21–22, 236; and the Seven Disciplines, 11

Myo, Jimmy, 51

mystics/mysticism, 130, 138, 147, 152, 166, 231

myths/mythologies, 7, 105, 143, 165, 232; as inconsistent with logic, 169; meaning of, 139; regarding Creation, 4–5, 34, 240; universality of, 140; and Wetiko archetype, 188, 193

N

Naga people, 152

Name-Giving Ceremony, 36, 39

Native Americans, as model for practice of natural freedom, 163

Native Peoples. *See* Indigenous Peoples

Native science: as celebration of renewal, 176; and Indigenous spirituality, 222. *See also* science/scientific thinking

natural law, 32, 42, 163; and respect for environment, 211

natural resources: conservation of, 19, 203; depletion of, 192, 218; exploitation of, xvi, 35, 57, 71, 82, 90, 170, 190, 247; and husbandry, 52; and mechanization, 191. *See also* natural world

natural world, xvi, 69, 125, 140, 153, 164, 166, 183; and activism, 201; degradation of, 175–76, 199, 218, 247; destruction of, 182, 213; dismal treatment of by Wetikos, 212; exploitation of, 156, 190, 194, 207, 214; as gift of Creator, 90; human dominance over, 164, 219; interconnectedness of, 172, 209; nurturing relationships with, 13, 27, 40, 84, 89, 214, 244; and positive cyclical growth, 222; protection of, 72, 181; reverence towards, 34, 103; as separate from civilization, 70, 240; as spiritual, 245; and stress, 241; as uncontrollable, 174. *See also* Creation; natural resources; physical world

Navajo people, 4, 30

near-death experiences (NDEs), 221, 223, 226–27

Nelson, George, 46–47

Nelson, Melissa, 237

New Testament: as containing elements of original spirituality, 136; and disasters to befall humanity, 137

New World, 86, 92–93, 103; colonization of, 94; European subjugation of, 98; Spanish exploitation of, 102, 142

111; and silence, 10; as thanking spirits, 68; as way of living, 127

prehistoric peoples. *See* primitive peoples

pre-literate societies. *See* primitive peoples

Presbyterian Church, and residential schools, 113

primitive peoples, 2, 73, 214; as excluded from civilization, 71; ideology of, 63, 65, 219; as Indigenous, 66, 219; knowledge systems of, xiv, 64; negative portrayals of, 66–68, 89; overthrow of, 240; significance of beliefs, xii; worldview and philosophy of, 219

private property, 104, 115; concept as virtually non-existent, 180; damage done by this concept, 116–17

Protestantism, 142–43, 155

pseudo-science, 168

psychic phenomena, 232

Pueblo people, 5

pyramids, 53–55

Q

quantum theory, 226, 229–30, 235

Quebec Act of 1774, 107

Quechua people, 58, 103

Quetzalcoatl, 26, 53–54, 99–100

Qur'an, 149–50

R

Ra (sun god), 133

racism, 91, 152, 182

rainforests, destruction of, 206–7, 216

rational thought: as divisive, 170; as guided by spirituality, 165, 172, 177; heathens as incapable of, 95; and humanism, 147; and Indigenous values, 167, 169, 177; and miracles, 49; as opposed to spiritual belief, 1, 130, 161, 164–66, 174; as promoting wealth and value, 181, 192, 249; regarded as

solution to challenges, 168, 175; rise of, 89–90. *See also* science/ scientific thinking; technology

reconciliation, xiii, xvi, 23, 91, 147, 236, 249; definitions of, 239; between Indigenous and non-Indigenous, 238

Red Road, 131

reincarnation, 143, 151, 221, 231–32; belief in, 224–26; cycle of, 84, 224; and learning through it, 9, 11; and pre-existence of souls, 138; research methodology for, 223

Reincarnation and Biology: A Contribution to the Etiology of Birth Marks and Birth Defects, 224

re-Indigenization, 249

relativism, regarding ethical truths, 129

Religion and Rational Theology, 161

religions, 80, 115, 155, 232, 241; as compared to spirituality, 79, 91, 115, 124, 127, 145–46, 249; cosmic archetypes in, 140; as failing to maintain overall harmony, 132, 184; as forced upon Aboriginals, 122, 184; as Indigenous, 122, 124, 145; as opposing Indigenous worldview, 83, 127–28, 137; as products of civilization, 130; and science, 229; and separation with state, 143. *See also* Abrahamic religions

residential schools, xi, xiv, 91, 109, 111; and brainwashing of children, 124; government apology for, 114; in Norway, 88; physical violence in, 113; removal of children to, 109

Resistance of 1885, 109

resources. *See* natural resources

respect, as virtue, 13–14, 35, 76, 81, 115, 117, 222

Rhine, J.B., 231

rituals: and consumerism, 182; for hospitality, 2; in non-Indigenous contexts, 86, 133, 138, 141–42,

175, 250; importance of, 95; methodology for, 235–36; principles of, 24; redefining of, 137; as religion, in pure sense, 188; and science, 176. *See also* Indigenous spirituality
spiritual knowledge, xiv, 53, 74, 154, 168, 170, 175, 219
Standing Rock Indian Reservation, 210
Starblanket, Noel, xiii, 40, 225
Stevenson, Ian, 223–26
stewardship, of natural world: as human responsibility, xv, 19, 27, 57, 90, 156, 234, 247; as Indigenous value, 120, 192, 214, 241; as promoting better relationships, 13
storytelling, 52, 60
Sublimus Dei, 102, 142
Sumerian civilization, 71, 132
Sun Dances, 26, 38, 109
the supernal, 33, 57, 71, 175, 250; as aiding healing, 51, 115, 246; and authority, 129; belief in, 29, 128; connection with, 51, 91, 117, 138, 245; and discovering one's mission, 36; existence of, 235; as fundamental, 94; messages of, 37, 95; as opposed to rational thinking, 161; revelation by, 7, 22; wisdom of, 16, 218, 226; world of, 12. *See also* the transcendent
Suzuki, David, 211, 215
Sweat Lodge Ceremonies, 12, 32, 237
Sweetgrass Way, 131

T

Taino people, 100
Tanak, 80, 82, 150
Tawa (Creator), 25–26
technology, 56, 175, 193, 207; as creating modern civilization, xvi, 173; as demythologizing world, 105, 168, 190; and domination of nature, 194; failure of, 184; as great panacea, 221; growth of, 157, 166, 182, 184,
212–13, 215; and Indigenous innovations, 234; negative effects of, 176, 195–96, 203, 211, 217; as safe when combined with supernal wisdom, 218. *See also* rational thought; science/scientific thinking
Tecumseh (Shawnee leader), 107
Ten Commandments, 135, 137
Tenochtitlan, 54, 61, 100–101
Teotihuacan, 53–54
terra nullius, 95, 125
Tezcatlipoca, 99
The Theory of Moral Sentiments, 191
Theory of Natural Slavery, 76
Thirst Dance Ceremony, 32, 38
Tlaxcalan people, 100
tobacco, 34, 36, 151
Tootoosis, Ernest, 29
Tootoosis, Wilfred, 148
traditional communities: beliefs of, 130, 250; and healing, 124; and medicines, 117; as more in tune with nature, 182; spiritual practices of, 94, 127; as stressing positive relationships, 237; value systems of, xii, 151; virtues of, 13, 15. *See also* Indigenous communities
traditional cultures, 33, 87, 171, 242, 247. *See also* Indigenous cultures
traditional knowledge, 17, 168, 211, 216. *See also* Indigenous knowledge
the transcendent: connection to, xvi, 21, 36, 49–51, 93, 117, 138; denial of, 128; education about, 33, 37; effect on by colonists, 137, 147, 163, 165; guidance of, 15, 229; Indigenous beliefs about, xiii, 18, 47, 221, 241; as real, 170; relationship with, xii, 17, 39, 167, 242, 246; respect for, 173; as ultimate authority, 2, 129, 140. *See also* the supernal
treaties, 95, 107, 109, 182, 214; negotiations, 42–43, 106, 108; rights of, 125
Tree of Knowledge of Good and Evil, 76, 135, 159, 188

Eden, 222; and dismal treatment of environment, 212; by products of, 194–95; as scarcity-based, 185

Wetiko/Wetikoism, 167, 180, 187, 240; as archetype, 188; characteristics of, 94, 247; as disease/psychosis, 61, 183, 185–86; as force of greed, xvi, 23, 61, 66, 156, 171, 175, 183; global influence of, 157, 184; as preying on people, 25, 60

Where Reincarnation and Biology Intersect, 224

Whisperers: The Secret History of the Spirit World, 131

White Buffalo (the sacred), 165

White Man, 43, 46, 110, 148, 188, 198–99; as carrying disease of greed, 189; lack of regard for Indigenous Peoples, 111

White Man's law, 115

Wicce (healers), 84

Widdowson, Frances, 168

Winago (evil), 25

Windigo (in Anishinaabemowin), 25, 60–61, 183

Wîsahkecâhk, 5–6, 26, 34, 145

wisdom, 84, 139–40, 174, 226; acquiring of, 12, 14, 40, 234, 244; in African spirituality, 118–19; definition of, 15, 159; as foundation of knowledge/science, 52, 154, 172, 176, 190, 218, 247; Indigenous view of, 168, 175, 180, 183, 195, 211, 240, 242, 249; as one of Seven Virtues, ix, 13, 77, 81

Wi Taski Win (living on the land in harmony), 108

witchcraft, 86, 144, 166

With or Without God, 143

World Commission on Environment and Development, 216

world population: and growth of non-Indigenous persons, 69, 89, 181; as mostly Indigenous, 68; as optimal, 213

The World We Used to Live In: Remembering the Powers of the Medicine Man, xii, 48

World Wildlife Federation: Living Planet Index, 205

Wu Chi, 152

Y

Yowa (Creator), 25

Z

Zoroastrianism, 72, 83, 124

Zuni Medicine Man, 50

About the Author

ALEXANDER BLAIR STONECHILD is professor of Indigenous Studies at the First Nations University of Canada in Regina, Saskatchewan. He is of Cree, Saulteaux, and Métis heritage, and is a member of the Muscowpetung First Nation. Blair attended Qu'Appelle Indian Residential School and Campion Collegiate, obtained his bachelor's degree from McGill University and masters and doctorate degrees from University of Regina. In 1976, Blair became the first faculty member at First Nations University and has been dean of academics and executive director of development. His major publications include *Loyal Till Death: Indians and the North-West Rebellion* (1997); *The New Buffalo: Aboriginal Post-secondary Policy in Canada* (2006); *Buffy Sainte-Marie: It's My Way* (2012); *The Knowledge Seeker: Embracing Indigenous Spirituality* (2016); and *Loss of Indigenous Eden and the Fall of Spirituality* (2020). Blair is married to Sylvia and has three adult children.

CPSIA information can be obtained
at www.ICGtesting.com
Printed in the USA
LVHW030334300323
743017LV00016B/107